SURVIVAL

GUIDE

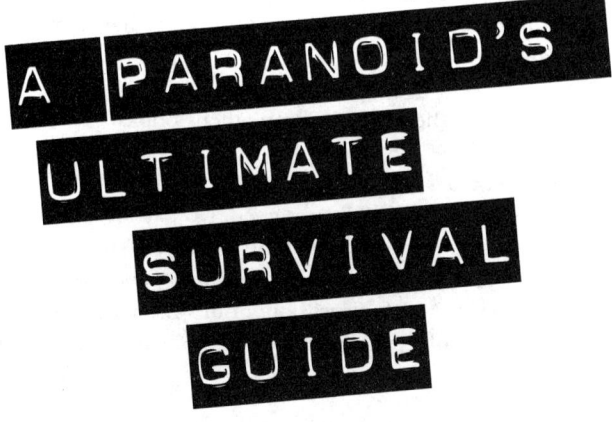

A PARANOID'S ULTIMATE SURVIVAL GUIDE

PATRICIA BARNES-SVARNEY & THOMAS EUGENE SVARNEY

Prometheus Books

59 John Glenn Drive
Amherst, New York 14228-2197

The material and information for this book were developed to best of the authors' knowledge. The authors are not responsible for disease or harm resulting from the use of the information in this book.

Published 2002 by Prometheus Books

Inquiries should be addressed to
Prometheus Books
59 John Glenn Drive
Amherst, New York 14228–2197
VOICE: 716–691–0133, ext. 207
FAX: 716–564–2711
WWW.PROMETHEUSBOOKS.COM

06 05 04 03 02   5 4 3 2 1

Library of Congress Cataloging-in-Publication Data

Barnes-Svarney, Patricia L.
    A paranoid's ultimate survival guide / Patricia Barnes-Svarney, Thomas Eugene Svarney.
        p. cm.
    Includes index.
    ISBN 1–57392–971–9 (paper : alk. paper)
    1. Survival skills. I. Svarney, Thomas E. II. Title.

GF86 .B36 2002
613.6'9—dc21

2002018982

Printed in the United States of America on acid-free paper

CONTENTS

6

CONTENTS

CONTENTS 9

PREFACE

"... It can be a dangerous place. ..."

—Commander Jeffrey Sinclair,
referring to the space station
on the TV show *Babylon 5*

*F*unk and Wagnall's *Standard College Dictionary* defines the word *danger* as "exposure to evil, injury, or loss; peril; risk." That is an apt description of the world in which we live—although most of the time, we don't realize that danger constantly surrounds us. We've learned that there's a good reason for this: Many of the dangers that beset humanity are hidden from sight, consciousness, or knowledge.

But in the backs of our minds, there's that vague feeling of unease, probably a remnant from our distant ancestors. Catchphrases—"The world is a dangerous place." "Be careful out there." "Watch out." "Don't take any chances." "Stay safe." express our nebulous, generalized fear of the world around us. There is even a word for this concern: *paranoia.* From the Greek word for madness, paranoia is usually used to describe extreme states of fear and the nervousness brought on by fear. The general consensus is that paranoia is distorted thinking. But as we all know, even paranoids have enemies. And sometimes the dangers poised out there are so large, so intense, that the word *paranoia* seems inadequate.

In the last hundred years or so, the field of scientific inquiry has made great strides in unlocking the mysteries of the universe. The downside is that we now know more about its hidden dangers that we could have imagined. With new tools ranging from the scanning electron microscope to the Hubble Space Telescope, we have the ability to determine just what dangers lurk out there—from the extremely tiny to the extremely large, from inside our bodies to inside our homes, and even to those associated with our planet, solar system, galaxy, and universe. And as we become more and more sophisticated, we'll no doubt discover even more in the future.

Fortunately, with this knowledge has also come power. With our new awareness of previously hidden dangers, we can avoid them, prevent them, or be prepared to cope with them—or all three.

A Paranoid's Ultimate Survival Guide presents the latest scientific findings on dangers that can confront you and your loved ones. It is a fallacy that just because our society has become more urbanized, sophisticated, and removed from the natural world, we no longer need to be concerned about the dangers around us. Nothing could be farther from the truth.

If anything, modern science has revealed more dangers that the universe has cooked up for us. This book reveals many of those hidden dangers—and an occasional not-so-hidden danger—explaining the science behind them. We'll tell you what the danger is, where it can be found, what most likely causes it, who's at risk, and what can be done to survive it—if anything.

Each danger is introduced by explaining why a certain event or thing is considered a danger. This is usually something you don't know about—something you never saw coming. We'll even let you know if it's something worth being *really* paranoid about.

"Judging the Danger" will explain why some dangers are not to be worried about, while others need to be thought of as distinct possibilities. Should you be concerned about the West Nile Virus? The Sun? Or even your sweet, lovable cat, Mr. Tinkles?

And finally, "Minimizing the Danger" will give you a brief synopsis of what you can do to possibly protect yourself from the danger listed. Beware though: No matter how knowledgeable and prepared you are, sometimes it's still not enough.

So sit back and enjoy the ride. With a large dose of cutting-edge science, a little lightheartedness, and some practical, real-world tips, we hope *A Paranoid's Ultimate Survival Guide* will educate you, entertain you—and maybe even save your life or that of a loved one.

THE VIOLENT EARTH

Not everything on Earth
is as innocent and calm as it seems.
Just ask anyone in
Southern California or Japan . . .

As we drive to work each day or settle into bed at night, we assume that the ground beneath us is firm, solid, and "steady as a rock"—timeless, unchanging. Nothing could be farther from the truth. The earth beneath our feet, indeed the whole planet, is constantly moving and changing. We're essentially living on the skin of pudding—and Nature chooses the flavor. The inside remains hot and mushy, while the thin crust dries and breaks into plates. However, unlike a bowl of pudding, our planet's crustal plates are in constant motion, driven by the molten interior.

Earth's shifting crust was first recognized in the early 1900s by the great German scientist Alfred Wegener, but it wasn't confirmed until the 1960s and 1970s. Wegener believed that millions of year ago, all the land masses formed one supercontinent called *Pangaea.* Over time, the continents slowly moved into the positions we recognize today. And the motion continues at tortoise-like speeds of

15

less than one inch per year. Over millions of years, this means millions of inches—movement that eventually makes quite a difference. But humans? We don't live long enough to detect the slow, continuous continental movement occurring all around the world.

The movements and interactions of the plates give rise to the many phenomena that can come out of nowhere, such as earthquakes and volcanoes. Take 1996, a year of 600 major natural disasters. There were about 200 storms, 170 floods, and 75 forest fires, but there were also 50 earthquakes, 30 volcanic eruptions, and 75 landslides. Those numbers are up about 400 percent from three decades ago. And each year, we lose an average of eleven thousand people worldwide from these natural disasters—many of the deaths caused by this shaking, eruptions, and shifting of the earth's surface.[1]

You never know when one of these sudden hazardous shifts will pop up—or where. But can we be prepared?

EARTH SHAKING

Earthquakes: Shake, Rattle, and Roll

The earthquake that struck Turkey in August 1999 was devastating. Measuring magnitude 7.4 on the Richter scale, the quake occurred at the western end of an about 750-mile long tear in the crust—a fault resulting from the slow-motion collision of crustal plates associated with Arabia and Eurasia. More than twelve thousand people were killed as buildings collapsed, and the amount of damage was in the billions of dollars. In Armenia in 1997, a massive quake killed more than twenty-five thousand, with damage greater than $20 billion. Neither of these quakes surprised scientists. Both places are major earthquake regions, places where the earth's crustal plates are either slamming together or tearing apart—ripe regions for such quakes.

We see the pictures on the news: streets full of rubble, houses in ruins, bodies everywhere, people crying or in shock. Another earthquake has struck, bringing misery and death to untold thousands. What's going on here?

Judging the Danger

Earthquakes are just vibrations (actually waves) reverberating through the planet. These oscillations occur as chunks of the crust called *plates* slide, push, or pull at each other. When the plates get stuck together and can't move, they build up large amounts of energy. When they become unstuck, they release energy—just like a stuck window that finally gives, usually catching your finger in the process. Vertical and horizontal waves form, both shaking the ground with enormous energy. Depending on the severity of the earthquake, it can destroy just about everything close to the epicenter—the spot on the surface above the earthquake's origin. Few people die from the ground shaking alone, however. Most deaths and injuries occur as a result of falling objects, such as windows, buildings, bridges, roadways, rocks, and trees.

Although the movement of the plates has been studied and the major faults mapped, scientists still cannot predict where and when these major catastrophes will strike. They seem to come out of nowhere, triggered by forces beyond our control, announcing their imminent arrival in ways we can't sense.

Minimizing the Danger

Unless we can somehow stop the earth's crustal plates from moving—which has as much a chance of happening as Woody Allen competing for the welterweight title—it's best to be aware and be prepared. The Federal Emergency Management Agency has some pretty sensible hints about how to handle yourself during and after an earthquake. Here are their recommendations, along with some of our own.[2]

When an earthquake hits:

✦ Stay inside and take refuge in a safe area. This can be under a desk, inside a door frame—in other words, use something sturdy to shield yourself from falling debris. Grab something sturdy as the room shakes. Pray that your contractor was good and your concrete walls aren't made of oatmeal.

✦ If you're caught outside, move into a safe area, away from potential falling hazards. Remember, flying debris causes most earthquake injuries. Things dropping from several stories up can act like falling missiles.

✦ If you're caught driving during an earthquake, stop in a safe area, if possible, away from falling debris and larger items such as telephone poles. Stay in the car until the shaking stops—if you're a safe distance away from falling objects. Remember, you can't "outrun" an earthquake. There's nowhere *to* run.

After the earthquake, here are a few more hints:

✦ Be prepared for aftershocks. These are normally of lower magnitude than the original shock, although some have been known to be equal or greater in magnitude.

✦ Treat all your and others' injuries; call for help if you need it. Keep in mind that emergency services may be taxed to the limit.

The Loma Prieta earthquake in Oakland, California, struck in October 1989. It was strong enough to topple this part of a highway. (Michael Nevins/U.S. Army Corps of Engineers)

Why Southern California Rocks

Everyone knows that California is the Earthquake Capital of the United States. It's the most at risk for quakes for a good reason: It lies on the site where two of Earth's crustal plates grind together. It's also filled with cracks generated by the grinding area—faults at the surface or deeply buried. Put it all together and it spells "shake me."

The two major valleys in southern California—San Gabriel and San Fernando—also have another strike against them. According to a study done by the United States Geological Survey, both valleys sit on basins of sediment once laid down by ancient seas and rivers—which means it's not solid bedrock. Add to that the depth of the sediment-filled basins—one to a half times deeper than previously thought.[3] If there is an earthquake, the basins shake "like big bowls of Jell-O," as one researcher so aptly said. But this is not your average strawberry flavor—this gelatin means all those buildings, structures, and people are in for quite a shaking during an earthquake. In fact, the San Fernando Valley was the site of the 6.7 magnitude 1994 Northridge earthquake, which killed more than fifty people and caused some $15.3 billion in insured losses.

✦ Listen for emergency information on the radio or television, if they are still on the air. Usually, the radio is the best bet—it often will have emergency broadcasts. Those irritating warning signals of the Emergency Alert System (formerly the Emergency Broadcast System) are practiced for just these occasions.

✦ Stay out of damaged buildings—earthquakes can crack a house or other structure. A step inside could shift the balance, causing the building to crack more or even collapse—with you inside.

✦ Check for gas leaks and clean up any small flammable spills. If you think there are any leaks, toxic chemicals, or large flammable-liquid spills around, call emergency services for help.

✦ Check for electrical system damage. Don't touch any sparking or downed power lines. Call emergency services for help.

✦ Check for water system damage. Any seepage or problems with water pipes could indicate or lead to contamination.

✦ Open cabinets and cupboards cautiously. Nature loves to shuffle things around during a quake. Your iron frying pan may be at the edge, waiting to fall on your head when you open the cupboard door.

Earthquakes Revisited: Quakes Out of Nowhere

The area centered around New Madrid, Missouri, where the Ohio and Missouri Rivers meet the Mississippi River, was a peaceful place. There were the usual farms, trading posts, saloons, churches, and country grocery stores. But for three months during the years 1811 and 1812, the people of this region were shook to the bone by earthquakes. They experienced three large shocks estimated to be greater than magnitude 8; aftershocks included around two at magnitude 8, five at about magnitude 7.7, and ten at about magnitude 5.3—and more than eighty-nine at magnitude 4.3. The earthquakes at New Madrid, about four hundred miles south of Chicago, became known as the greatest, most powerful earthquakes ever experienced in the United States. And these quakes didn't occur at a plate boundary—they occurred in the middle of the North American plate, along a long, rupturing underground fault.

The New Madrid quakes were not the only hidden ones. Quakes have occurred in such unlikely places as New York City (two at about magnitude 5 in 1737 and 1884) and Charleston, South Carolina (a magnitude 7 quake happened there on August 31, 1886, killing sixty people and damaging most of the buildings in the city). There is one culprit "at fault" for these two quakes, too: The Cameron's Line, a fault running through the Bronx, down the East River, past Gracie Mansion, through Staten Island, and down to Charleston, South Carolina.[4] Imagine if that crack came unzipped.

Judging the Danger

The idea that an earthquake can occur in non-earthquake-prone areas is jarring. Take this November 1999 study from the University of Colorado at Boulder: Scientists there suggested that the potential for a large earthquake along the New Madrid seismic zone in the central Mississippi Valley was "serious"—and it is only one of many places where quakes can come seemingly out of nowhere.[5] And what about in December 1999, when scientists from all over the world presented the first global earthquake hazard map—a map developed by five hundred scientists over seven years.[6] Some parts of the map showed few surprises: Places like southern California, Iceland, Turkey, Taiwan, and the India-China border were sites of major earthquake hazards. But there were also some surprise zones that caused consternation: Much of the world's population lives on potentially shaky ground. The map highlighted places where quakes are not usually a concern, but now have the potential. This included Missouri, upstate New York, parts of southern Africa—and even New York City. (In fact, only two states have not had an earthquake with a magnitude greater than 4.5 within their borders—Maryland and Wisconsin.)

What would happen if one of these out-of-nowhere earthquakes occurred in a populated area—an area not prepared for the shaking by a quake? During the New Madrid earthquakes of 1811–1812 some people in the area of the quakes felt their effects, but there was little damage because there were few structures in the

Faulting Cities

We all know California is the United States's poster state for earthquakes. But FEMA recently used earthquake data from the United States Geological Survey to work out how bad the damages would be to areas not thought of as earthquake-prone. They collected data about not only 150,000 earthquake hazard points from across the country, but also about local building inventories, economics, and other details to estimate potential fatalities and economic losses if the earth begins to tremble.

Which cities would face the highest potential loss? Try this list: Memphis, Tennessee; Seattle, Washington; Portland, Oregon; New York, New York; Salt Lake City, Utah; St. Louis, Missouri; Tacoma, Washington; Las Vegas, Nevada; Anchorage, Alaska; Boston, Massachusetts; Reno, Nevada; Charleston, South Carolina; Albuquerque, New Mexico; Newark, New Jersey; Honolulu, Hawaii; and Atlanta, Georgia.

While the chance of being in an earthquake has remained pretty much the same in these cities over the years, the risk of damage has increased substantially. The main reason has to do with humans, of course: Urban areas have grown considerably in the higher seismic hazard areas—and old (and some new) buildings standing in these spots are not build to withstand a shaking.[7]

The concern is valid. In the United States, FEMA estimates property damage from earthquakes at about $4.4 billion annually. That makes it a major player in the country's overall annual natural hazards costs: From 1898 to 1998, the National Weather Service estimates that annual flood losses averaged $5.2 billion; the National Climate Data Center estimates $5.4 billion for hurricane losses during that same period.

affected area. But in Vermont in June 1973, a magnitude 5.2 quake (originating in western Maine) cracked plaster, moved chimneys away from walls, and cracked many road surfaces. In other words, big and little cities with many non-earthquake-resistant buildings and structures exist all along these potential quake zones. There are pipelines and underground cables to shift. There are bridges and overpasses to crumble. A major movement along the New Madrid fault—or a similar area—would be disastrous.[8]

Minimizing the Danger

If you live in an area such as southern California, you already know your risk! If not, consult the new earthquake hazard maps mentioned above to get an idea of how your region fares. Then follow the tips recommended by the Federal Emergency Management Agency (FEMA) if you're in an prime earthquake hot spot—or even if your locale has potential:[9]

+ Correct any home hazards:
    —Strengthen overhead light fixtures.
    —Put large and/or heavy objects on lower shelves.
    —Put breakable items, such as glassware, dishes, and bottles, in closed, latched cabinets.
    —Hang heavy items such as mirrors away from places where people normally sit.
    —Store flammable materials in closed, latched cabinets.
    —Secure shelves to walls.
    —Have any structural, electrical, water system, or fuel line defects repaired.
+ Identify places of relative safety for your family:
    —Under strong, stable furniture such as a heavy table.
    —Against an inside wall.
    —Away from windows and places where heavy items could fall.
    —If outside, away from power and telephone lines, trees, and other buildings and structures.

✦ Make sure family members know how to:
  —Turn off the water, gas, and electricity.
  —How to call for emergency help (9-1-1 in most parts of
   the United States).
  —Find emergency radio stations for more information.
  —Use any emergency communication plans.
✦ Stock up on emergency supplies such as:
  —Water and canned food.
  —First aid kit.
  —Flashlight and extra batteries.
  —Appropriate clothes.
  —Battery-powered radios.
  —Cash, credit cards, and critical medicines.

And here are some tips from the *Los Angeles Fire Department
Earthquake Handbook*:

When you feel an earthquake, duck under a desk or sturdy table.
Stay away from windows, bookcases, file cabinets, heavy mirrors,
hanging plants, and other heavy objects that could fall. Watch out
for falling plaster and ceiling tiles. Stay undercover until the
shaking stops, and hold onto your cover. If it moves, move with
it.[10]

Tsunamis: Let's Give a Big Wave

You're sitting on the deck of your beachfront house on a beautiful
day. There's no danger in sight, just the sound of the surf hissing back
and forth across the sand. True, the ground did seem to rumble a
while ago, but it might have been a passing truck. Suddenly, without
warning, you notice the sound of the surf stop. The water starts to
recede faster and faster, uncovering a large portion of land that is
normally underwater. Strange . . . that's never happened before. It's
so quiet now. Why are the neighbors all running inland? What's that
moving far off on the horizon? It's getting closer. It's a wall of water
one hundred feet high. And it's the last thing you'll ever see.

"It" is a tsunami: a huge ocean wave generated by a seismic event

Big Wave Alert

The Pacific Ocean is a hotbed not only of political coups, but of tsunami activity. Because of this, the National Weather Service operates the Pacific Tsunami Warning Center (PTWC) near Honolulu, Hawaii. The group monitors seismic activity, evaluates the potential for tsunamis, and issues watches and warnings for all U.S. territories and states bordering the Pacific Ocean. There is also the International Tsunami Information Center, a group of twenty-six member countries that monitor the PTWC for the sake of their respective countries in the Pacific.[11] Just listen to the reports and everything is well in hand. There's plenty of time to get ready. Right?

Scientists recently rediscovered a mechanism that can generate local tsunamis close to shore with little or no warning. In July 1998 an earthquake measuring 7.0 on the Richter scale occurred just off the northwest coast of Papua New Guinea. There was no time to issue any warnings—mainly because the earthquake immediately triggered an underwater landslide, generating a fifty-foot tsunami. The wave struck the coast within ten minutes, killing approximately three thousand people.

What's even scarier? After further studying this tragedy, scientists believe underwater landslides can be generated not only by major earthquakes, but by a variety of other factors, such as small earthquakes that aren't big enough to create their own tsunamis, the movement of water, or just an unstable rockbed. The resulting local tsunamis can form very close to shore, striking with little or no warning. This greatly expands the coastal regions at risk for tsunamis.

Because of Papua New Guinea, scientists are now checking areas with underwater landslide potential or that show evidence of a landslide in the recent past. For instance, there were the sketchy reports from Santa Barbara in 1812 about a landslide-generated tsunami; Puerto Rico and the Virgin Islands each experienced two in the mid-to-late 1800s and early 1900s. And the records go on. Now scientists have a new at-risk list: Places like British Columbia, Oregon, Washington, and northern California could experience localized landslide-induced tsunamis. With time, scientists hope to map all the coastal areas with potential for landslide-induced tsunamis. Until then, keep those running shoes close at hand.[12]

such as an earthquake, volcanic activity, or an underwater landslide. Erroneously referred to as "tidal waves" (they have nothing to do with the tides), the name comes from the Japanese words *tsu* (harbor) and *nami* (wave). In the open ocean, these waves may have a height of a few feet, with wavelengths on the order of several miles—which means they're almost unnoticeable if you're in a ship. But as the tsunami approaches the shallows near a coast, the water begins to pile up, becoming deadly and destructive. First the ocean recedes in what is called a *negative wave*, then the tsunami, or *positive wave*, hits—often with many smaller sibling waves striking afterward. The larger tsunamis can measure more than 98 to 164 feet high, with some reported monsters at 200 feet. And they're not slowpokes—some waves travel faster than 150 miles per hour.

Judging the Danger

Following an earthquake, the next thing to hit might be a tsunami. Tsunamis are very destructive natural phenomena, with the potential for extreme numbers of deaths, injuries, and property damage. What areas are most at risk for these huge ocean waves? Naturally, if you live in the Midwest or high in the mountains, your risk for a tsunami is very low. About 80 percent of tsunamis occur in the Pacific Ocean. This may seem odd, but there is a good reason: A higher percentage of earthquake and volcanic activity, combined with the size of the Pacific, make it ripe for the formation of the huge waves. There isn't as much of a problem elsewhere—about 10 percent of tsunamis occur in the Atlantic Ocean, and 10 percent in all other oceans.

For those areas prone to tsunamis, it's a catch-22: Currently, we can't predict the events that trigger tsunamis, so we can't predict when one of these huge waves will strike a coast. A tsunami can happen anytime, anywhere, mostly invisible—except probably to the local fish population—until it reaches a coast. However, once an earthquake and then a tsunami occur, scientists can use sophisticated instruments to determine the areas at risk, approximately how large the approaching tsunami will be, and when it will strike. Of

This is a tsunami striking the coast of Hawaii in 1946. Note the arrow pointing to a man on the pier. He was never heard from again. (National Geophysical Data Center)

course, with all the variables involved, the science of tsunami prediction becomes analogous to that of the weather. Sometimes they're right on the money—and sometimes (much to the delight of coastal inhabitants), the wave fizzles. But don't take any chances. Assume the forecast is accurate and take appropriate action. Depending on the type and location of a triggering event, you may have anywhere from a few hours to a few minutes of warning before the wave hits—just enough time to start the car and peel out of there.

Minimizing the Danger

Tsunamis affect the coastlines and low-lying areas inland. If you live in these areas, stay alert and think like Boy and Girl Scouts: be prepared. Find out if your home or building is in a tsunami-prone area, and determine your height above sea level. Know the warning signs of a tsunami—from earthquakes and sizable rumbling of the ground, to the rapid rise or fall of the ocean water. Make sure your entire family knows evacuation routes; places to meet if separated; how to turn off the water, gas, and electricity; and especially how to call for emergency help (9-1-1 in most areas). And as for almost any situation, have emergency supplies such as water and canned food; a first aid kit; flashlight and extra batteries; battery- and/or solar-powered radio; and cash, credit cards, and critical medicines in case you have to evacuate your home.

There are some good resources from the government—including the following guidelines from the Federal Emergency Management Agency—to help you prepare for and deal with tsunamis. This is an extremely dangerous natural phenomenon, and should be taken seriously. Here are a few hints:[13]

+ Listen to TV or radio broadcasts to determine when and where a tsunami might strike. Don't fool around—be prepared to leave at once.
+ In the event of an official tsunami warning, or if you see signs of an approaching tsunami, use your evacuation route(s) and get to safe, high ground immediately.
+ Don't go to the beach to watch. If the water recedes, don't walk far out to gather sea shells. If you can see a tsunami wave approaching, it's too late to escape.
+ Do not return to the danger zone and/or your home until the all-clear has been sounded. There can be more than one tsunami wave.

After the tsunami, there will be work to do. Don't enter any damaged structure. If you can enter your home, the result will be similar to dealing with a flood: You may have to open the windows to dry out the home, plus shovel out mud. You'll also want to use bottled water until your drinking water can be tested for contamination. Don't forget to have a professional look for gas leaks, shorting electrical wires, and water problems. And be really thankful the wave didn't turn you into a tsunami death statistic.

Volcanoes: In the Land of Mordor Where the Shadows Lie

They call them "ticking time bombs." But these aren't your usual, bad-guy-style explosions with a couple sticks of dynamite. These bombs are actually natural volcanoes, found in places such as the northwestern regions of the United States. In fact, Mount Rainier in Washington—no, make that the entire Cascade Range—is actually a ticking time bomb of volcanics. There are other time bombs in the country, too—Yellowstone in Wyoming, Valles Caldera in New Mexico, and Long Valley Caldera in California. In other parts of the world, there are places like Mount Vesuvius in Italy. This serene mountain has been a dominant feature on the Italian landscape for centuries—and it has also blown its top on many occasions. Mount Vesuvius is currently a disaster waiting to happen: Scientists have discovered a "plug" of rock in the neck of the volcano. And it's only a matter of time before the cork blows.

There are close to twenty-five volcanoes erupting on Earth every day. Some scientists compare volcanoes to a lion that sleeps almost all the time, but is still alive. In the case of the volcano, it can "live" for many years in a sleeping state. Then one day—because of pressure buildup, movement of a crustal plate, or change in the lava movement within the volcano's hot, molten reservoir—the volcano erupts. And scientists still cannot predict how or when these sleeping giants will awaken and blow.

Judging the Danger

Volcanoes are another of those natural phenomena best taken seriously—very seriously. They are deadly to life and property—fully capable of spreading ash and toxic fumes over a hundred miles, throwing hot "bombs" more than twenty miles, and wiping out entire towns with mudflows, floods, and pyroclastic flows.

And of course, it's just not the volcano itself that's a killer.

They've been known to spawn earthquakes from the shifting of the ground as lava erupts; flash floods from the melting snow on top of the volcano; landslides and mudflows from mixing of water, ash, debris, and sediment from the mountain; thunderstorms, as the hot gases from the volcano can simulate a weather system; and tsunamis from the violent blast of the exploding volcano.

Minimizing the Danger

The first step in avoiding the danger of a volcano is simple: Determine if you live near a volcano—and if you do, is it active or dormant? What is its past history? What islands do you plan on visiting this year? Regular sacrifices of virgins to the volcano god are a bad sign.

If you do live close to a volcanically active area, the following guidelines adapted from the Federal Emergency Management Agency will help you deal with this extremely hazardous situation:[14]

Before an eruption:

+ Understand and prepare for disasters that may accompany a volcanic eruption, such as flash floods, thunderstorms, earthquakes, landslides, mudflows, and, near the coast, tsunamis.

+ Understand your community's warning systems when it comes to volcanoes. Geologists are often monitoring ground displacements around certain volcanoes with a global positioning system, which sometimes gathers enough data to alert the public to a possible eruption.

+ Make evacuation plans with a primary and backup route to higher ground. Be prepared to leave at a moment's notice— volcanic eruptions wait for no one. And don't forget a family emergency communication plan and have places where separated family members can meet.

+ Stock up on emergency supplies such as water and canned food; a first aid kit; flashlight and extra batteries; appropriate clothes; battery-powered radios; and cash, credit cards, and critical medicines.

+ Obtain a pair of goggles and a disposable breathing mask

(similar to what surgeons wear) for each member of the household—especially if you live near a place with fallout like Mount St. Helens. Remember the photos of people downwind from the volcanic plume after the 1980 eruption? There were so many breathing masks the entire town looked like a surgeon's convention.

What do you do during an eruption? Here are a few hints:

✦ Follow any evacuation order issued by emergency authorities. Do not stay at home and wait out the eruption. It is too dangerous. This is hot lava or lung-choking ash we're talking about. And in spite of what the actors did in the movie *Dante's Inferno*, you cannot outrun or out-drive an erupting volcano right in your own backyard. That's why they call it fiction.

✦ Avoid areas that are downwind of the volcano—that's where the dust and ash will fall.

✦ If you're caught indoors during an eruption, close all windows, dampers, and doors, put all your outdoor machinery inside a barn or garage, and bring livestock and other animals into closed shelters.

✦ If you're caught outdoors during an eruption, try to get indoors, if at all possible. If you are in a car, turn off the engine and try to get inside as soon as possible. If you are caught in a rockfall, protect your head by rolling into a ball with your arms around your head. Try, too, to avoid low-lying areas where poisonous gases can collect and/or flash floods may occur. Be especially aware of mudflows. These rivers of mud move faster than you can walk or run, and they are most dangerous in stream channels. Do not attempt to cross a bridge if a mudflow is approaching or moving beneath it— the power of the flow will often quickly destroy the structure.

✦ Don't linger around to watch a volcano erupt. A lateral blast can travel many miles—and flatten you faster than a toothpick in the wind. Get far away as quickly as possible.

Volcanic Oscars

If they gave Oscars for the best performance of a volcano, there would be too many contenders. After all, there more than six hundred potentially active volcanoes around the world at any given time. Which volcano would get the award for "most explosive volcano of the eons"? No one knows. Perhaps it was millions of years ago during the reign of the dinosaurs, or even before. Thanks to the rock records, we know there was a great deal of major volcanic activity in our past. And what star would be willing to give out these volcanic awards? Not many—there are probably few Vestal Virgins left in Hollywood.

Here is our shortlist for the Volcanic Oscar Awards. Which volcano would win the tallest? Right now, Mauna Loa on Hawaii is the tallest, reaching 13,677 feet from the ocean bottom to the peak. The winners for the most destructive or deadliest eruptions (in order of destruction) are: Mount Tambora, Indonesia, April 5, 1815; Krakatau, Indonesia, August 26, 1883; and Mount Pelée, Martinique, August 30, 1902. The most recent deadliest eruption award goes to Nevado del Ruiz in Columbia, where on November 13, 1985, the sleeping giant awoke.

Amazingly, the warmth of the eruption melted the mountain's snowcap—resulting in a *lahar*, a six- to fifteen-foot-high slurry of volcanic ash and soil (not to mention boulders and large rocks it picks up along the way). In all its fury, Nevado del Ruiz killed twenty-three thousand people in Amero, a city about two miles below the summit—a tragic catastrophe.

Finally, our Volcanic Oscar for "making it past all that flak" goes to the pilot of an Australian airliner on January 21, 1951. As the plane flew over Mount Lamington in Papua New Guinea, the dormant volcano—and scientists were unaware it was anything but dormant—suddenly blew, sending pumice and stone thirty-six thousand feet into the air. The pilot kept control, even though the hot rocks pounded against the plane's wings and fuselage. He managed to get the aircraft to safety—but can you imagine being on that plane? "Folks, this is your captain speaking. We'll be experiencing some . . . er . . . turbulence heading our way. Ignore the hot lava slamming into your windows. Oh, and is there a volcanologist on board?"

After an eruption, keep calm. Listen to your battery-powered radio or television for the latest emergency information. If you must go outside:

✦ Stay away from volcanic ashfall, and don't drive in heavy ashfall. It can clog up your engine and stall your vehicle. For that matter, don't run any outdoor machine, if possible.

✦ Cover your mouth and nose to avoid inhaling ash. Wear goggles to protect your eyes and keep your skin covered to avoid burns or irritation from the ash. If you have a respiratory ailment, avoid contact with ash and stay indoors until health officials advise it is safe to go outdoors.

✦ If at all possible, clear your roof of ashfall. It can be very heavy and can cause buildings to collapse.

And finally, if the city council wants to rename your town Pompeii—move.

Volcanoes Again:
Smoldering in a Backyard Near You

Picture tending your cornfield in central Mexico on a hot, sunny day. All of the sudden, something starts smoldering in the field. As it grows larger, it gets even hotter. Suddenly, your cornfield is gone—but you're the hit of the town. No one else has a volcano in *their* backyard. That's how the cinder cone called Paricutín was born back in 1943. The volcano never reached the size of a Mount Fuji in Japan or Mount Kilimanjaro in East Africa. It reached only 1,345 feet—but with long, extensive lava fields around it. Most of the ash, cinders, and lava were produced in its first few years; then it fizzled out in 1952.

Now think about hot spots. By this we mean places where volcanoes occur that are not on crustal plate boundaries, but in the middle of a crustal plate. Many scientists believe this is where a magma plume forms close to the surface, then shows itself as either volcanoes or eruptions of water or steam.

There are two other perfect hot spot examples. The first is the

Hawaiian Islands—volcanic islands built on a conveyor belt. Yes, "Paradise" was formed when the Pacific Ocean crustal plate rode over a hot spot that spit out enough lava to form the islands. The results are a string of small islands and submerged seamounts (volcanoes with their heads worn off) stretching out for about thirty-seven hundred miles. At the top of the hot-spot chain, Kure and Midway formed about 27.7 million years ago; the northwesternmost inhabited Hawaiian Island started about 5.5 million years ago; the most current, growing "island" is still about six thousand feet above the seafloor and close to the surface—Loihi, a young volcano building up southeast of Hawaii.

The second example is Yellowstone National Park in Wyoming. In this idyllic land, groundwater is heated by the close-to-the-surface magma. This action causes the periodical release of steam in the form of Old Faithful (about every fifty to one hundred minutes, faithfully) and about 150 to 200 other geysers in the park. There are also bubbling pools of mineral muck called mud pots and just over one hundred percolating hot springs. Dig down about 250 feet and you'll find temperatures in excess of 400°F (204°C). And if you have

This is the volcanic cinder cone Paricutín that grew in a farmer's backyard. (National Geophysical Data Center)

Why You Shouldn't Go Back Anymore

Some folks who apparently had extra time on their hands counted the number killed by volcanoes in recorded history. The number came to about 275,000 people, according to a scientist with the National Museum of Natural History in Washington, D.C.[15] But there was more. Each of the past three centuries has shown a doubling of fatal eruptions. Add that to this fact: Recent decades averaged only about three such eruptions per year. Population growth is one culprit—but there is another.

Yes, many victims succumbed to pyroclastic flows—those hot plasma flows that travel down the slopes of a volcano like a hurricane. Even volcanic-induced tsunamis killed people over the years. But the researchers also discovered something strange: Although many

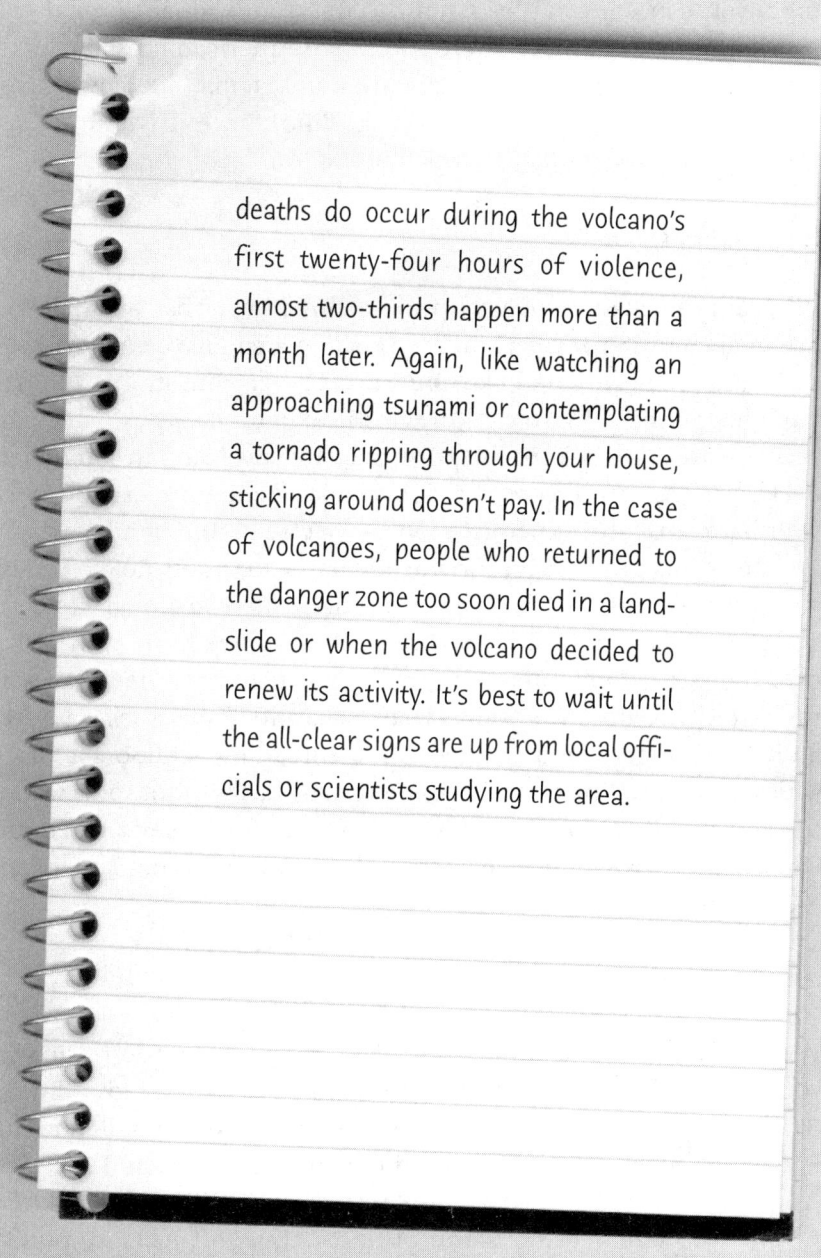

deaths do occur during the volcano's first twenty-four hours of violence, almost two-thirds happen more than a month later. Again, like watching an approaching tsunami or contemplating a tornado ripping through your house, sticking around doesn't pay. In the case of volcanoes, people who returned to the danger zone too soon died in a landslide or when the volcano decided to renew its activity. It's best to wait until the all-clear signs are up from local officials or scientists studying the area.

time, you can count at least ten thousand individual thermal features in the park. This is where the North American crustal plate is riding over an active continental chunk of magma; the Snake River volcanic plain is an earlier offspring. One day, tourists at Yellowstone may get more than they bargained for.

Judging the Danger

What are the chances of a volcano starting in your backyard? If you live in an active or formerly active volcanic area, maybe a bit higher than someone living on Lake Ontario. (Then again, stranger things have happened.) In volcanic regions, magma can push through weak fissures or cracks in the crust, creating a volcano in someone's backyard. (And you were concerned about someone else's dog in your backyard!) Informed caution is what we recommend.

Hot spots are a different story. What's the good news? Unless you're in a hot-spot area, there shouldn't be too much concern about volcanic dangers. Only about 122 hot spots have been active over the past 10 million years—including such renowned places as the Azores, Reunion, Easter, Galapagos, and Canary Islands. Iceland—the huge island located on a spreading seafloor, a place where two crustal plates are ripping apart—has two hot spots where the lava keeps coming. Not only do these places take centuries upon centuries to grow, but they represent less than 1 percent of all Earth's volcanic activity.

Minimizing the Danger

We're going to tell you up front: If there is a volcano growing in your own backyard, just move. Contrary to what you read in books or see in the movies, you, the local sheriff, the town councilmen, the Federal Bureau of Investigation, the National Guard, and the U.S. Army will not stop a volcano with growth on its mind. Just ask the people who watched the island of Surtsey, just off Iceland, punch through the ocean in 1963. It kept growing until 1967.

What about a hot spot? Pay attention to your local volcanologist or geologist if he or she says the carbon dioxide readings or temperature of the local waters are quickly rising. For those of you who scout the oceans, start thinking in terms of your future: If you spot an island growing above a hot spot on the ocean floor, see if you can buy the soon-to-be prime real estate before the natives find out. Your island may need to cool off for a few hundred or thousand years, depending on the size—but your progeny will thank you for buying an investment that grows.

THE DOWNSIDE OF DOWNSLIDES

Landslides: Soil in a Slump

It was not the first rumbling in the city of Seattle—but it had been a while. In March 2001, a fault zone thirty miles below the Olympic Peninsula slipped, resulting in an earthquake that measured 6.7 on the Richter scale. The Seattle quiver was in the same ballpark as the 1994 Northridge quake in Los Angeles—but much less intense than the 1989 quake in San Francisco that measured 7.1 on the scale. There was property damage—about $1 billion worth—including one problem that often strikes areas shaken by a quake: A huge landslide took a giant bite out of Highway 101 in eastern Washington.

Earthquakes aren't the only way to shake some soil. In April 1999, villagers living below Lake Kasu in Papua New Guinea said the lake exploded. Scientists knew the lake was at the top of a dormant volcano—one that had been asleep for ten thousand years. Researchers visited the site and found what they suspected. It wasn't an eruption, but a massive landslide that nearly emptied the lake—and created a landslide-induced tsunami wave about fifty feet high. Not only did the wave knock down houses and trees in its path, but it left a huge mudslide in its wake. Eleven people were seriously injured, with one resulting death.

Judging the Danger

Landslides can form anywhere and anytime—especially around loose soil or steep slopes. Along a creek near the authors' own backyard, there are several spots where waterlogged soil—mostly unconsolidated sediment left over from Ice Age glaciers—has slipped down the steeper slopes. Add an earthquake or volcano nearby and we bet some of our land might be traveling downstream in a big hurry. Or add another El Niño–type year of torrential rains and we could say good-bye to our friendly sediment.

Not only do torrential rains bring landslides, but so do other circumstances. Slides occur in places that have high bluffs—broad, rounded cliff faces that overlook a plain or body of water, such as along the Mississippi and Missouri Rivers. Wildfires can wipe out soil-hugging vegetation, giving rains a good chance to cause landslides and debris flows; this occurs most frequently in western states, such as Colorado, New Mexico, and California. Steep coastal and high mountain areas are also prime targets for slides—along with earthquake-prone areas, such as coastal California. You may want to consider this you're riding along Highway 1 during a downpour.

But volcanoes wrote the cookbook on landslides. First, volcanic slopes are usually very steep and highly unstable—after all, most of the deposits come from the air in bits and pieces, so most volcanoes are just piles of rock and rubble. Add the fact that volcanic rocks weather to clay rather quickly, making the slopes that much more slippery. Next, the top layer is always being broken down by sulfuric acid belching from the volcano. Finally, throw in a snowpack on top—one that melts at the first sign of eruption—and you have a great recipe for disaster.

A great example of highly populated areas in danger of landslides are the housing developments spreading east from Seattle toward Mount Rainier. Sure, there are the occasional quakes, but there are also volcanoes, with their accompanying steep slopes and lakes. Take away vegetation and expose the ground to water (which is plentiful in that part of the country) as housing developments do, and the area becomes a natural slip-and-slide.

Minimizing the Danger

Who should pay attention to landslides? Everyone. According to the United States Geological Survey, landslides occur in all fifty states and all U.S. territories—with at least half of the states suffering significant landslide problems. The slides can cost between $1 to $2 billion annually, wreaking havoc along highway and railroad lines, destroying homes, wrecking utility lines, polluting rivers and streams, and even covering up animal habitats. Worldwide, they cause about six hundred deaths annually, with twenty-five to fifty occurring in the United States.[16]

For those near smaller landslide sites, there are some steps being taken to ward off disaster. In our area, town transportation workers try to stabilize the steeper slopes with rip-rap (large stones often contained in wire to stabilize the slope); retaining walls (if the area is small); vegetation (like crown vetch); or filling in with more sediment (which doesn't work in some soils—rain causes gullies that take away much of the loose soil). For an even smaller site in your backyard, vegetation—from trees and smaller shrubs to thick-rooted flowers or ground cover—or retaining walls are the best bet.

For people near dangerous landslide areas, keep alert. And here are a few hints adapted from the Federal Emergency Management Agency (FEMA) on how to tell if a landslide may be heading your way:[17]

✦ If doors or windows stick or jam suddenly, or new cracks appear in your foundation, brick, plaster, or tiles. Watch, too, if sidewalks, porches, outside walls, or patios suddenly start pulling away from a building (this is definitely different than frost heave).

✦ If you notice some developing cracks in the ground, sidewalk, or street that slowly widen. Or if your fence, retaining walls, utility poles, or trees begin to tilt or move.

✦ If underground utilities or water pipes suddenly break or rupture (although this could also be from old age or other problems).

✦ If you see ground bulging at the base of a slope—this could indicate the toe of the landslide.

The Toll of Tumbling Rocks

Some scenic views can turn into a nightmare—and there's really no way to tell when. Sometimes all it takes is a few ancient rocks and several days of rain; other times, it's a clear, sunny sky and just weathered rocks. A landslide can occur when you least expect it—and in the nicest places. True or false?

For those of you who said true, you're right. One common place to watch rocks fall—albeit from a distance, please—is Yosemite Valley.[18] Here, the natural cracking and shearing of the rocks make the views breathtaking. But at the same time, it makes certain areas and hiking trails that much more dangerous. Back in June 1999, about 525 tons of falling rock fell near Curry Village at Yosemite National Park, killing one rock climber and injuring several others. In fact, employee housing in the valley continues to be threatened by rock slides—and the entire valley lies on the debris of prehistoric rockfalls. The place was carved by glaciers, with the bowl-shaped valley surrounded by walls of pure granite. (Living up to its heritage, the park's Glacier Point was the site of the most recent rockfalls.) But granite weathers over time—physically and chemically—causing rocks to fall. And no amount of planning will change that natural geologic fact.

As with most natural hazards, the only way to keep track of these scenic but sometimes nasty places is through monitoring—especially using global positioning systems (GPS) to determine sudden or slight movements along potential land-slide sites. And for you who travel, hike, or enjoy the wilderness, the best way to stay safe in these areas is to pay attention to the warnings issued by park personnel. They get their information from the scientists with the spiffy GPS devices.

✦ If you hear faint rumbling that increases in volume, it may be a landslide. If you're close, the ground may start shifting in a downslope direction.

If you find yourself in a landslide, FEMA says to stay in the building if you're already inside and take cover under a desk, table, or other sturdy furniture. If you're outside, it doesn't mean you'll have to hike with a football helmet on. First, try to get out of the path of the mudflow or landslide and head for the higher ground. If you can't get out of the way fast enough, run for a large barrier— a group of trees or a building—that can protect you from the flowing mud and debris. And if you can't do any of the above, curl into a tight ball and protect your head.

But here, too, as with most things in life, luck and logic often prevail. The best way to protect yourself from landslides is to stay away from slide areas.

OCEAN AND CLIMATE FEARS

Who was it who compared the earth to a bathtub without the rubber ducky?

Our planet is a water planet—more accurately, an ocean planet. Over 75 percent of the earth's surface is water, giving it the characteristic blue color when viewed from outer space. The ocean produces food for us, generates our weather, and controls our climate; it provides coastal places to live and makes a great vacation destination. Right now, nearly two-thirds of the world's population live along the oceans; by 2025, there will be some 6.3 billion humans living along the narrow coastal belts of the world. That will put smiles on the faces of people with beachfront property.

Or will it?

All is not always rosy at that beachfront property. By their very nature, the oceans contain many hidden dangers for land-dwellers. The waves pound relentlessly, eroding the beaches and tearing apart—either gradually or all at once—structures we try to build. Oceans flood coasts, especially during hurricane and cyclone seasons. Most of us are viewed by many ocean animals as food. The oceans also control our climate, something that seems so stable, so eternal, but can actually be enormously hazardous—and maybe more so in the near future.

Face it. We're the interlopers in the watery world. We can be either fodder for a sharp-eyed shark or the number one recreational target for jellyfish. It's time we realized it.

THE OCEAN IN ACTION

Rip Currents:
The Riptides That Bind—and Hurt

Rip currents are silent killers needing only a nice breeze, perpendicular to the shore, to get them stirred. Add the winds and water from a hurricane and they can become more of a danger. We've all heard about swimmers and surfers caught by a relentless riptide along many coastal surf areas. It's estimated that 80 percent of all water rescues across the nation are precipitated by rip currents. And in Florida alone, more people are killed annually by rip currents than hurricanes, tornadoes, and lightning combined. Maybe it *is* a good thing to be a landlubber.

Judging the Danger

We have all sorts of names for rip currents—*riptides, rips, run-outs,* and the erroneous term *undertows.* No matter what you name them, they are always the same: strong, narrow surface currents of water that usually flow from inside a near-shore sand bar into deeper water. They occur when opposing currents swirl together, then flow seaward. Contrary to popular belief, the rip current doesn't drag a person underwater, but moves them—about twice as fast as a walking pace—into deeper water. It's there where people panic and try to swim directly toward the shore. Eventually exhausted, the swimmer can drown. Even strong swimmers or people who can touch the bottom and try walking back have no luck against the moving water.

A Most (Un)Charming Rogue

If there's one way to ruin your day at the beach, it's getting washed out to sea unexpectedly. No way, you say. You'll just hike along the beach with your dog, Spot, and not even go near the water. In fact, you won't even be near the water's edge. It doesn't matter. But remember—sometimes Nature likes to send a larger than normal wave crashing against the shore, sweeping unsuspecting hikers and seashell seekers out to sea. Just for a change of pace, no doubt.

These large waves are known as *sneaker waves*—aka *rogue waves*—and have nothing to do with your Nikes.[1] These sneakers can appear with little or no warning, even when the ocean appears calm. A number of interacting factors cause the huge waves: Waves from faraway storms encountering areas of shoaling; strong currents flowing out of harbors that amplify incoming waves; under-

[continued on next page]

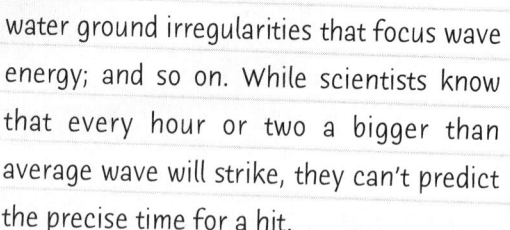

water ground irregularities that focus wave energy; and so on. While scientists know that every hour or two a bigger than average wave will strike, they can't predict the precise time for a hit.

How do you prevent you or Spot from taking an unexpected sea cruise? First, be aware that sneaker waves exist. Second, find out if your chosen destination has a history of these types of waves. Local rangers, park service personnel, or the local Coast Guard are just some of the sources you can consult. Keep a watchful eye on the conditions of the ocean at all times. Be knowledgeable of the tides, and realize that times of high surf and high tides call for extra precautions. And don't let a sneaker get the jump on you—so never turn your back to the ocean. Even a second or two advance notice may give you time to head for safety.

Minimizing the Danger

The best way not to come in contact with these strong currents is to stay away from the deepest water—just wade or gaze at the ocean from afar. Pick sea shells along the sandy beach. Read a book under your beach umbrella. But don't go in the water.

But this isn't practical for those of us who like to cool off in seawater. Here are a few hints while on the beach:[2]

+ Pay attention to the signs. That means obeying posted warning signal flags, signs, or other displays. Listen to the beach patrol personnel or lifeguards; there's a reason they're called "lifeguards"—because they know the warning signs. For instance, rip currents often show up at the surface as a brown-colored plume, foam, bubbles, or a stretch of seaweed extending seaward from the breakers. They can also be identified by the lower height of the breaking waves.

+ *If you do come in contact with a rip current:* Most deaths from rip currents occur when people panic and try to swim toward shore. This only causes the swimmer to become exhausted. In such cases, Nature wins. She has the stronger currents against the swimmer's puny breast stroke. So *don't panic.* At this point, you can wave your arms in the air and call for help—but it will take most lifeguards time to get out there. So again, *don't panic.* Because the current is normally about only ten to thirty yards wide, swim or wade parallel to the beach, across the current. Then, when the tug of the current dissipates, swim toward shore at an angle away from the current. Another way is to float with the rip current—most extend about fifty to two hundred yards offshore—beyond the breakers. Again, when the current weakens, swim back to shore at an angle away from the current.

Beach Erosion: There Goes the Neighborhood

The beach. Those two words are often spoken with a sigh or a smile—or both. It means sun, surf, and sand. It means time off for most people, and huge mansions with scenic views for celebrities. It also means a place where more than one-half of the U.S. population live and work within fifty miles of the coastline, which represents only around 11 percent of the nation's land. And it's those people who plunk down a house on the beach that often get the biggest surprise: watching their beach change—and their beach house wash out into the sea.

Beach erosion is nothing new. It's been going on since before the dinosaurs roamed Gondwanaland. It's Nature again, moving not just one sand grain at a time—but a gazillion all over the world. After all, Nature is the ultimate exterior designer. Take some of the places she's worked over: She's stripped beaches in southern California of sand, and some are already down to the bare rock. Humans have helped, too—replacement sand originally came from river sediment, but damming and water removal have cut off much of the supply. Then there's part of the North Carolina coast where over the years, Nature has worn away about 1,300 feet of beach. With the waves only 150 feet away, the 208-foot tall Cape Hatteras Lighthouse—there since 1870—recently had to be moved back about a quarter mile.

The nor'easter of *The Perfect Storm* fame breached a seawall in Monmouth Beach, New Jersey, in October 1991. (U.S. Army Corps of Engineers)

And don't forget the recent estimates: About 328 miles of sandy beaches—about 40 percent of the 825 miles along Florida's Atlantic and Gulf coasts—are classified as critically eroded.[3] The list goes on.

Judging the Danger

Sure, geologists tell us how sundry items on the earth gradually move over time. But there are always exceptions, like erupting volcanoes, earthquakes—and beach erosion. In almost a geologic nanosecond—or literally overnight—a beach can change. The quickest way to ruin a beach is by a major storm, longshore drift (currents parallel to a coastline), and sand pulled into deep water by natural water erosion. Heracleitus of Ephesus (c.540–480 B.C.E.), the Greek philosopher and pantheist, once said, "No one can step twice into the same river, nor touch mortal substance twice in the same condition." Maybe he really meant a beach.

One of the biggest culprits in beach erosion comes all at once in the form of huge storms—hurricanes, nor'easters, typhoons, or cyclones, depending on the beach location. Hurricane Floyd slammed into the coast of North Carolina in September 1999, not long after Hurricane Dennis had made its mark. Both destroyed sixty-five buildings between Currituck and Sunset Beach, and dragged tons of sand out to sea. And during the famous El Niño times—when the waters off the South American coast are warm enough to change worldwide weather patterns—storms can be devastating. During a harsh 1992 storm near Westhampton, New York, seawater broke through a barrier island, destroying about 190 of the area's 246 homes. The long, man-made barriers (called *groins*) erected along the shore didn't help—in fact, they probably helped cause the breakthrough.

Minimizing the Danger

Not all beach erosion is bad. It really is Nature's way of moving sand around to produce beaches, dunes, and highly productive (in terms of wildlife and plantlife) estuaries and bays. And as we all know, they're great places to get a good shot of sunshine, fresh air, and saltwater taffy.

If you do find yourself watching your backyard beach drift out to sea, there may be little you can do about it. Putting in a groin or beach barrier may help stabilize your beach, but it might erode the property next to yours. Grass will hold sand to a point, but becomes less effective the closer you get to the water. Pumping beach sand from the deep water to your beach is also an act in futility; the waves will have an easy time eroding the loose sand away. There is hope, albeit mostly temporary, as Nature always wins: Several states, such as North Carolina and Florida, have special state agencies that deal with such problems, and they are trying to find solutions. And as with the Cape Hatteras Lighthouse, sometimes the only solution is to retreat.

Beach Waste: Down at the Seashore, Picking Sea Syringes

It's a beautiful day at the beach. You unload the minivan while the kids run to the water's edge to explore. Sometimes living near the shore does have its advantages. And it's early enough to avoid the crowds, too. In fact, there's no one else on the beach as you spread the blankets and set up the chairs. Suddenly, one of the kids screams in pain and you run toward her. She's sitting down in the sand, crying and holding her foot. A syringe has punctured it. As you carry her back to the van, you finally notice signs saying the beach is closed due to "medical waste hazard."

Going to the shore used to be a way to relax and recharge. Beaches were clean and safe. But now it's often like visiting a wartorn country. Is the water polluted with human fecal waste bacteria—leading to illness? Is pesticide runoff from farms far inland draining into the water, causing serious diseases? Are there any viruses (from who knows where) that can infect you with potentially fatal consequences? And what about the junk you can step on—like the syringes on a typical day at South Beach in Staten Island, New York, during the late 1980s? Oil washed up from tanker spills seems almost benign in comparison—as long as you're not a shorebird or marine mammal.

So THAT'S Where We Left the Beemer

There are people who understand how we're all trashing our beaches—and they want to help. Some participate in the International Coastal Cleanup—an annual one-day event in which thousands of volunteers worldwide clean up the international shorelines.[4] Approximately 350,000 people pick up millions of pounds of debris from more than forty-five hundred beaches, underwater sites, lakeshores, and riverbanks. The type and amount of debris collected goes into a data bank, where it is used to educate the public and politicians (who we all hope will do something to help alleviate the problem).

What types of items are normally found washed up on shorelines? About 60 percent of the articles originate on land. They include common items such as plastic bottles, straws, metal bottle caps, and cigarette butts. The shoreline waste hunters have also found tires, lumber, syringes, fishing line, car parts, and glass bottles. More unusual items have included a chemical gas mask, a female mannequin, a BMW sedan, and a baby carriage filled with books. Go figure.

Judging the Danger

Coastline pollution comes from a large number of sources, such as storm water runoff, sewage treatment plant malfunctions, and sewer overflow. Each year, sixty-eight thousand tons of toxic metals and fifty-seven thousand tons of toxic organic chemicals from approximately 160,000 factories are dumped into the coastal waters of the United States. Sewage treatment plants annually add about 5.9 trillion gallons of wastewater into these waters. Don't forget oil—3.25 million tons of it drop into the ocean each year. Most it comes from street runoff—just add up all the drips of oil from motor vehicles. And add a few more items to the ocean dump equation: major cities that produce large amounts of garbage and sewage, farm pesticides, and ship spills of oil or waste can make it to our oceans.[5]

Anyone who thinks mathematically can see that the problem is huge. In the United States alone, only 10 percent of the coastline is tested regularly for polluted water—but this results in more than twenty-five hundred beach closures each year. It's enough to make you wonder about the other 90 percent.

And most of the time, we have met the enemy, and he is us. Take the coastal waters at the mouths of the major rivers in southern California: There may be a potentially harmful human virus lurking at these sites.[6] Although a recent study hasn't determined if this human adenovirus is virulent, it *is* considered a pathogen—and a member of a enteric virus group that includes hepatitis A. When ingested, this virus can attack the respiratory system or gastrointestinal tract, resulting in diarrhea, fever, sore throat, and nausea (but it is not hepatitis A). The really bad part? The very presence of this virus means human waste is making its way into the waterways and the shore. Normally, it's the measured fecal bacteria levels that indicate the presence of human waste and trigger beach closings. But this virus is showing up where bacteria counts are low, meaning no beaches close—and people are being exposed to health risks. More than one hundred viruses found in human waste survive as long as 130 days in seawater—which might make you want to bring along a water filter with your beach umbrella. And presently, no one routinely tests for this or many other viruses.

Minimizing the Danger

How can you find out if your day at the beach will be like *Baywatch* or *The Toxic Avenger*? Here are a few hints:

+ Recently, an annual National Health Protection Survey of Beaches has been instituted to monitor the quality of U.S. coastal waters, with government agencies collecting information on local beach health. These results are published by the Environmental Protection Agency and can be viewed on the Internet.[7]
+ Call the town you'll be visiting—but not the chamber of commerce. The best place to call is the sheriff or county offices. They should usually be aware if there are any closings.
+ Use your own judgment, too. Keep an eye on your kids at the beach. Don't let them stick anything in their mouths. If you find anything that looks like waste on a shoreline, let someone know about it. You may help yourself and many people from getting ill from a day at the beach.

OCEAN PARTY ANIMALS AND PLANTS

Jellyfish and Stingrays:
Reach Out and Sting Someone

Sometimes Nature plays tricks on us. She can make something deadly appear beautiful and innocent, or hide it under the sand where it can attack the unwary. We're talking about jellyfish and stingrays, respectively. But there's no worry, because you're not planning on any deep-sea diving. You're sticking close to shore. Maybe you'll do a little swimming, a little wading. No danger, right? Unfortunately, you don't have to go into the deep ocean to find these dangerous creatures. They can come right to you—and really mess up a day at the beach.

During a recent Memorial Day weekend at beaches in Orange

County, California, more than one hundred people were stung by sea nettles washed close to shore.[8] Some of these jellyfish were almost two feet in diameter with ten-foot tentacles. These people were fortunate, experiencing only itchy welts where the nettles stung. If they had encountered other species of jellyfish, there could have been more serious problems: The deadly sea wasp (*Chiromex fleckerit*) is among the most venomous of marine creatures. Found in the warm Pacific and Indian Ocean waters, this creature can kill you with only minimal contact. If a victim survives, he has to endure extreme pain and significant scarring. The Portuguese man-of-war is the most well known of these creatures—although technically, it's not a true jellyfish, but a very close cousin. The tentacles give a powerful, painful sting and can cause a fatal shock to humans. Again, the unlucky survivor gets to endure excruciating pain.

Around the same Memorial Day weekend, approximately twenty swimmers along Santa Monica, California, beaches were stung by stingrays. It must have been a convention: The creatures were no doubt resting on the shallow ocean bottom, submerged in sand—then stung people who accidentally stepped on them. In this case, it's best to let resting stingrays lie—undisturbed.

Judging the Danger

It may be hard to believe, but jellyfish are members of the same group as those beautiful corals (some of which also have a few dangerous secrets of their own) and cute sea anemones. Jellyfish drift idly along with the currents, their pulsing, mushroom-shaped bodies composed of almost 95 percent water. Long tentacles hang from their bodies, many with stinging cells that sting prey; afterward, the jellyfish pulls the poor sucker to its main body for digestion. Jellyfish venom, typically a neurotoxin, is found inside their tentacles in tiny mechanisms called nematocysts. These tiny tube-like projections filled with venom shoot out like cannons when prey comes by—including us, if we don't watch it. Thank ocean currents for that one—they often bring large numbers of jellyfish close to shore, where swimmers usually get stung. From there, waves bring

Jellyfish floating under Arctic ice. (OAR/ National Undersea Research Program)

the creatures into the surf zone and wash them up onto the beach, creating a hazard for humans wading or strolling along the shore.

When it comes to stingrays, they may look like innocent, flying diamond shapes, but not always. These marine creatures are in the same group as sharks and skates, but they differ from the other fish. The stingrays gently glide through the water with "wings" that are actually large pectoral fins on each side of the flattened body. They can be small or huge compared to a swimming human—ranging in size from one to five feet in diameter. And, of course, they retaliate when stepped on—the most common way humans get jabbed by stingrays.

What are the consequences of an up close and personal encounter with a jellyfish or stingray? Jellyfish tentacles can lay multiple stings on you, injecting their venom into your body. Your body's responses depend on the species of the jellyfish. You can end up with a mild itch, severe burning, excruciating pain, scarring, or trouble breathing. You might even end up dead. As for stingrays, certain species have a whiplike, stinging, poisonous tail with one or more sharp, barbed spines. The tail can cause deep wounds, profuse bleeding, and long-lasting extreme pain and swelling. As noted, some species of stingrays even deliver a fatal dose of venom.

Minimizing the Danger

How can you avoid getting stung by a jellyfish or stingray? Here are some hints:

+ The most simple advice is to avoid them. Check out the waters near the beach for signs of jellyfish. Ask the local lifeguards or marine safety officers if there are jellyfish in the area.

+ Keep alert when in the water, and look for signs of these creatures. Get out of the water immediately if you see one. See if you can get someone to determine whether the creature is poisonous. If no one is around, don't take a chance. Play in the sand instead.

+ Don't play with any stingray or jellyfish washed up on shore. They can still sting.

+ If you do get stung by a jellyfish, rinse the wound immediately with seawater, but don't rub it. Use a towel to apply a paste of salt water and sand or baking soda to any attached tentacles, then scrape them off. There are numerous concoctions, homemade and commercial, that will help to neutralize the poison. Some people recommend rubbing alcohol, vinegar, or meat tenderizer dissolved in salt water.

+ Unfortunately, stingrays are pretty good at hiding—until you step on one. In shallow water, shuffle your feet on the bottom. This will scare off any stingrays lying around. If you do get stung, wash out the wound with cold salt water, then use a towel to get out any spines still stuck in the wound. Soak the wound in very hot (approximately 105°F) water for at least thirty minutes. This will help break down the poison.

+ Seek medical treatment if you are stung—just to be on the safe side.

+ Consider taking your next vacation in the mountains.

Other Venomous Animals:
Not Quite Love Potion #9

Nothing beats wading in tide pools or diving down to coral reefs.
The diversity of life in the ocean is amazing. But just because there
are no large (and well-publicized) animals such as sharks hanging
around doesn't mean there is no danger lurking. Some of the most
deadly ocean animals are smaller and less well known—normally
hiding or staying camouflaged. The animals' poisons are usually
reserved for self-defense or to catch prey. Some bite, some impale,
and others use *nematocysts* (stinging capsules) to inject toxic substances into their hapless victims. Venom can come from anywhere—certain species of fish, some sea urchins, starfish, octopus,
and invertebrates such as fire coral and stinging seaweed.
Remember, these animals live in a harsh environment; in the ocean,
it's eat or be eaten. And that little organism has no idea that all you
want to do is take a closer look.

What can happen should you be unfortunate enough to interact
with one of these animals? The symptoms and consequences
depend on the species, but can include excruciating pain, swelling,
neuromuscular paralysis, heart failure, nausea, vomiting, or of
course, death. Not exactly what you originally had in mind while
innocently poking around at low tide.

Judging the Danger

Although we can't list every single venomous ocean fish in the sea—
the list would be a book in itself—we can tell you about a few of
these animals. Creatures in this list represent Nature's way of saying
"stay away":

✦ *Stonefish.* Don't even think about going near a stonefish. It has
   great camouflage—like an innocent stone lying on the ocean
   bottom. These warty-looking fish found in the Pacific and
   Indian Oceans and off Australia aren't normally aggressive;
   they only sting in self-defense. If the stonefish senses danger, it

raises its back and fin spines—bad for an unwary human who accidentally steps on the fish. The poison—enough to kill one thousand mice—causes excruciating pain over several hours, and can be accompanied by the swelling and death of tissues. The venom is often fatal if not properly treated.

+ *Scorpion fish.* Though not as deadly, some of the 330 species of scorpion fish can pack a wallop of a sting. Some look like rocks—and all have venomous spines. Included in this group are the lionfish, devilfish, and red rock cod.

+ *Octopus.* Not all octopi are bad. But there is a very small octopus found in tidal pools and shallow tropical waters that should be avoided at all costs: the blue-ringed octopus. It may only be about an inch to eight inches in size, and its bite may be painless—but it injects a neuromuscular-paralyzing venom. Nerve conduction is blocked, causing neuromuscular paralysis—then death. A victim might live if artificial respiration is begun before the major symptoms develop, but if you're alone . . .

+ *Cone shells.* Yes, some of the four hundred species of beautiful, multicolored cone shells—they really do look like small cones—may be dangerous. So try resisting the temptation to pick up these creatures along the seashore unless you've done your homework and know something about the species. Long favored by shell collectors, some cone shell occupants can inject venom, but only a few are really dangerous—including the textile cone. (The venom used to shoot the dinosaurs in the movie *Jurassic Park: The Lost World* was from a textile cone.) The snails and slugs that live in these shelly homes roam around the ocean floor looking for food. If one spots a good enough morsel—and unfortunately, a human hand can be included on the menu—the animal shoots out a venom-packed, barbed harpoon, hooking into and poisoning its prey. This could result in excruciating pain, paralysis, and respiratory failure, depending on the species encountered.

+ *Sea urchins.* Sea urchins are usually encountered in tidal pools or just below the low-tide line. The venomous spines of some sea urchins inflict mild to severe pain for a few hours. Contrary to some folklore, sea urchins don't throw their spines or leap on people as they pass; you actually have to pick up the little urchin or step on it to get stung. If pieces of the spine are left in the wound, a months-long infection is possible. Fatalities are rare—but several, including the flower-spined sea urchin, are highly poisonous. If you get stung, it's best to see a doctor as soon as possible.

✦ *Crown-of-thorns starfish.* Another animal whose spine pieces should be removed from any wound is the crown-of-thorns starfish. This animal is often found around coral reefs and measures almost twenty-five inches diameter, with thirteen to sixteen hard, sharp, spine-covered arms. Symptoms from its venom include severe pain for a number of hours, bleeding, and possible inflammation for weeks—or even more than six months.

✦ *Invertebrates.* Just because they don't have a backbone doesn't mean you should ignore them. There are certain marine invertebrates to be aware of—many of which have stinging capsules like the jellyfish mentioned in the last section. These nematocysts paralyze prey or are used for self-defense. Take the fire coral: It resembles a coral and is often found on coral reefs. If you get stung by the nematocysts on its microscopic tentacles, you may experience anything from minor irritation to excruciating pain. If it stings a large enough area of your skin, you may experience vomiting and nausea. Or try contact with stinging seaweed, an animal that looks like a fern. Such an encounter may give you pain ranging from mild to unbearable—with itchy pustules lasting for a week or more.

Minimizing the Danger

How can you avoid coming up close and personal with these venomous ocean animals? The best precaution is knowledge. If you're going to be mucking around a tidal pool or on the sea floor, find out beforehand what species of ocean animals in the local area are poisonous. Memorize how they look or take along a field guide.

Know where to find them so you can avoid them. Find out what options are available—including any first aid—should you get bit or stung. Take along a first aid kit with appropriate medication. And don't put off follow-up treatment; get help as soon as possible.

Let's take the highly venomous stonefish. The best way to not get stung is to know where they hide (often in the surge zone, where it anchors itself on rock); wear thick-soled plastic sandals or reef-walking shoes if you're near a known stonefish zone; and walk shuffling your feet to scare the stonefish away. But if you *do* step on this creature, here's the recommended first aid if you can't get to a hospital right away: Remove all pieces of the spines and wash the area with water. Don't stop any bleeding—it will help remove some of the venom. If available, immerse the wound in very, very hot water (not boiling, but as hot as you can stand without scalding) for approximately an hour, or until the pain decreases, with the site of the wound elevated. Then put on a clean dressing. Treat the wound with antibiotics such as bacitracin or neomycin, if available. An injection of an appropriate anesthetic will help reduce the pain. Get to a doctor or hospital as soon as possible—there is such a thing as stonefish antivenom. Now aren't you glad now you did all that research beforehand?

For those pesky invertebrates with nematocysts, it's best to see your doctor here, too. But here are some immediate first aid tips: Gently remove any tentacles still on the skin, then treat the affected area with a local anesthetic spray or ointment to alleviate any pain. Follow-up care includes continuing treatment with anesthetic ointments, and steroidal ointments for severe, longer-term itching.

Or maybe it's best just to watch all Jacques Cousteau specials again. And pay attention this time.

Sharks: We Need a Bigger Boat

The resort vacation was well worth the cost. The beach is fabulous, the sky blue, and the water crystal clear. Perfect for snorkeling. There are fish everywhere—all colors and sizes along the reef. Your loud bathing suit matches many of their colors, and the jewelry you're wearing sparkles and shines in the sunlight. Suddenly, out of the depths, a gray bullet streaks right at you, tearing a chunk of flesh out of your thigh. Blood fills the water. It attacks again, and the pain causes you to lose consciousness. You're fortunate. Nearby boaters pull you out of the water and you wake up in a hospital bed, groggy from blood loss—but still alive and mostly whole. The animal that attacked you was an indigenous tiger shark, smaller but more aggressive than the great white shark of movie fame.

Shark attacks are among the most feared natural marine dangers that can befall a human being. Part of it is realizing you really *are* a potential item on a shark's vast menu—and an item poorly adapted to the water, too. Another reason? You can't control a shark. Humans have hunted, eliminated, or isolated large land predators capable of eating us. But not so with sharks, whose watery world limits our influence on them. They come and go as they please—usually popping up without warning.

Sharks are classified as cartilaginous fish, along with skates, rays, and chimeras. Their skeletons are fibrous; they have paired fins, and jaws evolved from gill arches. These guys are old, too: Modern sharks have probably been around for more than 150 million years—so they know a few things, like how to be supremely adaptable ocean predators. About 370 different types of sharks, both large and small, live in the seas, including the sixgill, dogfish, nurse, dwarf, cookie-cutter, whale shark, and thresher. The vast majority of these sharks are considered harmless to humans—although you probably don't want to taunt them. Any of these sharks can inflict injuries if provoked enough.

Judging the Danger

Shark attacks are like airplane crashes: They're rare, but when it does happen, it can cause extensive injury and sometimes death. In the United States, you're thirty times more likely to be hit by lightning than attacked by a shark. But people do get hit by lightning—and people are attacked by sharks every year.

Unprovoked attacks by sharks come in three different flavors.

The most common type is the "hit and run," in which the victim, usually a surfer or swimmer in the surf zone, is bitten once. The shark is seldom seen and does not return. Scientists think these attacks are cases of mistaken identity under poor visibility, breaking surf, or strong current conditions. Befuddled by these conditions, the shark mistakes the splashing, colorfully swimsuited, and bejeweled human for its normal prey. After one bite, it realizes its tasteless mistake, spits out the victim like a bad-tasting chunk of chicken, and leaves. Such attacks usually leave small lacerations, usually on the leg below the knee.

"Bump and bite" and "sneak" attacks are less common, but they result in much greater injury. Most of the fatalities come from these types of attacks. These involve repeat attacks, with multiple severe wounds. They usually occur in deeper water, but in some areas of the world they occur in shallow water. In the "bump and bite" method, the shark initially circles the victim, many times bumping him or her prior to the attack. "Sneak" attacks, of course, occur without warning. These types of attacks are not the result of mistaken identity, but are feeding or antagonistic behaviors.

What sharks are most dangerous to humans? Although any larger shark (six feet or longer) can be a potential threat, three are the most common attackers of humans: the great white shark (*Carcharodon carcharias*), the bull shark (*Carcharhinus leucas*), and the tiger shark (*Galeocerdo cuvier*). These large sharks are found almost everywhere and normally eat large prey. Other species that attack humans include the shortfin mako (*Isurus oxyrhynchus*), Galapagos (*Carcharhinus galapagensis*), oceanic whitetip (*Carcharhinus longimanus*), great hammerhead (*Sphyrna mokarran*), and some reef sharks. It's hard to pinpoint sharks responsible for "hit and run" attacks, but a large number of species are thought to be involved.[9]

Minimizing the Danger

There are a number of things you can do to minimize your risk of being attacked by a shark. First, swim only on land in a pool. This is not very practical, or fun—and if you're a female there may be other types of "sharks" circling the pool. So here are a few choice hints adapted from the International Shark Attack File (ISAF), a clearinghouse for shark attack information affiliated with the Florida Museum of Natural History.[10] It's useful for those who go in, on, or near the water:

✦ If an area has sharks, don't enter the water. If sharks have been spotted in an area and you are in the water, evacuate immediately! If you do meet up with a shark, don't harass it. They have a definite advantage—they're used to being in the water.

✦ Sharks are more likely to attack a lone individual, so always stay in groups when you're in the water. And while you're at it, don't wander too far from shore. If you need it, assistance will be too far away.

✦ This is one the authors learned in Florida long ago: As we were just about to take a dip in a bay on a hot night in July, a park ranger ran over, yelling for us to stop. That's when we learned that sharks swim at night in certain areas—and can see much better in the water and dark than we can. After all, they do live in, and have learned to adapt to, the oceans. So don't go into the water when sharks are most active—this includes dawn, dusk, and the nighttime hours when some species move inshore to feed.

✦ Sharks like to hang out near steep dropoffs or in the areas between sandbars. Use caution in these areas.

✦ If you have an open wound or, for females, if you are menstruating, don't go into the water. Sharks truly are attracted to blood.

✦ Shiny jewelry is a no-no. Light reflecting off your jewels, gold, and silver resembles the sheen of fish scales—often the usual fare of the shark.

✦ Stay out of waters being used by sport or commercial fishermen, especially if there are signs of feeding activity or bait fish. The presence of diving seabirds is a warning signal that sharks may be in the vicinity, too. Also avoid areas with sewage or known effluents. Although it's not appetizing to us, sharks often find fresh meat (read: fish) hanging out here.

Best Bites

In 2000, the ISAF reported seventy-nine unprovoked shark attacks on humans worldwide. This was both good news and bad news. The good news? It really wasn't too many attacks when you consider the number of people in or near the water worldwide.[11]

The bad news? This was the all-time high for shark attacks since ISAF began gathering statistics in 1958. In contrast, 1999 had fifty-eight reported attacks; the annual average during the 1990s was fifty-four. Helping set this dubious record was an increase in U.S. shark attacks—from thirty-seven in 1999 to fifty-one in 2000. In particular, attacks in Florida increased from twenty-five to thirty-four in the same period, with Volusia County having the most attacks, at twelve. Other states and territories were as follows: North Carolina had five attacks; California had three; Alabama, Hawaii, and Texas each had two; and Louisiana, South Carolina, and Puerto Rico each had one. Worldwide, Australia had seven attacks; South Africa had five; the Bahamas had four; Reunion Island, Papua New Guinea and Tanzania each had two; and there were single attacks recorded in Japan, New Caledonia, Tonga, Kiribati, Fiji, and the Galapagos Islands. Of all these attacks, there were ten fatalities, up from four in 1999. Australia led with three fatalities, while there where two in Tanzania, and one each in Papua New Guinea, New Caledonia, Japan, Fiji, and St. Petersburg, Florida.

Why the increase in attacks? Scientists think there may be two reasons. First, there are many more people spending time in and around the ocean, especially well-heeled tourists in remote parts of the world. Sometimes these tourists enter waters the natives have learned—through tough experience—to avoid. Most sharks attack swimmers and waders—46 percent of the reported total. Thirty-two percent of victims are windsurfers and surfers, while divers and snorkelers make up 18 percent. Body surfers are 3 percent, and people just entering the water are 1 percent.

Another reason for the increase in numbers is that more shark attacks are being reported, thanks to increased communication technology such as the Internet and Web sites like the ISAF's (www.flmnh.ufl.edu/fish/sharks/isaf/isaf.htm). Victims of shark attacks worldwide can e-mail details of their attacks to the ISAF, including photo attachments of their injuries. Other reports come from the scientific community, as well as foreign radio and TV stations.

✦ Don't think that just because porpoises are present, sharks are not. Even though they're not buddies, they often feed on the same foods.

✦ Be extra cautious when your visibility is limited. And avoid bright-colored clothing or uneven tanning. Sharks can see contrasts particularly well—and you don't want to remind them of dinner.

✦ Don't engage in excessive splashing. And don't allow pets in the water. Their erratic movements may attract sharks.

✦ And our own warning: Never hum, whistle, sing, or otherwise replicate the theme from *Jaws* when swimming. You will scare yourself, and it makes the sharks—who don't get residuals from the movie—cranky.

COMING SOON TO A CLIMATE NEAR YOU

Global Warming: Earth As a Crock-Pot

It seems to be on the news every night. It's invisible. Some people believe it's real, and some don't. Predictions range from dire to benign. Everyone puts the blame on someone else. No, it's not the latest episode of *Survivor*. It's global warming—and no matter where you are, it will affect you in one way or another.

Global warming is simply the increase in the temperature of our planet's atmosphere over time; that warming, in turn, warms up everything else. The consequences of this warming are numerous, starting with changes in climate and leading to a host of related effects. But predictions of the consequences of global warming are as numerous and controversial as the causes. Some scientists believe it's merely a natural phenomenon; a few aren't convinced the atmosphere is warming. Others think human production of greenhouse gases—the industrial, mechanical, and sundry other mechanisms' belching of carbon dioxide, methane, and nitrogen oxides into the atmosphere—has helped exacerbate the warming of the world's climate. With this confusion in mind, would it be better to simply ignore global warming and hope it goes away? Not if you're really paranoid, and you probably wouldn't be reading this if you weren't.

Most of the data suggests our planet is indeed warming—in fact, it's warming faster that at any time in recorded history. Whether it's "natural," caused by humans, or a combination of both is not the point. Changes are coming and some of them will affect you. You may experience more severe storms, a drought for the first time, intense superhurricanes, or your coastal city may be inundated by rising sea levels, forcing you to move. Crops may fail, water supplies may run dry, pests may increase, and the temperatures may become oven hot or arctic cold, depending on where you live. There may be mass migrations of people and animals. Some flora and fauna could go extinct.[12] People may be at each other's throat. *Survivor* could be coming to a location near you.

Judging the Danger

What are some of the consequences of global warming? As with many things in life, there's the good news and bad news. The good news is that the United Nations Intergovernmental Panel on Climate Change (IPCC) recently released a one thousand-page report detailing many of the effects expected. The IPCC has been studying this problem since 1990, and has help from almost three thousand experts in dozens of countries. The bad news is what they predict will happen.[13]

According to this panel, the planet's average surface temperatures will rise approximately 2.7 to 11°F (1.5 to 6°C) by the end of the twenty-first century if we just sit around and do nothing. Worldwide melting of glaciers and the polar ice caps will help raise sea levels to between 0.09 and 0.88 meters, causing small oceanic islands, such as Samoa, Fiji, the Maldives, the Solomon Islands, and others, to follow the mythical Atlantis beneath the waves. Tens of millions of people living along the continental coastlines will be at risk from the rising sea levels. Coral reefs—havens for thousands of fish species—will be destroyed; rich farmland will be turned to desert; many species of plants and animals will go extinct; and flooding, drought, and disease will increase. Sounds almost biblical—but these things are predicted to happen over a longer time frame. And don't forget the global social consequences: The gap between the poorer and richer countries, and the poor and rich within each country, will widen—leading to more conflict and potential wars.

And now for the local report: The countries in the Northern Hemisphere will become hotter, leading to more deaths in the cities from heatstroke. There could be a influx of diseases normally restricted to the tropical areas of the world, such as malaria and various viral infections, reaching into countries not usually affected. There could be a rise in the incidence of skin cancer. Australia's agriculture could be threatened as drought spreads across the continent. Asia could experience more forest fires, and the spread of infectious disease could increase. Rising sea levels could swamp the mangrove forests that protect sea and river banks. The southern countries of Europe could experience an increased risk of water shortage and the soil quality could deteriorate, negatively impacting farming. The Middle East might see rivers drying out and water resources shrink, intensifying tensions between neighbors and increasing the risk of wars in already war-torn areas. The coastal cities of Africa could be inundated as the oceans rise, and disease could increase across this already poor, infection-ridden continent. Mexico and South America could see new diseases, a decline in crop yields, and shrinking deciduous tropical forests. The glaciers of the Himalayas might melt, causing massive flooding; without this source of water, 500 million people could continually face huge water shortages. Some of the more well known species of animals to fall into extinction include the Bengal tiger, the central African mountain gorilla, the polar bear, and penguins. The jury is still out on how humans will fare, but it's not going to be pretty.

Minimizing the Danger

It almost seems too big a problem to tackle. There is no magic formula to rid the world of global warming. But there may be two ways you can do something: politically and individually.

In the political arena, tell your representatives to stop squabbling and do something. One argument used to waffle about global warming is that the science is not perfect—and we may spend a lot of money for no good reason. Money is cheap compared to the effects of global warming. We can always print more money, but it's much harder to create a new climate and more farmland, or to hold back the rising ocean. And if the global warming doesn't happen, the money spent will still improve the planet.

We can also urge our government and the private sector to develop new, clean energy technologies and start planning for changes that may occur with global warming. Some of this "squeaky wheel" attitude has already paid off: In the United States, a program has been instituted called the National Assessment on the Potential Consequences of Climate Variability and Change.[14] There are twenty regional projects identifying the future impact of climate change, focusing on forests, water resources, human health, agriculture, marine resources, and coastal areas. New York City is one metropolitan area already using the results of this assessment to prepare for the future. Planners in the Big Apple are working to protect the eroding shoreline from increasing sea levels, seeking solutions to the rising salt levels in the water supply, and preparing for increased health problems.

Individually, you can learn about the general trends in future climate change for your area—and make plans accordingly. Maybe having a deeper backup well drilled would be a good strategy, along with some solar electric panels. Look at your basic needs, such as food, shelter, water, and clothing. How might they be impacted by the changes forecast in your area? Start to plan now so that you have a variety of options for heat, electricity, food, and water. Set up a local group to discuss matters and pressure local, state, and/or federal political figures. And help reduce emissions of greenhouse gases through strategies such as carpooling, bicycling, reducing energy use, and other means that are practical for your situation. Be aware of what's going on. Remember: until further notice, this is the only place we humans have to live.

Extremely Extreme Weather Events

During this coming century, as our planet undergoes climate changes, one of the consequences may be an increase in extreme weather events. Researchers at the National Oceanic and Atmospheric Administration's National Climatic Data Center and the National Centers for Atmospheric Research recently compared results for approximately twenty global climate models currently in use. These computer models take into account many factors, including ozone changes, solar variability, and greenhouse gases. The closer a model agrees with what's already happened to our climate—and most seem to do just that—the more likely it will predict future trends.[15]

In the twentieth century, the earth's average temperature rose approximately 1.1°F (0.6°C), while precipitation decreased in tropical regions and increased in the mid-to-high latitudes over land. Together, these climatic changes produce more extreme weather, such as an increase in very hot days for some areas, fewer frosts, and heavier rainfall over one or several days. What do many scientists predict so far? In North America, the southeast and central regions will become hotter and drier, while the West Coast will be less affected. Worldwide, the midcontinents will dry out more in the summer, leading to increasing incidence of drought. There is some disagreement over weather events such as storms—but most of the models indicate an increase in hurricane intensity. Warmer ocean surface temperatures in the eastern and central equatorial Pacific will add to El Niño events, bringing heavier rainfall to the central and eastern Pacific, with lighter amounts over Southeast Asia.

Why the concern? Global warming doesn't discriminate—so neither will these weather extremes. Take the United States: With an increase in population in storm-prone areas, the country will be more vulnerable to extreme weather events. In addition to more injuries and deaths, the economic costs will skyrocket over the next century from both private and business losses. And that's just a drop in the global bucket.

Rapid Climate Change:
The Great Climatological Houdini

We all know weather changes from day to day, but the climate? It's still the same as it's always been. Here in upstate New York, we get a little more snow in some years, and little less in others. Some summers are hotter than others, some colder. But it all seems to average out. And any changes that do happen to our planet's climate are gradual, taking hundreds or thousands of years to occur. Nothing major will happen in our lifetimes. Right?

Wrong. Just check out ice cores going back a few million years. Scientists recently found that the earth's climate has undergone rapid, dramatic changes—like a climatic yo-yo—for *at least* the last 1.5 million years. And when we say rapid, we're talking on a human scale, not a geological one. What it means is upstate New York and New England could change to a southern-Florida-like climate in a short time. Picture Burlington, Vermont, as sunny and warm as Miami. Not bad if you own property on Lake Champlain. But what happens if Miami ends up like northern Maine?

Needless to say, the consequences of this rapid and violent climate change would be staggering. There would be major changes in weather patterns. In turn, that would change the food and water supplies—including the extinction of some native plants that could not adapt. From there, animals and people would migrate to find better living conditions. And new habitats don't bode well for many unadaptable species, some of which would gradually or suddenly go extinct.

Judging the Danger

Only a decade ago, scientists had no idea our planet's climate could change so rapidly. They thought it was slow, nice, and smooth. But ice and ocean sediment cores tell a different story about the earth's past climate. There were rapid, large-amplitude fluctuations in climate during the past eight hundred thousand years in a time called the *Ice Ages*, when large glaciers advanced and retreated across the surface of the planet. The composition and chemical structure of fossils found in ice cores from Greenland and in worldwide ocean sediment cores gave them a clue. At first, the scientists thought these swings were from all that ice. That's because the most dramatic instabilities occurred during these cooler periods up until about ten thousand years ago. But those pesky glaciers are long gone, so it should be smooth (climate) sailing.

Researchers went literally deeper, gathering cores from the ocean floor—areas where deep water currents from Greenland rapidly accumulated sediment for millions of years. What they found was unexpected: Large-amplitude, rapid climate swings of as much as 18°F within a few decades, occurring not just during the last glacial periods, but all throughout the last 1.5 million years. This means rapid change may be a standard feature of our climate—not just an aberration that happened during the Ice Ages.

Minimizing the Danger

No one knows why this happens. Scientists realize climate changes are tied to changes in ocean circulation and heat transfer, but they can't explain the rapid changes. The scary part? It's the usual: because of our lack of knowledge, no one can predict when the next rapid change will occur. And because we're probably at the end of an unusually stable eight thousand-year warm period—combined with all the human factors such as the buildup of carbon dioxide and global warming—the climate may do anything at any time. So enjoy your climate while you can.

3 WEATHER WARY

"Everybody talks about the weather,
but nobody does anything about it."
—Mark Twain

M ark Twain was right on the mark. Nobody does much of anything about the weather except try to predict it and complain about it. We can't force an air mass to move north or south, drive away the rain, or stop a tornado from forming. Humans may know a great deal about the forces that drive our planet's weather and climate—but we also know they occur on a much grander scale than we could hope to influence. But look on the bright side. It could be much worse: We could live on Mars, with its thin atmosphere and miles-high dust devils; or on Jupiter or Saturn, with some of the strongest winds in the solar system. Instead, most of the time, our weather is relatively mild. But Nature does have some nasty tricks up her sleeve—and a good many of them are hidden, striking suddenly and without warning.

Heat Bursts: Are We Well-Done Yet?

Try breathing when temperatures suddenly rise precipitously in minutes, accompanied by dry winds. Now you know what it would be like to live in a blast furnace. Car radiators boil over. Trees topple. Grain and cotton fields become scorched. Roofs blow off buildings. People flee to bathrooms, covering themselves with wet towels and blankets. Those who have been through these bursts of heat and wind know it can ruin a perfectly fine evening.

Some heat bursts merely raise temperatures by a few degrees—just enough to feel the heat for a few minutes. But others are far more dangerous. In Glasgow, Montana, on September 9, 1994, the temperature was 67°F (19°C) at 5:02 A.M. Suddenly, a heat burst from a nearby storm sent the temperature up to 93°F (34°C) in fifteen minutes, tying the date's record high. By 5:40 A.M., it was back to 68°F (20°C), leaving behind frazzled nerves and property.

One of the most infamous—and longest—heat bursts occurred during the evening of May 22–23, 1996, in ten counties across Oklahoma. A massive burst of hot air raced downward from a dissipating thunderstorm and slammed into the ground at speeds of over one hundred miles per hour—raising the temperature from the 80s into the 100s (°F) in only a few minutes. Although the earth's surface friction eventually stopped the rampage, some people feared the world had come to an end.[1]

Judging the Danger

Heat bursts are insidious. They usually occur at night, when most thunderstorms fade away—as sunset takes away their fuel of moist, warm air. The gush of heated air is very hard to detect with weather instruments, so no one knows when or where a burst will occur until the oven "clicks on."

How do these natural barbecues form? It starts with a tall, dying thunderstorm as the sun goes down. As the warm humid air stops rising, rain falls into the cold air near the base of the cloud. This cools the air even more, making it heavier and heavier, until it plunges toward the ground, like the steep part of a rollercoaster ride. Physics takes over at this point, and as the cool air mass falls rapidly through the atmosphere—sometimes plunging more than twenty thousand feet—it is compressed by the higher air pressure near the ground. This dramatically increases its temperature and slows down the descent, but not by much. Hot air slams into the ground, sending the temperatures soaring in minutes, accompanied by shrieking winds, and the sound of crops, animals, property, and humans baking. Think of it as the world's largest hot air convection oven—and you're on the inside looking out.

Minimizing the Danger

Any tall, dying thunderstorm can produce a heat burst if enough cooling evaporation takes place above the ground. Because they occur relatively quickly, there is no real way to avoid them. The good part? They usually disappear relatively fast, too. And there is hope on the heat burst horizon: In places like tornado and thunderstorm-riddled Oklahoma, the weather service often keeps track of temperatures and winds every five minutes, and can sometimes detect a heat burst a short time before it occurs.

To cope with this danger, here are some helpful hints:

✦ Be alert to conditions as thunderstorms dissipate, especially after nightfall.
✦ Keep tuned to National Weather Service broadcasts.
✦ If you do find yourself outside in a heat burst, try to find cover. Get inside if possible. Wrap yourself in a wet towel and breathe through your nose under a wet cloth; use fans or get into air conditioning; and apply ice packs to the neck, wrists, or under the armpits to stay cool. And try to avoid the temptation to cover yourself with A-1 Sauce.

Downsloping Winds:
"Anything Can Happen . . ."

They may have called the wind Maria (pronounced mah-rye-ah) in the 1950s Lerner and Loewe musical *Paint Your Wagon*. But all over the world, downsloping winds have their own descriptive, usually less pronounceable, names: *foehn* in the European Alps, *zonda* in Argentina, *halny wiatr* in Poland, *koembang* in Java, and the infamous Santa Ana in California. And some winds probably have names that we can't repeat in this book.[2]

Meteorologists call these winds *adiabatic*, a less poetic but more descriptive term. They are typically hot, dry downslope winds formed where mountains stand in the way of strong air currents. Like the plunging heat of the bursts discussed in the last section, these winds first travel up and then plunge down a mountain, squeezed and thus warmed by atmospheric pressure, hence the name *downslope winds*. They are found in the mythology of many cultures—one of the most popular descriptions being "the mountains breathe fire."

But not all downsloping winds are hot stuff. The great downsloping winds called *katabatic*, or *fall winds* carry cold, dense air down mountains with the help of gravity. California's Mono winds are a fine example: They originate in the Great Basin, then travel nine thousand feet down the canyons of the Sierra Nevada—bringing 100 MPH winds that have been known to knock down huge one hundred-foot trees in their path.

Judging the Danger

The danger from seasonal downsloping winds are numerous, as the blasts of air can huff, puff, and blow many things down. There can be a high fire danger, wind damage to property, turbulence and low-level wind shear for aircraft, and high-wind dangers for boaters. For those people along coastlines, these winds can cause high surf conditions, such as during a Santa Ana event on the northeast side of the Channel Islands. On the plus side, the surfing can be awesome, dude!

The Mountains of Madness?

There may be another, more subtle danger when it comes to downsloping winds: A connection between these excessive breezes and human health. Take the chinook winds of the Rocky Mountains (named after Native Americans of the Pacific Northwest, where the winds originate). These warm, dry downslope winds can melt a foot of snow in less than a hour—and may cause the onset of migraines for many people. In a University of Calgary study, researchers found two scenarios that could trigger migraines: high-wind days—when wind speeds were greater than 24 MPH—and prechinook days.[3] Older patients were more likely to have an attack on the high-wind days. Just how these winds trigger migraines is still unknown. But if you live near chinooks—and perhaps other downsloping wind events—it may help to get out the migraine medications before the winds start.

Minimizing the Danger

For homeowners, days of rushing winds pouring down from the mountains can be wearing. Here are a few tips to help you cope:

+ Batten down the hatches, anchoring things in your yard that can become victims of high winds.
+ Use steel or composite fasteners to hold your roof in place.
+ Howling winds mean keeping an ear to the news for possible wildfires in your area—and to your local weather station to make sure prevailing winds are not swinging around in your direction. If so, follow the emergency services advice—especially if they believe a wildfire helped by the wind is heading toward your home.
+ Read *The Big Sleep* or *The Long Goodbye* to pass the time and you'll know why Raymond Chandler wrote, ". . . one of those hot dry Santa Anas that come down through the mountain passes and curl your hair. . . . Anything can happen."

Macrobursts: Batten Down the Hatches

On August 14, 1996, people in northwestern and western Phoenix, Arizona, experienced one of Nature's invisible dangers: straight-line winds equivalent to a category 3 hurricane, generated by a large thunderstorm. Trees and power lines were knocked down and air conditioning units were blown off of buildings. Many homeowners lost major parts of their roofs and some houses had structural damage. The highest wind gust, measuring 115 MPH at the Deer Valley Airport, broke an Arizona record. Two hours later, as the same straight-line winds reached Davis Air Force Base in Tucson, the record was again broken—with a 120 MPH gust. This was a classic macroburst: A gigantic downburst of air covering a swath just over two miles wide, with smaller microbursts popping out along its path. These straight-line winds may not resemble the spinning winds of a twisting tornado—but they can do just as much damage. Just look what they did to Helen Hunt in *Twister*.

When There's Too Much Wind in Your Sails

Boaters beware! You don't want to be caught out on the water in a macroburst (or maybe you really *do* want to be blown all the way to the Canary Islands). The best way to beat such a scenario is to listen to the current weather information broadcast—and if you are close to shore, look to see if any marinas are displaying lights or flags to indicate rough weather. Pay attention to the sky. Remember, whenever you encounter a thunderstorm, there is the chance of a macroburst. You might even be able to see a macroburst coming—it looks like blowing spray under or slightly ahead of the thunderstorm cloud. Get to shore if at all possible. If you can't get back to shore, point your boat's bow into the wind (and reef your sails, if applicable), secure all loose objects, and cover all openings. Finally, wear a personal flotation device and keep all emergency lifesaving equipment at hand.[4]

Judging the Danger

Macrobursts (also called *downbursts*) can be thought of as air on steroids—big, strong, unpredictable, and packing quite a windy punch in a big area. They form in thunderstorms where, deep within the clouds, rain-cooled air is carried up and down (updrafts and downdrafts) in yo-yo fashion. When conditions are just right—or just wrong, depending on your point of view—the updraft prevents the rain-cooled air from falling. This forms a large pool of cool air that eventually grows heavy enough to overcome and wrestle past the updraft. Falling like an invisible anvil, it races to the ground, hitting and spreading out strong horizontal winds at the surface. These winds can reach hurricane force, with damage similar to that of a tornado. And if minutes-long microbursts occur within the macroburst, the damage can be even more extensive.

Minimizing the Danger

The danger from macrobursts is pretty straightforward. These strong winds can cause major damage in only a few short minutes—so be alert as a thunderstorm approaches. Here are a few tips:

✦ Have a battery-powered weather radio handy to monitor thunderstorm watches and warnings.
✦ Anchor items in your yard that may be blown around by these winds.
✦ Stay indoors, preferably away from windows and doors. The cellar or interior rooms are best.
✦ Be prepared for a heavy-duty cleanup after the storm. Who knows what may blow into your yard.

Tornadoes: Welcome to Oz

Years ago, there was a common joke in our upstate New York hometown: Have an ice-cream social and you will always get a tornado watch. For some strange reason, ice cream and predictions of swirling winds seemed to go together. Maybe the meteorologists wanted all the ice cream for themselves. In reality, many times during those summer days, menacing clouds brought lightning and thunder—but few, if any, tornadoes. Things changed on May 31, 1998, as we were treated to tornado winds of 40 to over 158 MPH—cutting a sixty-mile swath in less than an hour. A one thousand foot television tower was twisted in two, and a large trash dumpster was thrown into two satellite dishes, then tossed about one hundred yards over an embankment. Tree tops were snapped or twisted off. A sport utility vehicle was rolled like a marble across the floor, as was a mobile home. The weird part? There was no ice-cream social that day.

Judging the Danger

We've all heard about the dangers of tornadoes—including stories of ruby slippers and the Wicked Witch of the West. But this phenomenon is definitely more dangerous than an army of flying monkeys. The property damage, personal injuries, and death they inflict is no joke. Sometimes they even destroy entire towns.

Tornadoes differ from microbursts in several ways: Their high winds are more concentrated, covering a smaller area along a usually longer path; they're also more destructive in smaller areas—and their cloudy, funnel shape is very distinctive.

Tornadoes peak in the south from March through May, with a second peak in some states in the fall; the north is treated to twisters in the summer—sometimes, but not always, during ice-cream socials. What makes them particularly dangerous is their randomness. No one is completely sure of the mechanism that spawns these deadly twisters. Violently rotating columns of air pop out of some, but not all, thunderstorms, carrying winds up to 250 MPH or more—four times the speed your car travels on most highways. They can cut a mile-wide path for more than fifty miles, or just touch down and disappear. Some bounce all over like a rubber ball, as if choosing spots to strike. And mobile-home parks appear to attract them.

Minimizing the Danger

Although they occur more commonly in the midwestern United States, don't let your guard down anywhere when it comes to tornadoes. One of the most important steps—whether you are at home or traveling—is to be aware of weather conditions. The National Oceanic and Atmospheric Administration's Weather Service radio stations broadcast around the clock in all parts of the country. There also are nifty weather radios that turn on automatically if a tornado watch or warning (or other dangerous weather) is issued. And the Weather Channel and many Internet weather sites also are good sources of information about severe thunderstorms—and the potential for tornadoes.

If twisters like to visit your area, be sure everyone in your family knows where to take shelter. Here are a few hints:[5]

+ *At home, school, or work.* Move to a predesignated shelter, such as a basement, in a home or building. If an underground shelter is not available, move to an interior room or hallway on the lowest floor and get under a sturdy piece of furniture. And one big but simple reminder: A major myth is to keep windows open to equalize pressure when a tornado strikes. Don't do it—you are just inviting in the damaging winds. Leave the windows alone and go to a safe place.
+ *Outdoors.* Don't try to outrun a tornado. You won't win. If you're in a car, get out and lie flat in a nearby ditch or depression. Try to hang on to something solid. (If you stay in the car, there is a chance you will be injured if the car is rocked—or thrown by the severe tornado winds.) And DO NOT take shelter under a highway overpass as a tornado approaches. You can easily be hit by debris—and the overpass can act like a wind tunnel, squeezing the air and increasing the already fast winds.

This Old (Safe) House

The Federal Emergency Management Agency (FEMA) is part of the government that wants to help you. Don't panic: it really can provide help from the dangers of tornadoes—whether you live in the middle of Kansas or in upstate New York. One of its major recommendations for homeowners is to have a *safe room*—a way of protecting youself and your family from injury or death from winds up to 250 MPH and projectiles traveling at high speeds. Should you build a safe room? Well, it depends on a number of things: Are you in a high-risk area? Can you reach safe shelter quickly if there are major winds? Would you feel safer with a safe room? And everyone's favorite: Can you afford to build a shelter? If you're at all interested, contact FEMA (through the mail or the Internet) for the shelter design—which includes size, retrofitting in existing houses, and ideal locations within a house. Construction plans, materials, and costs for a variety of situations are available. Tell them Dorothy and Toto sent you.

Hurricanes: Riders on the Storm

Most people are aware of the dangers posed by hurricanes: driving rain, high winds, property damage, personal injuries, cheesy B movie plots. But many don't know about the real killer that is an integral part of almost every hurricane: the storm surge—a massive raised dome of water, unstoppable and filled with power, driven inexorably over flat coastal areas by the action of these great storms.

The largest storm surge of the twentieth century in the United States occurred on August 17, 1969, when Hurricane Camille, a category 5 (the highest number for a hurricane), pushed a twenty-four-foot dome of water into Pass Christian, Mississippi. At least three feet of surge water hit places as far as 125 miles east and 31 miles to the west of Pass Christian, and more than eighteen thousand homes and seven hundred businesses were either destroyed or seriously damaged.[6]

What about surge potential? A category 3 to 5 hurricane's storm surge hitting near New Orleans or Florida's southwest coast between Tampa Bay and Everglades National Park would make residents wonder if they were living in Atlantis. New York City wouldn't fare any better. The East Coast starts to run west to east there, creating a "corner" that would only encourage a storm surge to run higher. In fact, one computer simulation showed more than ten feet of water over John F. Kennedy International Airport and Battery Park on the tip of Manhattan during a major hurricane.

Judging the Danger

No one ever mentions it, but over the years, hurricane storm surges have killed more people than the high winds. In 1900 Galveston, Texas, was decimated by a hurricane and accompanying storm surge that killed between six thousand and ten thousand people. Tragically, Bangladesh seems to be hit by one almost every year.

How does it work? A hurricane is nature's ultimate vacuum machine. The extreme low pressure system associated with these storms interacts with the ocean surface, pulling up a huge dome of

Tropical cyclone Litanne was in the southern Indian Ocean in March 1994—and has the typical look of a cyclone, another name for a hurricane. (NASA)

water in the center of the massive, rotating arms. Add howling winds from around the hurricane's eye and the water is forced to pile up even more, with the highest waters occurring on the right side of the storm in the Northern Hemisphere.

In the wide, deep ocean, this dome is not noticeable. When the hurricane approaches land, however, it's a very different story. The upward-sloping seafloor essentially piles up the water even higher, causing a huge influx of water along coastal areas, where large numbers of people just happen to live. The shallower the ocean offshore, the higher the storm surge. Add in the hurricane-force winds, perhaps a coincidental high tide, and POOF! . . . instant *Waterworld.*

Minimizing the Danger

The best way to deal with the hurricane and storm surge season is to be prepared. For most flood-prone areas, keep a stock of boards, tools, batteries, nonperishable foods, and other emergency equipment—especially if you live along the East Coast, where hurricanes like to hang out. And there is now high-tech help available called MEOW. No, it doesn't have anything to do with little Fluffy, but is the acronym for Maximum Envelope of Water. Local weather services along the coasts have a computer model to tell the MEOW, and can determine which areas should evacuate from the Gulf and Atlantic Coasts if a storm surge seems to be imminent.[7]

Here are a few tips if your area gets a hurricane and storm surge warning from the Federal Emergency Management Agency:[8]

+ Go to high ground if you live in a low-lying area—especially if a hurricane is imminent. Always know a safe evacuation route.
+ Stay at home if your house is sturdy and on high ground (and leave mobile homes for safer shelter—they seem to act like magnets to hurricanes and tornadoes). Stay inside when the hurricane hits.
+ Protect your windows with boards, shutters, or tape.
+ Make sure you have enough water to last several days, not only for drinking, but for sanitation.
+ Batten down the hatches and secure objects outside your home.
+ Make sure you have fuel in your car.
+ Never, repeat, *never* rent the movie *Key Largo*.

Dust Storms: The Grapes of Wrath

Dust storms bring to mind those grainy black and white images from the 1930s of the Midwest Dust Bowl, with families loading their pickups to move to the West Coast. These storms most commonly occur in arid places, but don't confuse them with sandstorms. A true desert sandstorm carries sand only a few inches to a few feet off the ground. Dust storms are much more massive—high winds carrying large amounts of loose soil into the air, sometimes miles high, reducing visibility to a just few feet. It's the soil that's the problem: Small clay and silt-sized particles are easily blown into the air when

Your Own Disaster Relief

Did you ever wonder what would be really, really handy during one of these weather-related hidden dangers? Try to stock the items on this list—not only in your home, but in your car, boat, motorcycle, or summer cottage:

+ flashlight and extra batteries
+ portable, battery-operated (or solar/battery/ generator-operated) radio
+ first aid kit and manual
+ emergency food and water
+ nonelectric can opener
+ jugs of water
+ essential medicines
+ cash and credit cards
+ sturdy shoes
+ extra thick rope
+ long-lasting candles
+ waterproof matches
+ blankets (especially space blankets, the ones that look like large insulated aluminum foil sheets.)
+ two sturdy buckets
+ compass

dry. And they don't easily settle back to the ground. This combination of dry soil from a lingering drought and blowing winds can trigger dust storms almost anywhere, bringing devastation to the land, people, and buildings—and, it is, unfortunately unpredictable.

In places like Arizona, for example, dust storms are most common where fields are being tilled—not just in the desert. In such areas, strong winds or thunderstorms pick up dust and blow it everywhere, most often across roads and highways, and into houses. These storms can happen in almost all dry, dusty areas of the world if the timing is right, including, but not limited to, the drier parts of the southwestern United States.

Judging the Danger

Summertime dust storms can make you a believer in the power of nature—and in the need for dust cloths. Imagine driving over a hill and coming up against a shimmering curtain of dust that instantly reduces your visibility to zero. The brown, churning wall looks like it was created by a giant playing with a pile of dirt, determined to dim or blot out the sun for minutes or even hours. Such a storm can turn a sunny, trouble-free trip to the next town into a hazardous journey. On high-speed, high-traffic roads or highways, dust storms can trigger accidents—often chain reactions involving many vehicles.

And don't think dust storms affect only your driving ability. Dust in the lungs is not easy on the body, either. In places where dust storms are a major problem, there appears to be a marked increase in respiratory infections, from dust and possibly from germs carried by the dust particles. Fortunately, breathing the earth's dust won't cause our eyes to start glowing blue like the people in Frank Herbert's science fiction book *Dune*.

Minimizing the Danger

One of the best ways to be safe during a dust storm—especially if you have upper-respiratory problems—is to avoid it. Be aware of weather conditions, especially if you live or travel in a dust-storm-prone area. If one strikes, get inside and close the windows. If you're caught outside, find a sheltering boulder, hill, tree, or any other structure. Stay low to the ground and cover your nose and mouth with a cloth. Make believe you're Lawrence of Arabia.

Many southwestern departments of public safety have a few tips of their own:[9]

+ If dense dust blows across or approaches a roadway, do not enter the area. Pull off the pavement (*Never* stop *on* the pavement) as far as possible and stop. Turn off your lights and keep your foot off the brake pedal. The object is to keep other motorists from hitting you from behind. With your lights on, there is a chance the other driver will think you are moving—and hit you in the rear.

+ If you decide to stay on the road or there is no room to pull over safely, reduce your speed, turn your lights on, and use the centerline as a guide—much like driving in a heavy fog. Sound your horn every now and then—just to let everyone know you are there.

LIGHTNING: WHEN NATURE FLASHES US

Lightning Strikes: Truly a Bolt from the Blue

A horror movie wouldn't be complete without lightning in the background. And there is a good reason why Hollywood uses the trick: We all have a primal fear of lightning. It is one of the most unpredictable, violent acts of nature, complete with blinding flashes of light and ear-pounding crashes of thunder. And in the United States, it causes more casualties annually than any other storm-related phenomenon. It's our ancestral right to be scared.

We also have the right to be fearful of "bolts from the blue." Like a thunderbolt thrown down from the Norse god Thor, a bolt from the blue—or *anvil lightning*—really does come from out of nowhere.

This lightning strike is typical—and deadly if you're in its path. (Grant Goodge/NCDC)

People standing on sunny patches of land have been struck or nearly hit by bolts from thunderstorms up to twenty-five miles away.[10]

Judging the Danger

The scenario for lightning is simple: Take a churning thundercloud that tosses air around like a bouncing basketball. Then notice the electric charges building up because of the up-and-down churn and carried through the cloud by raindrops, hail, and sundry other precipitation. In a short time, negative charges accumulate in the lower part of the thunderstorm and positive charges above. But these opposites don't attract, and as they build, they have to let off some steam: Negative meets positive in a split-second explosive display—that of a lightning bolt.

A bolt from the blue is like some craggy finger of fate—the lightning shooting out horizontally about two-thirds of the way up the cloud, then dropping to the ground miles away. Although we know a bit about how lightning forms, no one is certain why a thunderbolt develops the urge to expand its horizon and bolt away, unlike the more well-behaved lightning within or directly under the thundercloud.

Minimizing the Danger

Most bolts from the blue don't occur on mountain peaks, but on flatlands in the summer—perfect places that supply the fuel (heat from the sun-baked earth) to build up thunderstorms. In fact, the very flat state of Florida is not only the citrus capital of the world, it also has the dubious distinction as the lightning capital of the world—with about ninety to one hundred thunderstorms per year in east central Florida alone.

Here are some general hints to avoid being struck by an out-of-nowhere fickle finger of lightning:

✦ A lightning bolt is just about as thick as a pencil, but it's about three times hotter than the Sun's surface. So do not practice being a human lightning rod—you usually get only one try. Instead, if a thunderstorm rumbles in your direction—even if it's ten miles away—get inside a safe building. If you're outside, squat down and hug your knees—you'll be less of a target.

✦ Even being inside your car is better than out in the open, since the conducting outer surfaces carry away most of the electricity in a phenomena called the *skin effect.* Just make sure you're not touching any metallic objects connected to the outside of the car—such as window and door handles, steering wheels, radio dials, or gearshifts—when lightning is close by. The best strategy is sit quietly with your hands in your lap.

✦ We know it's great to sit or stand under a tree on a hot summer's day, but not before, during, or right after a thunderstorm. Lightning seeks out tall things.

✦ How do you tell if you're too close to the storm? If thunder booms just after the flash of lightning, you're probably about one quarter of a mile away from the storm. If it's a flash and immediate crack, it may be only a hundred yards away.

✦ Golfers, please get off the course if you see a thunderstorm coming. Don't hold your golf club to the heavens in defiance. Nature just loves those types of temptations—but you won't.

Ball Lightning: Great Balls of Lightning

Yes, this is one time science has named something accurately: Ball lightning is literally a ball of lightning—as large as a bus or small as a baseball—bouncing down a hill, running across power lines for yards, streaking through airplanes, and even darting through windows without leaving a trace. Their colors cover most of the spectrum, with balls that appear distinctly orange and blue seeming to last longer than average.

This type of lightning has been mentioned since ancient Greek times. And although about 5 percent of us have seen or know someone who has seen these light balls, scientists still can't explain them. Most of the time they are associated with violent lightning bolts, and they disappear with a pop or bang. Guesses as to their origins

Fastest Flash

Our eyes can register the sight of a good meal, but when it comes to fast things, we're lucky if we can see a bird fly past our window. We weren't meant to watch things that moved lightning fast, and now researchers have discovered there are even faster lightning flashes to worry about—lightning thousands of times quicker than anything ever observed.

Even if you didn't blink, you couldn't see this flash. Using a special sensor, scientists at the National Centers for Atmospheric Research discovered that these lightning flashes lasted no more than twenty-three microseconds, the instrument's limit of detection.[11] These ultra-quick flashes defy explanation so far, but they are thought to ignite from an extreme electric field within the thunderstorm. If so—and if someone can figure out a way to observe them from afar—they may be a way to judge thunderstorm severity. And a warning about such severe storms could save lives.

range from floating chunks of plasma from a thunderbolt or a chemical process, to a standing wave of electromagnetic radiation. No doubt someone has added space alien phaser blasters to the list, too.

Judging the Danger

Because it is so rare, ball lightning is not as dangerous to us as bolts of lightning during a thunderstorm. For one thing, a ball's lifetime varies widely, ranging from a few seconds to several minutes, with an average duration of about twenty-five seconds. They don't occur on mountain peaks, near high-rises, or at other high points that attract regular lightning. They also are harmless inside homes, buildings, airplanes, and even submarines that have a conducting frame.

Outside may be another story, although there has never been a verified report of a person being struck or hurt by ball lightning. The real damage seems to come when ball lightning disappears with a bang—with reports of electric connection boxes being blown off houses by these outdoor light shows.

Minimizing the Danger

The best way to prevent ball lightning from ruining your day is to be aware that electrical storms are not to be treated lightly.[12]

+ Ball lightning is more prevalent in flatlands—so beware when you are traveling or if you live in such areas.
+ Stay inside during electrical storms.
+ Don't use the telephone during a storm (lightning and ball lightning have both been reported to travel along phone lines).
+ Stay away from windows during the storm, as ball lightning has been known to enter homes through open windows. It's a good idea to stay away from windows during any electric storm.

Hail: Rain, Rain, the Hail's All Here

Take a couple of quacking ducks. Convince them to fly through a thunderstorm. Make them stay in the cloud for a long time, rising with the updrafts and falling with the downdrafts. The result? Duck á l'ice.

Ice-coated ducks really did fall from the sky in Worcester, Massachusetts, in 1933. As far as we know, no human has ever been treated to a natural coating of ice—although L.Col. William H. Rankin came close. He ejected out of a jet over Norfolk, Virginia, in 1959, plunging right into a severe thunderstorm—and was treated to the up-and-downdrafts for forty minutes before he finally fell to the ground, safe but shaken. These chunks of ice are even added as a footnote to the French Revolution: During the summer of 1788, severe hailstorms wiped out most of the crops around Paris, resulting in food shortages and civil unrest. Hail can also kill: the deadliest recorded hailstorm occurred on April 30, 1888, in which 246 people perished in the Moradad and Bareilly areas of India.

Judging the Danger

Hailstones are balls of ice that fall from spring and summer thunderstorms, formed as a particle or small piece of ice is continuously coated as it rises with updrafts and falls with downdrafts within a thundercloud. As the ice layers accumulate, the hailstone becomes heavier—eventually reaching a point of no return and falling to the ground. Such hail can damage or destroy crops, cars, animals, and buildings. For one thing, hailstones range from pea sized to the size of a grapefruit. Falling from great heights makes any size chunk of hail formidable. Remember the lesson we all learned in school: Drop a penny from the top of the Empire State Building and gravity does the rest. Just try dropping a heavy, golfball-sized hailstone from an even greater height.

The largest documented hailstones? Try a 17.5-inch diameter, 1.67-pound beauty that dropped on September 3, 1970, in Cof-

The Rainmakers

We all know the feeling: putting up with a long, rainy weekend only to see a sliver of sunlight peek through the clouds at Sunday's sunset. Does rain purposely show up to aggravate us on weekends? Apparently not—because we are the rainmakers without even doing a rain dance.[13]

It doesn't happen everywhere. Right now, research has centered on the East Coast. The reaction is like a good physics problem: The cause, pollution; the effect, heavier rainstorms on the weekends. Climatologists at Arizona State University noted a seven-day ozone and carbon monoxide cycle, peaking on Thursday and Friday, with low points from Sunday to Tuesday. Coordinating that data with ocean rainfall records from Florida to Canada, they found 22 percent more rain on Saturdays than Mondays. It's almost a give-and-take. We drive our cars and the car exhaust—not to mention industrial emissions—drive our rains. This is not a natural phenomenon, it's a man-made cycle—random chance because the calendar is a man-made creation.

feyville, Kansas. No one can confirm the 4-pound hailstone that reportedly fell in Germany in 1925. And such large hailstones can have deadly consequences: On April 14, 1986, 2.25-pound chunks of hail rained down on Bangladesh, killing 92 people.

Minimizing the Danger

If you do find yourself headed into a hailstorm, here are a few hints:

✦ The best way to protect yourself from hail during a thunderstorm is to get inside a solid structure. Cars are all right, but remember that larger hail can break windows. Your best bet is to get into a solid building. Nothing's wrong with grocery shopping during a storm.

✦ Where are the best places to see hail? About five hundred to seven hundred hailstorms occur each year in the United States alone, with the majority in "hail alley," an area that covers parts of eastern Colorado, Nebraska, and Wyoming; the High Plains, the Midwest, and the Ohio Valley get their fair share of the icy storms, too. Amazingly, even though hailstorms are associated with thunderstorms, Florida has the lowest hail rate in the country, along with the Pacific coastline.

✦ For world travelers, keep alert—especially in the downwind areas of large mountain ranges: Central Europe (Munich, Germany, holds the record for the most damaging hailstorm—in 1984) eastward to Ukraine, the Himalayas, southern China, Keriche, Kenya (132 hail days per year, one of the highest), and parts of South Africa, Argentina, and southeastern Australia.

✦ If you just have to be outside, don't forget a hard hat.

Snow: Not the Perfect Storm

The nor'easter of 1993 will always be remembered by those living in the northeastern United States. So will the Nantucket Effect that caused the Blizzard of 1996. And we won't forget the record lake-effect snows of November 2000 for a while, either. Blinding snow and plenty of snowflakes: It makes one pine for the crocodiles of Florida. At least it's warm down there.

Of course, the Northeast isn't the only region with the snowflake blues. The Midwest has its share of major storms, as do many mountain regions, such as the Rocky Mountains and Sierra Nevada. It's not that snow sneaks up on us—usually weather forecasters can predict a good storm—but it's the result of the white pileup that causes concern. Heavy snowfall can immobilize a region, paralyze a city, collapse a building, and, in the mountains, cause avalanches. Not every snowfall is skiing material.

Judging the Danger

Everyone in a snowstorm is potentially at risk—it depends on where you are when the weather system hits. (Someone once did some statistics about snowstorms and discovered most people hurt or injured during an ice or snow event are men; the injuries often result from shoveling.) And it's not just the heavy snows. Winter storms often come complete with windy blizzard conditions—blinding, wind-driven snow; severe drifting; and dangerously low wind chills. Other storms drag along extreme cold in their wake, creating conditions ripe for hypothermia or frostbite. Not only that, freezing rivers can disrupt shipping and ice jams can cause floods. A winter storm may also be as gentle as a lamb, coming in as rain, but falling on already frozen ground—with the heavy, thick ice coating electrical wires, bringing down trees and communication towers.

Minimizing the Danger

Here are a few hints if you're stuck in a major snowstorm:

+ If you are outside, find shelter. If you can't get inside right away, try to stay dry and cover all exposed parts of your body—including the face. If you are caught farther away from civilization than expected, follow your animal instincts and protect yourself from the wind: Build a lean-to or snowcave. If possible, build a fire—complete with rocks around it to dissipate heat slowly—not only for heat, but to attract attention.

✦ Don't eat snow if you're trapped outside! No, the acid rain won't dissolve your tongue—but the cold snow will lower your body temperature, increasing the risk of hypothermia. Melt it first.

✦ If you have to travel during a snowstorm, don't think your car is your living room. Be prepared. Don't just put on a T-shirt—not even for a short drive to the store—but wear layers of clothing, especially clothes that breathe to let your sweat evaporate so you don't get chilled.

✦ If you are caught in your car or truck, stay there. Wind blows the snow in all types of disorienting directions, so walking to where you *think* the nearest exit is might be dangerous. Check to make sure your exhaust pipe is clear—then run the motor about ten minutes for an hour's worth of heat—but make sure you crack a window to avoid carbon monoxide poisoning. Make yourself noticeable to rescuers—maybe a piece of red cloth on your antenna, door, or window. Don't forget to move around now and then, to keep your blood moving and to stay warm.

✦ Always keep a "care package" in your car, filled with snacks and juices just in case you have to stay in your car for any length of time. Dehydration is a killer—you can't go without liquids (and we don't mean alcohol, which actually makes you colder) for more than three days. Food helps, too. One woman who skidded off the road during a major snowstorm in upstate New York wasn't found for a few days—and because she was hurt, she couldn't move. She lived off the snacks that she always kept in her car during the winter months. And at night, she licked the condensation off a nearby window to get enough water. Smart lady—and she is fine and healthy today.

Sneeze in the Breeze

Freak weather changes are becoming the thing of the future—and along with the strange weather extremes come health-related problems. Sure, there's been a great deal of study about weather-related deaths, but little has been done to study the connection between weather and health problems. But there seem to be some clues from a study recently done through Oxford University.[14]

Here's what researchers have found so far: A still, windless low-pressure system, usually in autumn, leads to low clouds—and that often leads to an increase in flu, as seen in the great British flu epidemic of 1989, which broke out after four days of low clouds. Some speculate it's the damp air that helps the virus to proliferate, and without the wind to disperse the virus, an outbreak occurs. And be careful around thunderstorms—not just because they can carry lightning and hail. The researchers also found a link between thunderstorms and asthma attacks. One great example: One day in 1994, within an hour after a major thunderstorm, 640 people were treated for asthma attacks in London hospitals—six times more than normal.

HAZARDOUS
SPACE
STUFF
4

Space. Some say the final frontier.
Others say the only frontier.
We say it's a place to watch.

I t sounds so poetic. Humans observing and dreaming about space for thousands of years. They chart the passage of the stars and planets through the nighttime skies. And in the last century, our species finally broke the bonds of Earth—traveling out into this vast region and sending probes deep into the solar system and beyond.

What we're only now realizing is that outer space reciprocates. A vast armada of "stuff" comes to our planet from "out there." Some, like heat and light, are essential for life. But there are darker things that bombard us regularly, or lie in wait, hidden and ready to strike. Many of these phenomena have the potential to create havoc with our lives, our society, our planet—even our very existence.

No, we're not alone. We're just sitting ducks.

THINGS TO WATCH NEARBY

Space Weather:
Something Wicked This Way Comes

Coronal mass ejections (CMEs) can be thought of as solar "burps." But instead of the pepperoni-and-cheese burps from the pizza you just ate, the Sun sends out a huge discharge of electrified, magnetic gas from its outer atmosphere, called the *corona*. Made up largely of hydrogen, with a little bit of helium and other elements, a CME is hurled from the Sun at speeds that can reach 1,250 miles per second. In this scorching region, atoms separate into negatively charged electrons and positively charged protons, turning into a plasma. Other things come along for the ride—a piece of the Sun's magnetic field, high-energy particles, and X rays. And we don't even want to think about the cannibal CMEs, huge ejections that gobble up smaller CMEs.[1]

Sometimes the magnetic field dragged along with a CME interacts with our planet's own magnetic field—the shield that guards us from the Sun's solar particles (aka the *solar wind*). This changes the shape of our shield; if the visiting magnetic field points southward—opposite the direction of our planet's magnetic field—watch out, Earth! In such a case, the CME dramatically alters our magnetic field and creates a strong electric current. Take, for instance, January 11, 1997: A CME pushed our magnetosphere below the altitude in which geostationary satellites orbit—exposing many communications satellites to a constant barrage of solar particles—all recorded on the craft as large jumps in energetic particles. Earthlings were lucky—the only effect was interference of radio communications with Antarctic research outposts.

But remember, there are now approximately two thousand communications satellites in orbit. And we're a society overdependent on computers, automatic teller machines, cell phones, and a host of other electronic equipment. If a CME makes it to Earth, there is a potential for communication loss and an assortment of computer glitches. The next time you can't get Zimbabwe on your cell phone,

This major solar flare occurred in April 2, 2001—the largest X-ray flare on record. It hurled a CME into space—but luckily not toward Earth. (NASA)

there's a problem with your airline flight, or your credit rating suddenly goes south, it may be a CME. This definitely gives "sunshine on your shoulder" a new meaning.

Judging the Danger

Earth has a magnetic field, called the *magnetosphere*, and an atmosphere that protects us from CMEs. There is no direct danger to our health as long as these "shields" remain in place. Admittedly, in the majority of cases, space weather—including CMEs—doesn't directly affect public safety in the same way as weather on the surface of the planet. But it does affect our tools and techno-toys.

Typically, it takes a few days for a solar CME ejected in our direction to reach Earth—where it can create techno-havoc. Besides causing problems with our satellites, such solar storms can affect the electrical grid on the surface. When a CME changes the shape of our magnetosphere, Earth's magnetic field moves slightly, and long pieces of wire (such as those of telephone lines and power grids) can act as electrical generators. There are examples: On March 13, 1989, one of the largest recorded solar eruptions generated a CME. The particles battered Earth, causing a major hydropower plant in Quebec to shut down. The entire province was thrown into a blackout—almost causing a cascade effect that would have shut down all electric output in eastern Canada and the northeastern United States. And in July 2000, a large CME dumped almost fifteen hundred gigawatts of power into the atmosphere, about four times the amount generated by the entire U.S. power grid.[2] The frying effect damaged two large power transformers and shut down voltage-regulating devices along the East Coast. Face it, without electricity, our modern society shuts down. All of it.

Minimizing the Danger

At present, scientists are only beginning to understand the mechanisms behind solar wind and CMEs. So far, there is no way to predict when the Sun will spit out a chunk of particles in our direction. Right now, there is a small cadre of satellites (with more in the works) that monitor and track the Sun when it does decide to burp. With time, more satellites and better computer models will allow astronomers to predict if and when CMEs might strike Earth—and the potential dangers. A few hours' notice allows controllers to put their communications satellites in a safe mode and alerts power companies as to potential problems. There is even a space weather bureau associated with the National Oceanic and Atmospheric Administration—the Space Environment Center—that monitors and forecasts space weather events.

We probably won't be able to stop a CME any time in the near future—and no one wants to throw away their latest satellite dish—so be prepared for interruptions of electrical service in the future. Having backup systems—such as candles, hand pumps, woodstoves, and solar panels—is probably a good idea, especially for people in the northern regions of the world. A browse through an all-nonelectric catalog or similar publication (such as the Lehman's Non-Electric, Cumberland General Store, or Real Goods catalogs) may make you feel better about the possible loss of your television remote.

But the spitting out of the Sun's CME's isn't the only problem we encounter with our Sun. There is also its future—and just how hot and big it will get.

Stellar Brightness: Our Sun's Idea of Fun

The Sun, our only star, dominates the solar system. With a diameter more than one hundred times that of Earth, it is the key to our survival. Simply put, sunshine begets warmth and light, begets plants, begets animals, and begets humans with sunburn. And face it: Without it, there would be no *Baywatch*.

Most scientists believe the Sun has a long way to go before it fizzles out. Based on what astronomers know about stars, ours won't burn out for another 5 to 6 billion years, give or take a few hundred million. But in the meantime, some astronomers believe that our Sun will increase in brightness in the next billion years or so. And if our planet is still in its present orbit, what will our flora and fauna descendants be? Simple. They'll all be toast.

Judging the Danger

The reason we have sunshine is at the core of the star: A nuclear powerhouse where hydrogen nuclei are smashed together and welded into heavier nuclei. Lighter particles and high-energy gamma rays are thrown off. The hydrogen particle consists of only a proton; these small things wrestle with each other, colliding to form something that sounds like what the android Data would say on *Star Trek*: nuclei of deuterium, or *deuterons*. These smack into other protons, eventually forming helium 3, which then smash into other helium 3, get into a headlock, and form helium 4. Then two protons are released.

But in about a billion years, something will cause this internal smacking to go berserk, and the Sun will become over 10 percent brighter than it is today; in 3 billion years, it will increase by 40 percent. As our star becomes brighter, it will cause a moist greenhouse reaction on Earth—years and years of unrelenting rain, almost like living in Seattle. With more sunshine will come a runaway greenhouse, almost like living in Seattle if it were on Venus—where the near surface temperatures can reach close to 900°F (482°C).

Minimizing the Danger

All right. So you and I won't be here then. But we want to help future generations with their paranoia. So if humans are still around the planet and haven't cloned or blown themselves out of existence, scientists suggest the best way to protect our species is *not* to hide behind a near-Earth asteroid. One idea is to use the "gravitational slingshot" technique now used to send spacecraft to the outer planets—and reposition Earth to keep it one step ahead of the Sun's hot rays.

Here's how our descendants would expand Earth's orbit outward from the Sun: First, they would find just the right, about sixty-two-mile-wide, near-Earth asteroid. Then they would direct the rock (by towing or nudging with spacecraft—we suggest giant rubber bands) toward Earth. From there, as the asteroid flies past Earth, it would transfer some of its orbital energy to our planet. If our descendants were great at orbital gymnastics, the huge rock would then fly out to Jupiter, gain some more energy, and then fly by Earth again, imparting energy to our orbit. This would be a good time to have their instruments calibrated, too—it would be more than embarrassing to have the asteroid hit Earth.

According to some of the scientists who worked on this—Don Korycansky, University of California; Gregory Laughlin, NASA; and Fred Adams, University of Michigan—our descendants would have to make sure the asteroid encounters Earth every six thousand years, or about every 240 generations.[3] We'd like to be in the family who passes down the "business" of keeping track of that asteroid. Talk about job security.

And if scientists and engineers of the future got really tricky with the asteroids, they could even move moons and planets to make new Earths. They'll have to do something. After all, messing up Earth's orbit will also destabilize the orbits of Venus and Mercury.

We know all our way-in-the-future descendants now reading the above paragraphs are having a good laugh. Because by now, you've invented transporter technology, are living on Titan, surfing on Europa, and skiing on the polar caps of Mars.

Near-Earth Asteroids: Someone's Knocking at the Door

Dinosaurs, those ancient reptiles we all know and love, lived on this planet for well over 200 million years. Many scientists now believe that the creatures unceremoniously became extinct because of one or many large chunks of rock: not just any old rock you find in your backyard—but one or more estimated to be six to twelve miles in diameter. The alleged impact on our planet and demise of the dinosaurs took place about 65 million years ago (and it wasn't the only huge impact throughout geologic history). So far, evidence points not only to a same-age impact crater measuring 150 miles wide, but to Earth's rock records. They indicate that a catastrophic, global event killed off many forms of life, including the above-mentioned dinosaurs. That's extinction in every sense of the word.

This rock and others like it are called *asteroids*—large bodies orbiting in our solar system, mainly between the orbits of Mars and Jupiter. However, over millions of years, some asteroids stray from the fold, ending up in orbits that come close to or cross Earth's orbit. Such asteroids are referred to as near-Earth asteroids (NEAs), for the simple reason that they come provocatively close to our planet.

NEAs range in size from a boulder to 0.6 miles (one kilometer) in diameter, and can be stony, metallic, or carbonaceous. And because

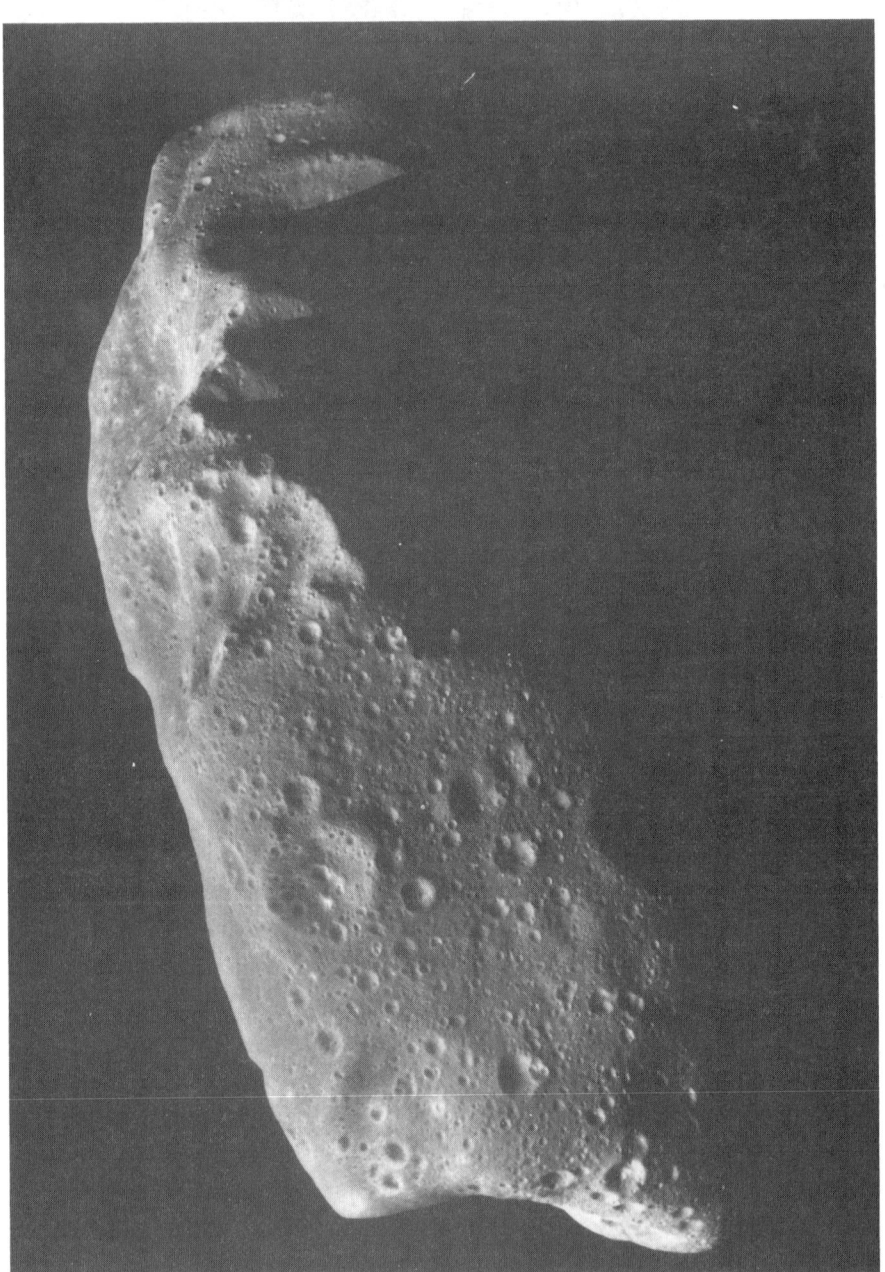

The asteroid Ida was the second such small body visited by a spacecraft. Ida is a member of the main belt of asteroids; it is not a near-Earth asteroid. But most near-Earth asteroids no doubt look similar. (Photo courtesy Dr. Peter Thomas, Cornell University)

asteroids can't be seen with the naked eye, they can, and do, come perilously close to Earth without warning. If they enter our atmosphere, the small ones burn up or hit the surface with little impact, no pun intended. But the larger ones are another story. They are capable of causing havoc ranging from huge destruction and global climate change to extinction of many species—including humans.

Judging the Danger

What are our chances of being impacted by a large enough asteroid to cause extinction? How about its chances of causing general death and destruction? For the last few years, astronomers who telescopically scan the night skies have found that the news is not good. Current observations and computer models estimate too many big ones "out there"—enough to scare us into sprucing up ye olde bomb shelter out back. In fact, there may be anywhere from nine hundred to eleven hundred asteroids larger than six-tenths of a mile in diameter with orbits crossing or coming very close to Earth.

So what's the big deal about an asteroid that size? This just happens to be the "magic size" astronomers use to differentiate between smaller asteroids that cause localized destruction—and larger ones capable of global mayhem. Take our "magic" asteroid six-tenths of a mile across. Now have it strike land or shallow water. The impact would throw huge amounts of dust into the atmosphere—creating a cascade of events: It would block the Sun's rays enough to darken the skies, disrupt weather and climate, create a mini-ice age, and inhibit plant growth for at least a year. There would be a rapid cutoff of the food supply, and within a few months the possible loss of a quarter of the world's population.

And don't even think about an asteroid greater than three miles in diameter—not even Mad Max could survive that one. Such a impact would destroy most of the plant and animal life on Earth, and that includes us. Even a midocean hit would have huge effects. One computer simulation showed that such a strike in the Atlantic Ocean could produce a huge tsunami spreading out in every direction. These large and powerful waves would completely inundate the upper East Coast of the United States, all the way to the Appalachian Mountains. Western Europe would suffer the same fate.

Although the numbers bounce around depending on what group puts out the data, there is a general consensus that NEAs are a credible threat. Astronomers have determined the orbits of about four hundred NEAs over the magic size. That leaves around seven hundred unknown, stealth NEAs that haven't been determined yet. And nothing hurts worse than being smacked from behind by a sneaky asteroid.

Near misses and true strikes are definitely part of our recent past. In 1996 an asteroid about a third of a mile across was detected only four days before it came within 280,000 miles of our planet—a very near miss in astronomical terms. Between 1991 and 1994, four asteroids came closer to Earth than half the distance to the Moon. In 1972 a small, one-thousand-ton asteroid skimmed our outer atmosphere. One of the most famous visited on June 30, 1908, when a small asteroid one to two hundred feet wide exploded about three miles above the ground near Tunguska, Siberia. Although this object had a grazing trajectory instead of coming straight down, it still released energy equivalent to a nuclear bomb, destroying hundreds of square miles of remote forest lands.

Minimizing the Danger

Figuring out when an asteroid capable of global devastation will impact Earth is tricky business, since only about 40 percent (maybe) of them have been discovered so far. And of those whose orbits are known, calculations are only accurate for the next hundred years or so. After that, it's possible something in the solar system will perturb a huge rock's orbit, sending it hurling directly toward Earth. On top of that, the remaining 60 percent might be difficult to find. They might be too far from us or in regions of the sky difficult to observe. You can't calculate what you don't know.

But there is good news:

+ Right now, there is an effort afoot by NASA—through, of all things, a congressional mandate—to discover 90 percent of all NEAs a half mile or larger in diameter within the next ten years. This may give us anywhere from five to one hundred years' warning about an impending large asteroid impact. That way, we can develop methods to stop the interloper, by breaking it up into smaller pieces.

✦ A new risk-assessment scale was recently developed that assigns a numerical value to currently known and yet-to-be-discovered NEAs. The scale, called the *Torino Impact Hazard Scale*, created by Richard Binzel at the Massachusetts Institute of Technology, runs from 0 to 10, with 0 or 1 representing no risk of damage to our planet and 10 meaning a certain global catastrophe.[4] This system takes into account the probability that a specific asteroid will hit Earth, as well as its speed and size. So far, no asteroid found has ever carried a ranking greater than one.

✦ For those of you who slept through statistics, we'll figure it out for you: It appears that the probability of dying in an aircraft accident is one in twenty thousand; from an asteroid impact, one in twenty-five thousand; from a flood one in thirty-thousand; and from food poisoning one in 3 million. Las Vegas should have such odds.

✦ Want more statistics? The actual probability of Earth being hit by a large asteroid is very low. Although we are constantly bombarded by the small stuff, most scientists believe that an impact from an asteroid just over a half mile in diameter or larger happens only once every five hundred thousand to 10 million years (although some believe it happens as often as every one hundred thousand years). And an impact capable of global extinction from an asteroid about six miles wide happens only every 100 million years or so. The probabilities are low, but they are still like the odds at a horse race. Sometimes the dark horse wins. Let's hope none of these big boys do.

Comets: What a Tail

Along with asteroids and meteoroids, comets can also be referred to as near-Earth objects (NEOs). Once harbingers of doom and gloom, comets are now known to be leftovers of the formation of our solar system and reservoirs of data about our past. But they are also objects that can cross Earth's path—with the potential to hit, causing destruction and mayhem just like asteroids.

Asteroids and comets seem like evil twins. They were apparently born at the same time (at the beginnings of our solar system's formation); they live in the same place (the evil solar-system empire); and have a propensity to orbit (in all fairness, so does Earth). But they do differ: Comets don't always stick around and they are made of more dust, ice, and gases than an asteroid. This makes their arrival and departure that much more likable. Who wouldn't like a dusty, icy, gassy guest that didn't come back for two hundred years?

Judging the Danger

Unlike rocky asteroids, comets are a collection of dust, gases, and ice. Think of them as your not-so-average icy mudballs orbiting the Sun—composed of carbon dioxide, frozen water, methane, ammonia, and materials such as silicates and organic compounds. We all know about comets from literature—their tails often become visible to the naked eye as they approach the Sun and the solar wind blows material from them. Short-period comets orbit the Sun every few to two hundred years and are thought to originate from the Kuiper Belt, a disk of cometlike objects that probably exists beyond the orbits of Pluto and Neptune. Long-period comets travel into our solar system in orbits that take from two hundred years to thousands of years—some returning, others not. These comets are thought to originate in the Oort Cloud, a theoretical mass of comets surrounding the solar system about one hundred thousand astronomical units from the Sun (for comparison: Earth is one astronomical unit from the Sun).

One of the problems with NEOs in general—and asteroids and comets in particular—is that many of them have not been discovered yet. This leads to speculation about the comet population and their potential to strike us. To date, some scientists estimate that only 7 to 10 percent of all comets have been found. Again it's hard to make predictions about something you can't find.

Comets are thought to be fairly common in our solar system, and the chances of seeing one are good. Of course, the really spectacular ones become visible to the naked eye, such as Comet Hyakutake in 1996 and Comet Hale-Bopp in 1997. More ominous was Shoemaker-Levy 9, a comet that fragmented into at least twenty-one pieces, eventually impacting Jupiter from July 16 to July 22, 1994. This was the first time humans witnessed the impact of a space object on another planet. Luckily, Earth was not in the line of fire, or you likely wouldn't be reading this book right now. The comet chunks—some with diameters estimated at over a mile wide—would have obliterated life on Earth.

Minimizing the Danger

How do you stop a comet? As with an asteroid, no one really knows. If only we truly had phasers, maybe we could melt a too-close-for-comfort one.

No one is ignoring the potential danger from comets—and other NEOs, for that matter. There is a worldwide effort to search for these interlopers, from the United States to the United Kingdom:

+ A recent study put out by the U.K. Task Force on Potentially Hazardous Near Earth Objects, and prepared for the United Kingdom's Ministry of Science, urges national and international steps to discover potential NEO hazards; find ways to get rid of potential troublemakers (NEOs, not in the Ministry); and keep us, the public, informed. The group also identified 258 potentially hazardous NEOs that orbit within 4.6 million miles of Earth and are at least close to five hundred feet across.[5]
+ There are places that attempt to track NEOs for the rest of us without big or fancy telescopes. Although most of the groups concentrate on near-Earth asteroids, they still find many comets in the process: Lincoln Near-Earth Asteroid Research (LINEAR); Near-Earth Asteroid Tracking (NEAT); Spacewatch; Catalina Sky Survey; Lowell Observatory Near-Earth Object Search (LONEOS); and the UK and Japanese Spaceguard groups.

That Old Devil Moon

We've always suspected that a full moon has a weird influence on people and animals. Other than making really bad Hollywood movies possible, why else would the werewolf legend exist? And haven't you noticed that things really do feel a little different during a full moon—a little more frantic, funky, and a bit loony? In fact, increased traffic accidents and incidence of insanity have been reported on full-moon days. And now another one has been added: animal bites.

A recent study surveyed 1,621 animal-bite patients from 1997 to 1999 at the accident and emergency department of Bradford Royal Infirmary in England. The incidence of animal bites were two times greater on or around days with a full moon, pointing to some association with animal behavior. More studies are being

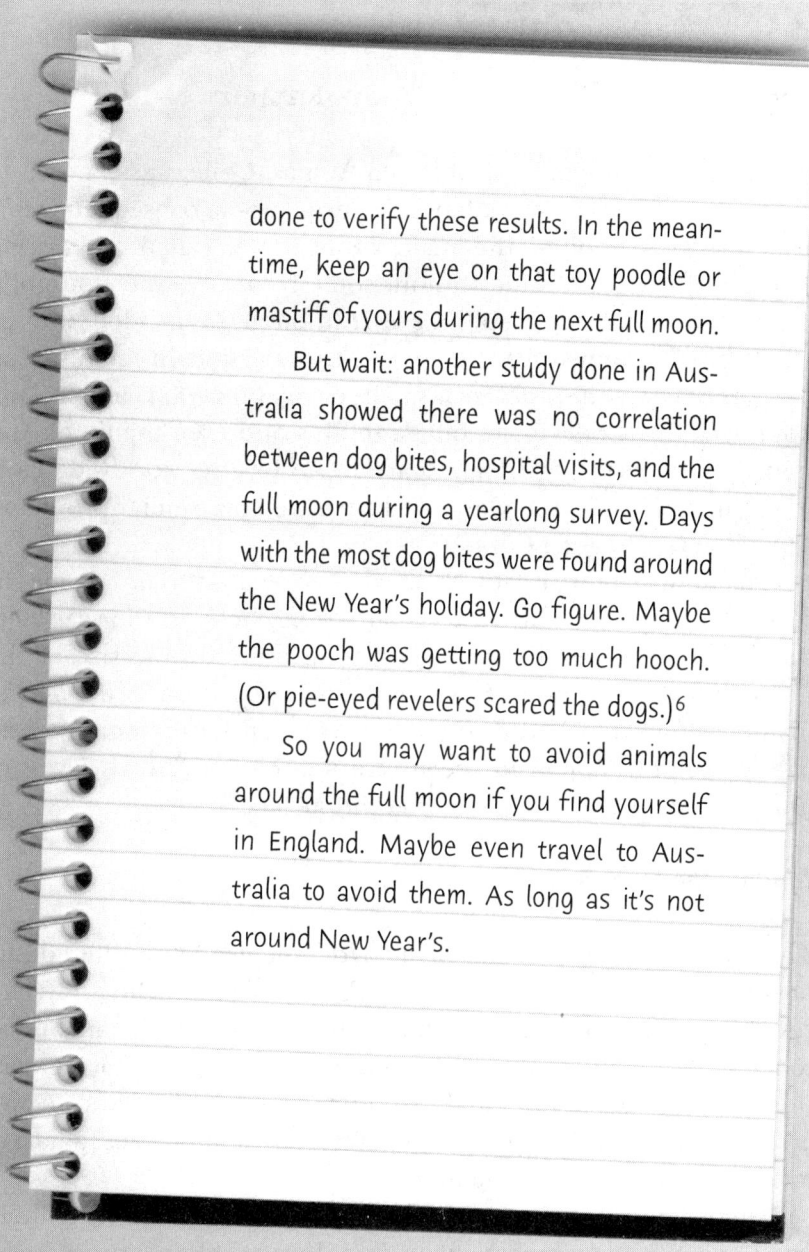

done to verify these results. In the meantime, keep an eye on that toy poodle or mastiff of yours during the next full moon.

But wait: another study done in Australia showed there was no correlation between dog bites, hospital visits, and the full moon during a yearlong survey. Days with the most dog bites were found around the New Year's holiday. Go figure. Maybe the pooch was getting too much hooch. (Or pie-eyed revelers scared the dogs.)[6]

So you may want to avoid animals around the full moon if you find yourself in England. Maybe even travel to Australia to avoid them. As long as it's not around New Year's.

THE OOZING OZONE

Ozone Loss: It's Not Your Father's Tan

In the fall of 2000, the city of Punta Arenas, Chile, was exposed to high levels of ultraviolet radiation for two days—a consequence of a wandering offshoot of the main ozone hole, called a *filament*.[7] Anyone who went outside without some form of protection got a sunburn in as little as seven minutes. Although this incident was relatively brief, scientists fear longer ones are possible in the future as the Antarctic ozone hole grows. They believe these filaments will not only affect Chile again, but Argentina and even the tip of Australia, South Africa, and New Zealand. And as the worldwide layer thins, other areas of the planet will begin to have similar problems. This is no way to get a Coppertone tan.

Filaments are a relatively new discovery, with no rhyme or reason to their spinning off the main ozone hole. In the year 2000 the ozone hole was the largest ever—three times the size of the United States, with over 50 percent ozone depletion. A wandering filament finally reached a populated area—giving the world a taste of what might happen in the future if (or when?) high levels of ultraviolet rays reach our bodies at the surface.

Judging the Danger

The ozone layer protects our planet from the deadly, unfiltered rays of the Sun—particularly ultraviolet (UV) radiation. These rays are responsible for that symbol of the modern good life, the tan. Spend too much time sunbathing and you can get a bad burn. Fortunately, the ozone molecules that make up our planet's invisible protective layer act as a filter, absorbing most of the Sun's ultraviolet radiation and preventing it from reaching us.

Unfortunately, this protective layer is exposed to a variety of influences, many of them human-made. Emissions of chlorofluorocarbons, nitrous oxide, and methane by human activity all act to reduce the number of ozone molecules. This causes a thinning of the already ten-

Singing in the (Electron) Rain

As if human-made chemical compounds didn't deplete the ozone enough, now scientists involved in the Solar-Atmospheric Coupling by Electrons (SOLACE) study at NASA have discovered a natural mechanism. It's "raining" free-electron particles. And this is one rain in which we can't use an umbrella.[8]

Yes, they may be free, but this is no deal. The free electrons raining from Earth's magnetosphere can create significant amounts of nitrogen oxide. And that, in turn, contributes to the depletion of the ozone layer. Billions of electrons normally spiral back and forth between Earth's magnetic poles in the magnetosphere—the region protecting our planet, and us, from the Sun's particle emissions, called the *solar wind*. When the solar wind fluctuates, as it does in an eleven-year solar cycle, it can interfere with the magnetosphere. This causes some of these electrons to fall, or "rain," into the upper atmosphere—naturally creating chemical compounds that help deplete the ozone layer. Lucky for us the cycle peaks only once every eleven years.

uous ozone layer, allowing more UV radiation to penetrate. Since scientific monitoring began in 1985, the worldwide ozone layer has been steadily thinning. And in Antarctica, the dreaded "hole" forms during each southern winter, allowing a larger percentage of UV radiation to reach the surface and surrounding ocean.

Although some people will appreciate the convenience of a quick tan, too much UV radiation can cause skin cancer in humans. Already, New Zealand and Australia—two countries close to the seasonal ozone hole—have the world's highest rates of skin cancer. And melanoma, the worst form of skin cancer, can kill you. The UV radiation also affects the DNA of plankton, the tiny plants and animals at the bottom of the ocean's food chain—and can eventually kill them. This, in turn, reduces the number of commercially harvested fish—fish that feed on the plankton to survive. If the ozone hole and its filaments continue to grow, agriculture and livestock will be affected. Tourism will be cut considerably; the vacationer will opt for the slower tanning beds versus minutes grilling in the Southern Hemisphere countries.

Minimizing the Danger

What can we do to avoid overexposure to ultraviolet radiation? Here are a few hints:

+ Obviously, limit your exposure to the direct rays of the Sun, especially between 10 A.M. and 4 P.M. Wearing protective clothing and applying sunscreen are good short-term solutions.
+ Moving to more northern, cloudy climates may help—but may also be depressing.
+ None of these things address the long-term problems with health, agriculture, fishing, and tourism. For this we need to boost up the thinning ozone layer worldwide. And to do this we need to reduce the amount of ozone-depleting materials that we emit into the atmosphere. Like going off cigarettes, laying off the bad, smoky stuff we put into the atmosphere will allow the ozone layer to recover naturally.

✦ You can also help on a more local level: Buy and grow organic produce, avoiding the use of methyl bromide, a toxic soil fumigant and one of the more ozone-depleting chemicals still in use; keep home and garden chemicals and solvents tightly sealed to prevent gases from escaping into the atmosphere; improve energy efficiency in cars and lawnmowers to reduce carbon emissions, or bike to work and use a manual push mower; recycle fire extinguishers that contain ozone-depleting halones; and check air conditioning and refrigerators for leaks.

✦ Although there has been good progress in reducing emission of industrial chlorine-containing compounds—such as those used in aerosol sprays, solvents, and refrigerants—other ozone-depleting materials have been harder to reduce. Large amounts of methane are produced by agriculture, and automobile catalytic converters and airplanes burning jet fuel emit nitrous oxide—both contributing to ozone depletion. Not that everyone around the world agrees—but with efforts and legislation such as the Montreal and Kyoto Protocols, the release of ozone-depleting chemicals is beginning to level off somewhat. But it could be decades, even centuries, before the ozone layer recovers, if it does at all. It may be time to invest in companies that make sunscreen and protective clothing.

THINGS TO WATCH OUT THERE

Killer Cosmic Clouds:
When Interstellar Dust Gets in Your Eyes

Killer cosmic clouds. Just the name sends a chill of fear up and down the spine. We picture roving gangs of glowing cloud formations speeding our way, ready to obliterate life on Earth. In truth, we can't see these clouds—but that doesn't make them any less dangerous for us. Our Sun produces a constant outpouring of energetic particles, known collectively as the *solar wind*. This wind, in turn, produces a protective bubble around our solar system (the *heliosphere*), keeping nasty items such as galactic cosmic rays at bay.[9]

When our solar system is cruising through a relatively empty, low-density part of interstellar space, as we have for the last 5 million years, this bubble stays intact, making life possible on Earth. And what is empty space? It's interstellar space that contains less than one atom per cubic inch. Space, however, is full of clouds or regions containing ten to one hundred particles per cubic inch. It's called *local fluff*, and we could bump into one of these gassy clusters almost anytime. Existing instruments cannot detect these extremely small clouds. Even if we somehow sail around these local clouds, we're not out of the galactic woods yet. A large cloud region located toward the Aquila Rift is headed our way—and due to collide with us within the next fifty thousand years. That's something to drop on your guests at your next cocktail party.

Judging the Danger

How can a collision with something we can't even see harm us? It's as simple as an encroaching thunderstorm—something else you can't stop. As the solar system enters the cloud, the heliosphere will start to collapse. This will allow neutral hydrogen atoms to strike our atmosphere, possibly causing large and catastrophic climate changes. Be ready for a new ice age or an increased greenhouse effect. The number of high-energy galactic cosmic rays hitting the planet would increase. This is not good, since such rays are fatal to humans. But we won't be the only ones—other forms of life will die, making this scenario a good illustration of a mass extinction.

Minimizing the Danger

Currently, there is no way to detect when, or even if, we will encounter a killer cosmic cloud. And there's not a big enough fan to wave the cloud in a different direction. Plus, there really is no way to avoid one. The first signs of collision will be an increase in neutral hydrogen hitting our atmosphere. Then there will be a rise in the level of galactic cosmic rays. After that, it's time sell off that land in Arizona and take the next shuttle to the Andromeda galaxy.

Cosmic Ray Jets: Any Relation to the Jetsons?

Scientists have come up with a relatively new theory about cosmic rays and extinction. Our galaxy is home to neutron stars, extremely massive remnants left behind after some stars become supernovas, or exploded stars. Some are present in pairs, slowly spiraling into each other. When they finally do collide, they briefly form a brilliant disk and emit huge jets of cosmic rays. Unfortunately for those in the way of a jet, they're fatal to most forms of life.

Judging the Danger

What would happen if our planet were less than three thousand light years away from a pair of colliding neutron stars—and we just happened to be in the path of a jet? First, you could count on large amounts of cosmic rays flooding Earth for up to a month. The rays would cut like a knife, penetrating the water and ground for hundreds of yards. Many species, including humans, would have their central nervous systems destroyed—another way to cause a mass extinction. But it wouldn't be over: Chemical compounds formed by these rays would deplete the ozone layer, allowing more ultraviolet radiation to reach the surface, killing many plants. The food chain would be disrupted. And much of the planet would become radioactive. This would not be good. Life as we know it would end.

Minimizing the Danger

If a cosmic ray jet were heading our way, the organisms and species sheltered deep—and we mean *very* deep, in caves, underground, and underwater—would survive. Land and shallow water species would not—except for some radiation-resistant species such as insects and some plants. The cockroach would survive, but we already knew that.

Where could we hide? Underground or underwater living spaces would be best, although pretty boring. The good part is that some scientists believe that the radiation from these jets could create mutations in life that would survive. And that would lead to new species and a new flowering of life on Earth. Bring on the two-headed trout and five-winged bats.

What are the odds of this happening? Scientists have so far identified five pairs of neutrons stars in our galaxy. Only two are within three thousand light years of us. And since it will be several hundred million years before they collide, we're set. True? Unfortunately, these are only the ones currently known. Some estimates put the number of neutron star pairs in our galaxy in the hundreds. If and when one of these unknown pairs collide, we will still have lots of time—on the order of hundreds of thousands of years—to prepare.

Time to start building that starship.

Black Holes: Gobbling Up Everything

M87 is not the name of a new automatic rifle. It's a galaxy only fifty light years—a mere jog to the store in astronomical terms—from our own Milky Way Galaxy. Thanks to the sharp-eyed telescopes of the orbiting Hubble Space Telescope, scientists also think this island of stars has something insidious lurking at its center—an object about 3 billion times the Sun's mass all crammed into a spot no larger than our solar system. You guessed it: a huge black hole.

No one knows for certain how black holes start, but they do qualify for the vacuum-in-space award. In general, the theory is that black holes were once large stars that burned out their nuclear fuel and then collapsed—the mashing so violent that all the atoms were crushed out of existence. From there, these "stars" were squeezed into an amazingly small size, with mega-increases in their densities and gravity. And they probably grow in size. After all, black holes just love to suck in other stars that get too close to their boundaries—called *event horizons*. So billions of years could mean billions of stars down the gullet of many black holes.

Judging the Danger

We know now that black holes exist—or if they don't, something out there comes pretty close to mimicking them. In 1994, M87 was one of the first to be found. Since then, others have been inferred, based on the reaction of other stellar phenomena around them.

You wouldn't want to get too close. Once inside a black hole, everything is reduced to a singular point in space and time—or a point of infinite density. Here, space and time are turned to mush. Of course, there are people who think they may be able to develop a desktop black hole. We're way ahead of them. Our desktop already has one. It eats pencils and pens.

Minimizing the Danger

Big black holes? Medium black holes? Mini-black holes? Should we be afraid? At this stage of the game, not really. And here's why:

+ For one thing, we still don't have any solid evidence (as if you could ever get such data) of a black hole. But many scientists believe we do have solid circumstantial evidence.
+ We've also apparently been living around one for a while with no visible effects. Scientists believe there may be a big black hole in the middle of the Milky Way Galaxy, where we reside—but it's toward the center, and we're on one of the galaxy's spiral arms.
+ We should also let go of the notion that our Sun will become a black hole. There's just not enough stuff in the star to even consider a mutation to a black hole.
+ And although we've heard the rumors, there is not a black hole around Pluto.
+ What we *should* be paranoid about are the people trying to make an analog to black holes—something called a *desktop black hole* (also called an *optical* or *sonic black hole*). Recently, researchers reportedly brought light to a standstill—which is thought to simulate the physics behind a black hole. They

are attempting to trap light in a vortex, trying to replicate some of the true black hole behavior—hopefully without sucking everyone in the lab into an alternate reality.

✦ There are others who believe there are miniature black holes—and that one day, we'll be able to create these small suckers. Why we would want to do it is another question.

5 TRAVEL-TIME TERRORS

"Leaving on a jet plane,
don't know when
I'll be back again . . ."

T ravel is an experience, a process, and a way to learn and grow. Most of the time, the lessons are positive: a new culture, new language, different food, another way of looking at life and the world, new friends. You come back changed for the better. Sometimes, though, we forget that travel has a dark side. In spite of our best efforts to sanitize, homogenize, and safety-ize the process, there are still inherent dangers—and not just the airline food.

Some of these dangers are obvious. Most people realize certain spots around the world aren't suitable for general travel. You don't want to take the kids on a trip to a country embroiled in a war—holy or not. You and your spouse don't want to drink champagne in places rampant with terrorism. And you certainly don't want to take a day hike in a country with a brutal dictatorship or with complete anarchy.

No form of travel is completely safe, either. Trains, buses, and automobiles all have accidents at one time or another, leading to injury and death. But when traveling to a faraway destination, most people choose the airplane, which has its own unique dangers. And assuming you deplane at your remote destination safe and sound—whether it's Timbuktu or the heartland of America—there are numerous diseases waiting to strike. They lay hidden in your food and water, or in the insect that bites you.

Yes, you may be leaving on a jet plane. And you really *won't* know when (or if) you'll be back again—if you're not careful.

LEAVING ON A JET PLANE

Deep Vein Thrombosis: Getting There Is Only Half the Fun

It's been a long flight and the plane is on final approach. The movie wasn't too bad and the food was decent. All in all, a good trip.

Could taking off on a plane be fun—or are there hidden dangers everywhere? (NASA)

Strange, though: one of your legs looks swollen. Very swollen. So swollen that the attendants have to carry you off the plane in a wheelchair. An ambulance rushes you to the hospital, where you're prepped for immediate surgery. What's going on here?

The link between long airline flights and deep vein thrombosis (DVT)—or blood clots—has only recently been rigorously studied.[1] But the evidence continues to mount: There was the tragic death of a young woman who collapsed minutes after a twenty-three-hour flight from Australia. Another case occurred when a father of four complained of breathing difficulties on arrival in Australia from Great Britain; after falling into a coma for five days, he died when a blood clot made its way into his lungs. A middle-aged executive almost died from DVT during a flight from New York to Switzerland. Former Vice President Dan Quayle is one of the most famous victims of DVT, suffering an attack while on a flight in 1994. And the list goes on.

Deep vein thrombosis is a blood clot in a major vein, usually in the legs and/or pelvis. The incidents on long-haul airline flights have led to the nickname "economy-class syndrome," but the risk isn't only for those in the "cheap" seats—it can also reach those in the first-class section. There are more incidents in economy class simply because more people fly that class, and there tends to be less space to move your legs. In fact, the British government wants airlines to issue health warnings to all passengers on long flights about the dangers of these serious and potentially fatal blood clots.

Judging the Danger

Although the link between long airline flights and DVT has just been recognized, the problem is not new. A study in England found that approximately 100 airline passengers with blood clots are admitted to hospital emergency rooms near London's Heathrow Airport each year. And of the approximately 142 patients a year who die from DVT in hospitals around Gatwick, many are thought to be passengers on long airline flights. Some doctors believe that this economy-class syndrome has claimed hundreds of lives over the last few decades—no doubt many times without anyone realizing the connection.

Scuba and the Friendly Skies

What's the dangerous connection between scuba diving and airplanes? People wearing dry suits instead of wet suits? Actually, the danger occurs not in the water, but when you travel on an airplane too soon after diving. And with millions of recreational scuba divers in the United States alone—many of whom travel to exotic, far-away places like Australia's Great Barrier Reef or the Hawaiian Islands to see the (underwater) sights—this becomes a real danger.

We've all heard of the "bends." During a dive, the body (especially the lungs) experiences higher than normal pressure due to the water weight above. During a rapid ascent, the pressure drops off and your lungs expand because of the air inside. Because the air you breathe while diving is compressed in a tank, it further expands and can rupture your alveoli, the tiny air-filled sacs in the lungs. Escaping gas bubbles travel through the surrounding blood vessels, then throughout the body, lodging in small arteries everywhere—including your heart and brain—a condition known as arterial gas embolism (AGE). If bubbles lodge in the heart, they can cause shortness of breath, chest pain, or even a heart attack. Those in the brain can cause mild confusion, unconsciousness, or stroke. This is why divers do not return rapidly and directly to the surface, but stop at specific depths for certain periods during the ascent. The only treatment for AGE is recompression therapy in a chamber, which must be administered as soon as possible.[2]

But what, you say, does this have to do with airplane travel? If you're like most divers who have traveled to an exotic locale, you want to dive as much as possible—including the day you have to take that big bird back home. Bad move. An airplane is a low-pressure environment, while your dive takes you to a high-pressure one—and this change in pressure could cause AGE. The greater and more rapid the change, such as going from the deep below into the great blue sky, the greater the risk. Remember, commercial airplanes do not carry recompression chambers. So try leaving at least a full day between your last dive and your plane trip. Relax and get your body used to sea level pressure. During this period you can sip cool native drinks, check yourself for any signs of AGE from the dives, and watch episodes of Sea Hunt.

Long-distance flights present passengers with a combination of risk factors for developing blood clots in the legs: high altitudes, cramped conditions, and even the cabin air. One recent study confirmed the risk: Twenty healthy men where placed in a chamber simulating an air pressure of seven thousand feet above sea level, the same pressure found in modern airplanes. They were told not to exercise, and after eight hours, their blood samples were analyzed. There was an increase in the compounds associated with clotting—in fact, between two and a half and eight times the initial levels. The researchers concluded that exposure to airplane cabin pressure helps activate coagulation, increasing the risk of serious or even potentially fatal DVT.

But it's not only the pressure—it's the cramped position and air. Sitting for many hours in an economy-class airline seat can reduce the circulation in your legs by 50 percent. The seats are smaller and recline less, making it easier for the blood to become more static. Add to this the dry air in the cabin—which causes the blood to hypercoagulate, or become thicker—and it's a perfect setup for the formation of clots.

Minimizing the Danger

What can you do to decrease your risk of getting these blood clots on long airline flights? Doctors recommend performing leg exercises regularly, including stretches. No matter how much the person sitting in the aisle seat stares and grumbles, periodically get up and walk around when it's safe. In fact, warn them of the DVT and see if they want to get up and stretch (but pay attention to seatbelt signs—just in case any turbulence begins and you need to get back to your seat). If you can, elevate your legs a bit by putting your feet on a small piece of carry-on luggage under your seat. And even though one study showed that alcohol thins the blood somewhat, it's still better for your system to lighten up on the drinks; better yet, only drink nonalcoholic beverages. If you take any blood-thinning medication or aspirin, continue to do so.

And don't think planes are the only blood clot culprits while you're traveling. If you go from your long plane ride to a train, bus, car, or rickshaw, you're in a cramped position again. The best medicine for all these circumstances is to periodically stand up and stretch your legs when it's safe. Except in the rickshaw: it's a bit rickety—but the good news is it can't go too far on human power.

Disinsection: They Check In, but They Don't Check Out

Your overseas flight went smoothly and now the plane is taxiing toward the terminal. Before you can take off your seatbelt and reach for your carry-on, several local, official-looking people march down the aisles, spraying something from aerosol cans. Passengers start to cough and sneeze. The vapors reach you and you can't seem to catch your breath. What is this stuff they're spraying all over? And why has the air circulation system been turned off?

Congratulations. The airplane, you, your luggage, and all the other passengers have just been *disinsected*. It's a euphemism that sounds like what they do to frogs in biology class, but in this case, it means "sprayed with insecticides." You're probably familiar with insecticides—the kind of stuff you put on your backyard plants—with all the warnings and cautions. You know—the ones with labels saying things like "avoid breathing," "hazardous substance," and "wash hands thoroughly after use." The spraying is to prevent insects from being accidentally imported from one country to another or from carrying in various diseases. The consequence? Passengers have to breathe the fumes, aggravating any respiratory or other health conditions they may have in the short term. And of course, as with all those noxious chemicals some people put on their lawns, the long-term effects are still not completely understood.[3]

Judging the Danger

Not all disinsection procedures are the same. Sometimes flight attendants will spray down the interior of the plane just before it lands or after takeoff. Other times local authorities will spray after landing, while the passengers remain seated. Either way, these procedures occur when the plane is occupied. And don't be fooled into thinking your plane escaped any chemical infestation. Another way disinsection occurs is by residual spraying—or saturating an empty plane with pesticides every six to eight weeks. The material stays in the cabin, and passengers breathe the chemicals throughout the ensuing flights.

There is some controversy over the consequences of breathing these pesticides. The World Health Organization says the procedures are safe, while the Centers for Disease Control and Prevention caution the sprays may aggravate certain health conditions, such as allergies. Some people with high sensitivity to chemicals may end up with a variety of symptoms, such as dizziness, headache, coordination problems, and rashes. If you fly a great deal, there may be some longer-term health effects as well.

Not all international flights require disinsection. For example, the United States stopped airplane disinsection in 1979—mainly because it really didn't work well at keeping out foreign insects and diseases. But there are a number of countries that still don't get it, and require that incoming international flights be sprayed with pesticides. Most of them are located in the Caribbean, Latin America, Australia, and South Pacific regions. The U.S. Department of Transportation (DOT) keeps a list of countries that require pesticide spraying. According to these records, you and your fellow passengers will probably be sprayed on flights ending in places such as India, Madagascar, Australia, New Zealand, Kenya, Mozambique, the United Kingdom, Fiji, Trinidad, Panama, Argentina, Jamaica, Grenada, and Barbados. Places that allow residual spraying include Panama, New Zealand, Fiji, Australia, and Jamaica.

Minimizing the Danger

How can you avoid ending up feeling like a roach in a Raid commercial when flying overseas? First, contact your travel agent or airline and ask whether spraying will occur on your specific flight(s)—with or without passengers onboard. Consult the DOT for an up-to-date list of countries that require disinsection. Consider taking an alternate route to those destinations, such as boat, car, or camel caravan.[4]

Don't Pass the Air Bag

You've survived the disinsection after takeoff and are thwarting economy-class syndrome with frequent stretches. Good for you. Unfortunately, there are still more hidden dangers that await the airline passenger. Take, for instance, the very air you're breathing. You may assume that it's pure, fresh, and adequate.

But it might not be. Fresh air is a big expense. An airline can save approximately $40 million in fuel costs every year if 50 percent of the air in each of its planes was recirculated. But the higher the amount of recirculation, the worse the quality of the air. Proposed new standards call for further reducing the amount of fresh, outdoor air in an plane cabin from fifteen cubic feet per minute per person to just five cubic feet. This could greatly increase the level of toxins in the air, such as hydraulic fluid, lubrication oil, and carbon dioxide. And you guessed it: this could lead to greater risks for passengers with heart conditions and asthma, and a better way to spread diseases such as tuberculosis. It might even make people more irritable, triggering incidents of air rage—as if waiting in line for tickets wasn't enough.

[continued on next page]

What can you do? If you're feeling a little stuffy, ask the flight attendant to ask the pilot for "full utilization of air." They may (or may not) adjust the cabin air—which reduces recirculation and adds more outside air. And try flying on newer airplanes with better, more up-to-date cabin air circulation systems.

On the subject of cabin air, we all know it tends to be very dry. A human is most comfortable with approximately 50 percent humidity. Deserts tend toward 20 to 25 percent, while airplane cabins are less than 10 percent—sometimes approaching 1 percent on long-distance flights. This means you will begin to resemble (inside and out) one of those sun-dried fruits you're snacking on. This is serious dehydration, and can cause dry, wrinkly skin, bloodshot and scratchy eyes, an overwhelming thirst, constipation, and a desire to see *Flight of the Phoenix*.

To avoid ending up like a raisin, drink plenty of water en route. That's water, not alcoholic beverages or coffee—diuretics that lead to more water loss. Bring your own water, or order bottled water from the attendants. Splash

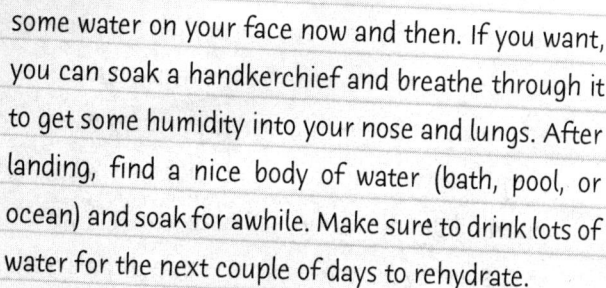

some water on your face now and then. If you want, you can soak a handkerchief and breathe through it to get some humidity into your nose and lungs. After landing, find a nice body of water (bath, pool, or ocean) and soak for awhile. Make sure to drink lots of water for the next couple of days to rehydrate.

Finally, when flying at higher altitudes, you're leaving behind part of the atmosphere's protective layer. As a consequence, the amount of X rays (photons) and energetic particles (neutrons, protons, electrons, muons, and pions) our bodies receive from "out there" increases, but it's a small amount for each flight—a bit more than the normal amount you get each year on the ground. And it's not much of a risk unless you fly quite frequently. In fact, some scientists advise people who fly seventy-five thousand miles per year (at altitudes averaging about thirty-five thousand feet) or more should become more educated about their exposures, especially women who may be or plan to become pregnant.

But the Sun's output is not always the same. Our

[continued on next page]

star becomes more active every eleven years during its natural twenty-two-year sunspot cycle—and the amount of exposure to cosmic particles can increase significantly. The National Oceanic and Atmospheric Administration estimates that in an eleven-year solar cycle, there can be up to three events that produce a much higher dose of particles per hour at airliner altitudes. And there was such an event in November 2000, near the peak of a cycle: The Sun generated one of its most powerful solar radiation storms in twenty-five years, earning it a severe rating on the government's space weather scale. Although we couldn't see or feel it, passengers on airplanes flying near Earth's poles received radiation estimated to be equivalent to ten chest X rays.[5] And you thought everyone on the flight was glowing with good health.

You can also ask the airline for an exemption to being sprayed on arrival—but you'll need a doctor's note. Circumstances for an exemption include an allergy to pesticides, pregnancy, or asthma. Be sure to ask again for the exemption when you confirm your reservation *and* when you check in at the airport. If you can't get an exemption, find out from the flight attendants when (and if) spraying will occur. It may look strange, but prepare yourself by covering up with a blanket to reduce the amount of pesticide that gets onto your hair and clothes. This will also limit the amount of pesticide absorbed by your skin. If inhaling pesticides is a major health issue for you, consider carrying a respirator. For those residual sprayed airplanes, make sure you wear a long-sleeve shirt and pants to minimize the amount of pesticides absorbed from the seat cushions into your skin.[6]

SICK "IN-COUNTRY"

Insect-Borne Diseases: Dodging the Bites

To paraphrase the late Carl Sagan, there are billions and billions of them. But we're talking about insects, bugs, and creepy crawlies here—not stars. The world traveler—whether he wanders out into the wild areas of the country or cowers inside an air-conditioned, urban hotel room—will sooner or later meet up with the native insects. It's inevitable. And it's not just the gross factor or the itchy bites. In some parts of the world, certain insects carry hidden dangers—such as infectious agents they transfer to the unwary human, with often devastating results. Many times the tiniest of insects travel unseen, making this a double hidden danger.

What happens if you're in the wrong place at the wrong time—and get bitten by a disease carrying insect? Symptoms are disease specific, of course, but can range anywhere from mild discomfort, diarrhea, vomiting, fever, and chills, to very bad stuff like heart and brain inflammation. All from a bite, sting, or chomp.

Judging the Danger

What insect-borne diseases might the traveler encounter? Here's just a sampling from the Centers for Disease Control and Prevention (CDC). (In fact, this list should induce you to buy shares in companies that make insecticides—the very ones you ducked away from on those airplanes so as not to breathe them in. The stronger, the better.).[7]

Disease	Location	Agent/Carrier	Symptoms
African sleeping sickness (African Trypanosomiasis)	Tropical Africa	Protozoa/Tsetse fly	*Eastern Trypanosomiasis*: fever, headache, malaise; possibility of death in two to six weeks *Western Trypanosomiasis*: skin ulcer; after dormant period: headache, swollen lymph glands, tremor, fever, rapid heartbeat, then a stupor leading to death
Bartonellosis (Carrion's disease, Oroya Fever)	Peru, Ecuador, Colombia	Bacteria/Sandflies	Fever, pain in joints, bones, and muscles; possibility of skin eruptions and death
Chagas' disease (American Trypanosomiasis)	South & Central America	Protozoa/Assassin or Kissing bugs	Swelling at bite, loss of appetite, malaise, fever, heart irregularity and failure, limb swelling, rash, gastrointestinal problems
Chikungunya disease	India, Southeast Asia, Sub-Saharan Africa	Virus/Mosquitoes	Joint pain; potential for hemorrhagic symptoms
Dengue Fever	Asia, Central America, Africa, South America, Caribbean	Virus/Mosquitoes	First phase: headache, high fever, severe joint and muscle aches Second phase: nausea, depression, vomiting, diarrhea, light sensitivity, swollen lymph nodes
Encephalitis	Southeast Asia, Nepal, Eastern Europe	Virus/Mosquitoes & Ticks	Muscle pain, malaise, fever, sore throat, headache; then seizures, lethargy, and hallucinations; death in approximately 20 percent of cases.
Filariasis (River Blindness, Loiasis, Mansonellasis, Lymphatic filariasis)	Asia, South America, Central America, Africa	Round/Mosquitoes & worms/Biting flies	Headache; fever, vomiting; nausea; light sensitivity; abdominal swelling; inflammation in legs, abdomen and testicles; abscesses; rash; arthritis; and eye lesions that can lead to blindness

Leishmaniasis	Tropical & subtropical areas	Protozoans/Sandflies	Intermittent fever; anemia; enlarged spleen; skin lesions; ulcers in mouth, nose, anus, and skin
Loaisis	Central & West Africa	Loa Loa/Deer or parasite tabanid flies	Intermittent swelling under skin, heart and brain inflammation
Malaria	Africa, Asia, Middle East, Southeast Asia, Caribbean	Plasmodium/Mosquito parasite	Enlarged spleen, fever, chills in low-grade version; convulsions, kidney failure, hypoglycemia possible with more severe strains
Plague	Middle East, India, Africa, South America, Russia	Bacteria/Rodent-borne fleas; also ticks, lice, humans	Nausea, fever, swollen lymph nodes, diarrhea, abdominal pain, gangrene of the extremities
Rift Valley Fever	East Africa, Egypt	Virus/Mosquitoes; also infected livestock	Severe headache, weakness, light sensitivity, onetime fever, muscle pain, facial flushing, eye redness, diarrhea; also possible: retinitis, meningitis, blindness
Sandfly Fever	Africa, Mediterranean	Virus/Sandflies	Vomiting, light sensitivity, rash, fever, headache, chest muscle pain, eye pain, vomiting, joint pain
Trachoma	Asia, Africa, Middle East	Chlamydial/Flies Infection	Constant inflammation under eyelids, turned-in eyelashes, corneal scarring, blindness
Tularaemia (Rabbit Fever)	Worldwide	Bacteria/Ticks, deerflies, & mosquitoes	Rash, muscle pain, headache, chills, fever, enlarged spleen and liver, skin ulcers
Typhus Fever	India, Africa, South America, Southeast Asia	Rickettsia/Fleas, mites, lice, & ticks	Rash, muscle pain, fever, headache; advanced stages include: coma, kidney failure, and possible death
Yellow Fever	Africa, South America	Virus/Mosquitoes	Nausea, headache, fever, slow heart muscle pain, conjunctivitis; then delirium, black vomit, and lack of urination

Minimizing the Danger

If you want to travel, especially to Third World countries, don't despair. There is hope. A few sensible precautions will greatly reduce your odds of ending up as a case study for the American Medical Association.

By all means, consult your doctor long before you go anywhere overseas. Tell her where you plan to go and for how long, so she can advise you on preventative treatments, vaccines, and precautions to take. Listen to her advice. Even better is to have your doctor recommend a specialist in traveler's diseases—the more exotic the better. (The disease, not the doctor.) Follow his advice. Your doctor will probably want you to take some preventative medicines—such as a malarial prophylaxis or a vaccine for diseases like encephalitis, tularaemia, and yellow fever. Maybe all of them—as long as they don't work against each other.

There are also numerous sources available to the traveler who really wants to be knowledgeable and prepared. Check out *The World's Most Dangerous Places* by Robert Young Pelton (Harper Resource, 2000) for advice on all facets of world travel, including diseases. The CDC has a wealth of information about all types of travel-related diseases, including prevention methods and lists of the latest disease outbreaks. Be sure to have supplementary medical and evacuation insurance, just in case.[8] When you return from your adventure, have your doctor take blood, stool, and urine samples to see what, if any, nasty germs you may have picked up. It's always better to start treatment early rather than wait. With some diseases, later might be too late.

Once you're finally in-country, what's the best way to avoid these diseases? Simple! Avoid being bit by insects. To do that, use an effective insect repellent on your clothes and cover yourself up with light-colored long-sleeved pants and shirts. Protect your head and neck with a hat or bandanna. Wear high boots when walking in tall grass. Definitely avoid any areas of known infestation and be very wary of staying in native villages. When sleeping outside, take along and use a ground cloth and mosquito netting. Practice good personal hygiene. Don't forget to check periodically for insect bites and attached ticks. And avoid contact direct with other infected humans, and their clothes or towels.

If you should get bitten and start to develop signs of a native disease, consult a local doctor immediately for preliminary treatment. Most local doctors have seen and treated most of these diseases before. You may need evacuation at this point, too. You did remember to purchase that extra insurance, didn't you? While you're recovering in the local hospital, dream about returning home.

Then again, maybe before you go on your trip, you should read *The Hot Zone* by Richard Preston. You'll never say "Ebola" again without shivering.

Human-Borne Diseases: The Enemy Is Us

When you travel around the world—unless you limit your destinations to the most barren deserts or the highest mountaintops—chances are you'll run into people. Lots of people. And while getting to know other customs and languages is a good thing, the more people you run into, the higher the chances of picking up a disease from them. No, we're not talking sexually transmitted diseases (STDs) or acquired immune deficiency syndrome (AIDS) here, though they are a threat if you get too friendly. We're talking about diseases spread by direct contact, sneezing, or coughing: diseases such as polio, tuberculosis, meningitis, and diphtheria. In fact, diseases once thought to be eradicated make comebacks on the Centers for Disease Control and Prevention lists, and not just in Third World countries. These diseases can give you fevers, headaches, paralysis, skin lesions, deafness—or even kill you. Just remember that the next time you're on some hot, crowded bus with closed windows, elbow to elbow with the sneezing and coughing locals. They might have more than just a cold.

Judging the Danger

What are some of the top diseases on the list? Here is a rundown:[9]

+ *Diphtheria.* A toxin-producing strain of the bacterium *Corynebacterium diptheriae* can produce (in respiratory diphtheria) a low-grade fever, sore throat, and an adherent membrane of the nose, tonsils, or pharynx. Severe cases result in swelling of the neck. Common complications include airway obstruction, pallor, increased heart rate, and weakness, with a fatality rate of 5 to 10 percent. Cutaneous (skin) diphtheria results in infected skin lesions, with fewer complications and fatalities. This disease is spread by intimate physical and respiratory contact, with skin lesions playing an important role in transmission. Before a vaccine was produced, young children were the highest group at risk for the respiratory form of diphtheria. Now it has become a rare disease in the United States, with between zero and five cases per year, affecting mostly older children and adults. It's a different story in other countries, developed or developing, in which large populations are susceptible to this disease. For example, the countries that comprised the former Soviet Union have had an epidemic of diphtheria since 1990—affecting more than 150,000 people, mostly adults.

✦ *Meningitis.* Many types of bacteria, such as *Neisseria meningitidis*, produce meningitis. In meningitis, victims have a stiff neck, fever, headache, vomiting, and confusion; in meningococcemia, they develop a rash and blood infection. Meningitis cases have a 10 to 15 percent fatality rate, and 10 percent of victims who recover have permanent hearing loss or other serious consequences. It's spread through contact with the respiratory secretions of an infected person. Those at risk include infants and young children for the endemic disease; everyone during an epidemic; and refugees, military personnel, college students living in dorms, people living in the home of infected persons, and people exposed to passive and active tobacco smoke. In short, just about everyone is at risk. Although it has a worldwide distribution, meningitis as an epidemic is frequent in the so-called meningitis belt of Africa, and Nepal and Saudi Arabia. To give you an idea of the spread, between 1996 and 1997, 213,658 cases were reported in west African countries, with 21,830 fatalities.

✦ *Polio.* Poliomyelitis (polio) was once common. Regular epidemics occurred in the summer and fall in temperate zones, with outbreaks and recurrent cases worldwide. Caused by the poliovirus, this acute infection generally involves the gastrointestinal tract, but it occasionally attacks the central nervous system. Most people show no signs of the disease. But if they do, symptoms range from respiratory failure, acute paralysis of anywhere from a single limb to quadriplegia—and in some rare cases, death (5 to 10 percent of cases in children, 15 to 30 percent for adults). The virus is spread through fecal-oral transmission and effects both children and adults. Fortunately, the development of vaccines in the 1950s and 1960s dramatically reduced the incidents of this disease, with the last case in the Western Hemisphere associated with a wild poliovirus detected in 1991; unfortunately, several cases have since occurred in Haiti and the Dominican Republic.

The number of reported polio cases worldwide has dropped by more than 90 percent since the 1980s, and there are hopes for a complete eradication of the disease in the near future. However, the intrepid traveler should be aware of the approximately fifty countries where polio is endemic, concentrated in two large areas in south Asia and sub-Saharan Africa: Be careful in such places as Angola, Sudan, Liberia, Somalia, Ethiopia, Nigeria, Sierra Leone, the Democratic Republic of the Congo, India, Nepal, Bangladesh, Pakistan, Tajikistan, and Afghanistan.

✦ *Tuberculosis (TB)*. Tuberculosis is caused by the rod-shaped bacteria *Mycobacterium tuberculosis*, and is easily spread from person to person through the air. TB primarily affects the lungs, but can also affect other parts, such as the spine, kidneys, or brain. In general, a person with this disease has fever, night sweats, weight loss, and a feeling of weakness or sickness. Lung-associated symptoms include chest pain, chronic coughing, and coughing up blood. Untreated TB results in a fatality rate of approximately 60 percent after a period of two and one-half years. When a person with TB coughs or sneezes, the bacteria are expelled into the air. Anyone breathing that air may become infected, but not feel sick or have any symptoms; only later they may contract the TB disease with its attendant symptoms. They, too, become capable of spreading the disease. Those at risk include anyone who spends time with TB-infected people, such as coworkers or family members.

✦ *Leprosy.* The *Mycobacterium leprae* bacillus is the cause of leprosy, or Hansen's disease—a disease that has afflicted humanity since time immemorial. The bacteria multiply slowly and affect the skin, mucous membranes, and nerves. It's a chronic infection, believed by most scientists to spread from person to person in respiratory droplets, although there is still some uncertainty about this. There are two classifications of this disease: paucibacillary and multibacillary. Paucibacillary Hansen's disease is milder, and victims exhibit one or more skin spots. Multibacillary Hansen's results in thickened skin, nodules, and skin lesions, along with nasal mucus. Nerve damage, eventual loss of toes and fingers, blindness, and difficulty breathing are some other symptoms found in severe cases. Those at risk for leprosy include people living in countries where this disease is endemic, and those having close contact with active, untreated disease victims. Although ninety-one countries worldwide have been identified as endemic for this disease, travelers should be especially cautious in India, Myanmar, and Nepal—areas representing 70 percent of the worldwide reported cases. The United States had 108 cases of leprosy in 1999; worldwide the number was estimated to be approximately 640,000. Some 1 to 2 million people are permanently disabled worldwide as a result of this disease.

Minimizing the Danger

How can you avoid becoming a statistic with the CDC? What can you do to avoid these diseases while traveling? First, of course, is to check with the CDC for outbreaks and information about these diseases. Keep in mind—although not all vaccines are 100 percent effective (what is in life?), most are—so here are a few of the CDC's hints:

+ *Diphtheria.* The best way is to avoid this disease is to have the appropriate immunization, preferably at an early age. There is an antitoxin available should you come down with diphtheria, although it's a good strategy to avoid contact with people in areas where there are inadequate vaccination programs for this disease.
+ *Meningitis.* To fend off this disease, it is recommended to have a meningococcus polysaccharide vaccine shot before traveling. Avoid areas where outbreaks usually occur, such as the area from Ethiopia to Mali in the dry season. Penicillin G is the treatment of choice if you should come down with meningitis.
+ *Polio.* The best way to avoid this disease is to be fully vaccinated and to avoid areas where the disease is endemic or there is an epidemic going on. (Polio remains endemic in places with poor sanitation, crowding, and pockets of unvaccinated children.) A person is considered to be fully immunized if he or she has received a primary series of at least three doses of inactivated poliovirus vaccine (IPV), live oral poliovirus vaccin (OPV), or a combination, with IPV being the vaccine of choice in the United States (check with your doctor for details). An adult who has already received three doses, for example, in childhood, can receive another shot of IPV (booster shot) before traveling. The standard schedule of vaccination for unimmunized adults, or those whose vaccination status is in question, calls for two doses of IPV at intervals of four to eight weeks, then the third at six to twelve months after the second. If you just can't wait that long to visit sub-Saharan Africa, the CDC recommends the following alternatives (note: infants and children have a different vaccination schedule than adults, so again, consult your doctor):[10]

—If your trip is more than eight weeks away, three doses of IPV should be administered at least four weeks apart.

It's a Female Thing ... Sometimes

What's always in the back of our minds while traveling—be it by plane, car, foot, or donkey? Of course, it's the age-old question, "Where's a rest room?" Subconsciously, what we really want to say is, "What's the bathroom going to be like?" Let's face it, we don't always have at our disposal the luxury of a Ritz Hotel's private, sanitized rest room. Sometimes we have to use whatever is available—and when traveling, that can mean anything from no facilities at all to public, shared facilities.

Public facilities, though certainly more convenient than a hole in the ground, can unfortunately be a fertile source of illness-causing germs—especially if they aren't cleaned regularly. And they usually aren't. Surprisingly, the worst offenders are the women's rest rooms. Although men's rest rooms are usually messier and smellier, a recent study of fifty public rest rooms in Phoenix, Arizona, found twice the amount of a specific bacteria in the women's rest rooms as compared to the men's. The reason? Women are more likely to bring children into the rest rooms with them, and they also spend twice as much time inside as the men do. Maybe that freshly dug hole in the ground doesn't look as bad now.

Other than the women's rest rooms, where are all those nasty germs lurking? The same study found the worst offenders were public rest rooms in airports and bus stations. This is no doubt due to the large numbers of people using the rest rooms. The study also found the greatest number of germs in rest rooms with just one stall or more than four stalls. This seems strange, but the one-stall rest room is used by everyone, while one with more than four stalls is usually a high-traffic one. More people, more germs. The good news is that most men—and probably women, too—pick an end or middle stall, meaning the first one is probably the cleanest.[11]

What can you do to protect yourself from all these germs in public rest rooms? Good personal hygiene is the key. (And no, it's virtually impossible to catch diseases from toilet seats.) After urinating or defecating, don't touch your mouth, nose, or eyes—wash those hands with soap and water thoroughly. This will get rid of the germs before they reach your mouth, causing illness. The same goes for more primitive facilities. You did remember the toilet paper, water, and soap, didn't you?

   —If you have more than four weeks, but fewer than eight weeks until you need the protection, two doses of IPV should be administered at least four weeks apart.

   —If there are fewer than four weeks before you put yourself in harm's way, a single dose of IPV is recommended.

   —Any remaining doses of vaccine should be administered later at the recommended time(s), if the traveler is still at risk.

✦ *Tuberculosis.* The best way to avoid TB is to have the proper vaccination and/or isoniazid prophylaxis. But note: although the vaccine Bacille Calmette-Guérin (BCG) is the most widely used TB vaccine in the world, its efficacy in protecting against tuberculosis remains controversial. One of the main reasons for this is the emergence of multidrug resistant (MDR) TB bacteria, making the vaccine less effective. In fact, before MDRs, there was a 90 percent cure rate; with the MDRs, the numbers have dropped to 50 percent.

     Thus, it's best to stay away from people with known TB disease, avoid breathing their respiratory droplets, and drink only pasteurized milk from disease-free sources. If you suspect that you've been infected, get a tuberculin skin test. A positive reaction means only that you've been infected with the TB bacillus. Other tests will be needed—such as a chest X ray and phlegm sample—to determine if you have the TB disease. There are drugs available to treat the infection and stop you from developing the disease—or if you already have the disease, to potentially cure you—so don't put it off.

✦ *Leprosy*—There are several drugs recommended by the World Health Organization if you contract the disease—depending on which of the two types of leprosy is involved. Such drugs as rifampin, clofazimine, and dapsone are often used in combination, but never singularly. Eradication efforts continue worldwide, with improved detection of outbreaks. There are also medical groups providing victims in isolated populations with drugs and care.

Food and Water: Tainted Temptations

One of the pleasures of traveling is sampling new foods and drinks. But hidden dangers await in them, too. You and your newfound native friends are at a outdoor cafe, eating and drinking local specialties, watching the people pass by. Later, a band begins to play, and you dance the night away. Sometime during the early morning hours, your stomach starts to ache, your gut turns to water, and you become intimately acquainted with your toilet—for days.

Congratulations! You have a traveler's disease. If you're lucky, it will just be traveler's diarrhea (TD), also colorfully known as Montezuma's revenge or "the trots." Brought on by a variety of those infectious agents we all know and love—bacteria—and lasting anywhere from three to seven days, its symptoms include nausea, malaise, bloating, stomach pain, fever, and, of course, diarrhea. Most people don't die from this disease, they just feel like they are about to die. But TD is no laughing matter. If the diarrhea is prolonged, severe, or bloody, and accompanied by chills and/or high fever, or dehydration, things could get dicey.

And this is a mild disease compared to some that the intrepid traveler can acquire. As Rod Serling used to say, "for your consideration," a sampling of just a few other diseases that can smack you down when you travel—or even kill you—courtesy of the Centers for Disease Control and Prevention (CDC):[12]

Disease	Cause	Symptoms
Brucellosis (Undulant Fever)	Bacteria	Intermittent fever, rash, jaundice, sweating, enlarged spleen and lymph nodes
Cholera	Bacteria	Nausea, cramps, vomiting, and diarrhea
Ciguatera poisoning	Toxin in fish	Cramps, nausea, watery diarrhea, vomiting, skin rashes, hot/cold flashes, joint pain, weakness; severe cases may include paralysis, low blood pressure, low heart rate, blind spells
Dracontiasis (Guinea worm infection)	Waterborne nematode	Swelling around eyes, skin blisters, itching, fever, and wheezing
Hepatitis (A, Non-A, Non-B)	Virus	Nausea, fatigue, joint and muscle pain, sore throat, runny nose, light sensitivity, jaundice, liver enlargement and pain

Liver and lung flukes	Fish-borne flukes	Fever, pain, jaundice, obstruction of bile system, inflammation of pancreas; chest pain from lung flukes
Trichinosis	Worm cysts	Fever, nausea, diarrhea, and abdominal pain; untreated infection can lead to conjunctivitis, weakness, muscle pain, rash, and eye hemorrhages
Typhoid fever	Bacteria	Rash, enlarged spleen, headaches, and fever; advanced symptoms include intestinal hemorrhage and delirium

These make traveler's diarrhea look good, don't they?

Judging the Danger

What's the bad part of traveler's diarrhea and these other diseases? Most of the infectious agents lie hidden within your innocent-looking food and drink. You can't tell if that bowl of spicy stew or glass of ice water will keep you on the dance floor for hours, or on the toilet for days. Also be aware that you don't have to travel with the Crocodile Hunter in a remote corner of the world to pick up some of these diseases. Lunch at the corner diner just might make you feel like you've been to Central America.

So what are the risk factors that determine if you come down with traveler's diarrhea, or any of these other diseases? If you travel into areas that have lesser standards of hygiene than you're used to—from deepest Africa to the neighborhood fast-food restaurant—and partake of contaminated food or drink, there's a good chance of coming down with TD. And the worse the hygiene, the greater the risk. For example, the risk of infection is low if you eat in someone's private home and high if you ingest food from street vendors in some areas.

And depending on the part of the world you're visiting, the chances of getting one of the more dangerous diseases can increase dramatically. Third World countries in places like Africa, Central America, the Middle East, and Asia put the traveler at higher risk than, say, New Jersey or Arizona. But that doesn't mean that you will never come down with a disease in those lovely states. Remember, all areas—certainly throughout the United States—seem to have their own native diseases just waiting to strike the unwary traveler.

The biggest problem is that the infectious agents that bring on these diseases are invisible to the naked eye, ranging from different strains of bacteria or virus, to protozoan parasites, to toxins produced by dinoflagellates, flukes in fish, or worm cysts. And that covers only some of the known ones! These invisible pathogens end up in food and drink, and are then introduced into your body when you indulge yourself.

There are a number of ways these baddies get into the food and drink. There's fecal contamination through improper hygiene (which is why you see those "Employees must wash hands before returning to work" signs in restaurants). Hot food can be left out too long or improperly stored, allowing bacteria to multiply. And some pathogens are just naturally present in the water or animals of the local area.

Your trip to the beach may hold more than sun, sand, and surf. (Army Corps of Engineers)

Shades of Alien

Slow-moving fresh water can look inviting—especially during the heat of a tropical afternoon. A refreshing dip, perhaps, or maybe just splashing your feet in the shallows. It looks innocent enough, but that stream, river, or lake may hold a hidden danger, one that affects—and infects—approximately 200 million people worldwide. The danger comes from tiny, free-swimming larvae of the parasitic worms Schistosoma mansoni, S. haematobium, and S. japonicum. These larvae can penetrate unbroken skin and burrow into the body. Within several weeks, they grow into worms inside the blood vessels of your body, eventually producing more eggs. Some eggs travel to the liver, while others pass into the bladder and intestines. In rare cases, the eggs can also end up in the spinal cord or brain.[13]

The body's reaction to these eggs? Within days of infection, your skin may itch or a rash may develop at the site of entry. Two to three weeks after infection, the fever, diarrhea, cough, nausea, abdominal pain, lack of appetite, weight loss, and headaches begin, along with frequent, bloody, and painful urination and joint and/or

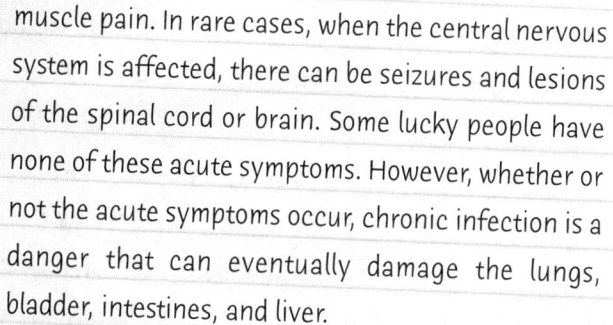

muscle pain. In rare cases, when the central nervous system is affected, there can be seizures and lesions of the spinal cord or brain. Some lucky people have none of these acute symptoms. However, whether or not the acute symptoms occur, chronic infection is a danger that can eventually damage the lungs, bladder, intestines, and liver.

How can you avoid getting schistosomiasis—aka Bilharzia? Avoid fresh, slow-moving water in the following areas: Africa (southern Africa, Lake Malawi, sub-Saharan Africa, Egypt's Nile River Valley), Southern China, the Middle East (Iraq, Iran, Yemen, Saudi Arabia, Syria), Southeast Asia (Japan, Laos, Cambodia, Philippines, central Indonesia, Mekong Delta), South America (Brazil, Venezuela, Suriname), and the Caribbean (Guadeloupe, Montserrat, Saint Lucia, Dominican Republic, Antigua, Martinique). To be really safe, avoid fresh water in any tropical or subtropical area where people are infected with this disease, where sanitation is poor, and where there are snails that can carry schistomosomes. Avoiding

[continued on next page]

means just that: no skin contact through wading, swimming, bathing, or washing. Since you'll probably want to wash at some point, make sure the water has been heated to at least 122°F (50°C) for five minutes, or treated with iodine or chlorine. If this cannot be done, let the bath water stand for at least three days, since the larvae rarely survive more than forty-eight hours. Boil drinking water for at least one minute and let it cool before you imbibe.

After returning from your adventure, have your doctor test you for the presence of this disease. The CDC has developed a blood test for this parasite. If you have contracted schistosomiasis, don't worry. There are safe and effective drugs available. Just get started as soon as possible, as this disease gets worse as time goes on—and the number of eggs in your system increases.

Minimizing the Danger

The best way to avoid getting a traveler's disease is to pay extreme attention to your choice of food and drink. Avoid raw food, such as uncooked vegetables, salads, and unpasteurized milk and milk products wherever sanitation and hygiene are suspect. That also goes for raw (or undercooked) meat, shellfish, and fish. Fruit peeled by you is all right, as are cooked and hot foods. Avoid cooked food that has been standing around at room temperature for several hours, unless it is *thoroughly* reheated.

It also helps to know what you're eating—especially the seafood in certain areas. Some species of shellfish and fish can contain poisonous toxins, even after thorough cooking. For example, avoid barracuda at all times. And tropical reef fish such as grouper, sea bass, amberjack, and red snapper can contain toxins at unpredictable times—especially in tropical and subtropical insular regions of the Indian and Pacific Oceans, and the West Indies.

In the United States, we take for granted that the water we drink is clean and pure. This is not a good assumption in many other parts of the world. Where sanitation practices and hygiene are not up to par, the traveler should be aware that water, drinks made with water, cups and glasses, and even ice may be a source of infectious agents. Avoid drinking or even brushing your teeth with suspect water. The only safe sources of liquids are beer or wine, tea or coffee made with boiled water, and bottled or canned carbonated beverages (soft drinks and bottled, carbonated water). Just be sure to dry any wet bottles or cans before opening, since that water may be contaminated, and wipe clean the areas to be in direct contact with your mouth.

Another option is to treat the water yourself using a variety of methods. One way is to bring the suspect water to a vigorous boil for one minute, then allow it to cool before drinking. Adding a pinch of salt or pouring it from one clean container to another will help the taste. Numerous chemical disinfectants, such as chlorine or iodine, are available. Be sure to follow the manufacturer's directions carefully—you don't want to poison yourself. There are also a number of portable water filters on the market that provide different degrees of protection against microbes. Some can remove bacteria and protozoa, but not viruses, while others can get rid of all three. Some are small and easily carried, while others are larger and more expensive. The traveler should do careful research on the various types, including their efficiency, operation, care, and maintenance. Needless to say, you should follow the manufacturer's instructions so you're not put out of commission on your once-in-a-lifetime trip.

BACKYARD

6 PERILS

Tiptoe through the tulips . . . ouch . . .

You expect danger, hidden or otherwise, when you travel to far-flung lands. But in your own backyard? No way! That's the place for relaxation, gardening, lawn mowing, sunbathing, swimming in the pool. Unfortunately, backyards—whether city, suburban, or country—can carry innumerable dangers, most of which are very well hidden indeed. So the next time you're outside, look around and have some respect. Because most of us live in "civilization" (read: cities), we think we're completely safe. Wrong. Even something as innocuous as a walk in some backyards could lead to being bitten by a tick: and not just any tick—but one that might carry a debilitating or even fatal disease. And wildlife—or a wild life—is everywhere, even in the midst of cities, making disease an ever-present possibility.

When it comes to backyard dangers, knowledge is power. So here's some power . . .

THINGS IN THE YARD

Trees: Revenge of the Ents

A world without trees would be unimaginable. Among the most beautiful living features of our planet, the right kind of trees can enhance any dwelling. They provide shade in the summer, windbreaks in the winter, a place to hang a hammock or swing—or great structures to climb or just sit under in quiet contemplation. And contrary to what former President Ronald Reagan once said, trees do not pollute. If anything, we should be thankful. Without them, oxygen would be a thing of the past.

But these living organisms can also be deadly. That stately old oak tree in front of the house may be just waiting for the opportunity to drop a limb on you or your car. That pine in the back? It's ready to fall on your house. And don't forget that elm tree in the median—it just might fall down while you're driving by. Like everything else on this planet, trees should be enjoyed, but also respected as a potential risk.

Things that can make a tree hazardous include structural defects likely to cause all or part of the tree to split, break off, or come crashing down. When you consider the targets a tree is capable of striking—homes, buildings, vehicles, or places where people congregate, such as picnic tables, backyards, decks, streets, or park benches—you can see that consequences range from property damage and personal injury to death. Although trees can cause damage at any time, severe weather seems to bring out the worst in them. High winds, thunderstorms, ice storms—in other words, your usual and sundry maelstroms—put stress on healthy trees. And for trees with defects, it's when the most damage seems to occur.

Judging the Danger

Not all trees are hazardous—even if they're dead or cracked. Many trees living far from any targets can be useful, especially those in a forest. Some are used by woodpeckers, owls, and other wildlife for shelter or food (woodpeckers usually seek ants in dead wood); others are home to fungi, bacteria, and all sorts of critters who turn the wood into vital nutrients for the woodland floors.

But what about that splendid pine tree you planted when the kids were young—could it take out the back deck? The best way to judge the tree-damage potential is to inspect them yearly, looking for seven major defects. (Remember, any or all of these defects may be found on any one tree. The more defects a tree has, the more dangerous it is—no matter how healthy or magnificent it seems.)[1]

+ *Dead Wood.* No, dead wood in this case isn't your coworker, whose only job is to staple a few papers together. It's real wood that is really dead, which means it can break or fall at any time. You'll know it by the look: dry, brittle, no leaves. A dead branch or tree is the most dangerous defect—needing immediate attention, especially if it's near a target in your backyard. The best thing to do is cut, chop, or saw it down—depending on the size. It's a good solution for you, and such sensible pruning is often good for the tree.

+ *Cracks.* A crack is a deep split extending through the bark and into the wood of a tree. This type of defect is also very dangerous because it indicates the tree is failing. There is a good chance for a problem if a crack extends very deep into or completely through the stem, if multiple cracks occur in the same general stem area, if a crack contacts another type of defect, or if a large branch has a crack.

+ *Weak Branches.* If your tree has places where the branches are not strongly attached, you can have a weak branch union. Unlike the AFL-CIO, these branch unions—in which two or more similar-sized branches develop so close together that bark grows inside the union—are bad. Like a union buster, the bark in the junction may even act as a wedge and force the two branches to split apart. They often occur on the main stem or are seen with other defects.

+ *Decay.* Decay—on your teeth or on your trees—is not good. One you solve by going to the dentist; the other is tougher. In the early stages, this condition doesn't mean the tree is truly hazardous, but it's a good indicator that a problem is brewing. Watch out for the advanced stages of decay—you may see fungus (like mushrooms, but don't eat them—it's hard to tell which are poisonous); soft, crumbly, light, or punky wood; and deep cavities. You may also notice an abundance of wildlife visiting the decay—it's a great site for the little insects woodpeckers eat. And if advanced decay is present around any other defects, remove the branches as soon as possible.

◆ *Cankers.* Cankers—parts of stems or branches on which the bark is missing or sunken—are actually diseases or wounds. Such weak spots increase the chances of the stem or branch breaking, especially if it's connected to another defect. You *know* you have to take action when a single canker or multiple cankers affect more than half of the tree's circumference. This can mean anything from cutting down the offending branches—to losing the tree if the disease is severe.

◆ *Severe Root Problems.* Trees with severe root problems can fall over without warning—sometimes just from the weight of the leaves. Windstorms take their toll on these trees, as do torrential rains that can loosen the soil around the roots. (Farmers often let these trees fall in the fields, cut the roots from the rest of the tree, and slip them side by side to use as fences. But most of us don't have that luxury.) Root problems are mostly hidden underground, but fortunately, there are a few above-ground signs to let you know it's time for action. Watch out for leaning trees with fresh root exposure, soil movement, or mounding. Advanced decay in the base roots, or *root flares*, or a large number of cut or crushed roots indicate a dangerous tree.

◆ *Strange Trees.* Face it. We've all seen strange-looking trees. The odd shapes can be due to anything from prevailing winds or storm damage to improper care or poor growing conditions. But the odd shapes can also mean a structural imbalance or weakness. These trees may be inclined to eventually incline too much and, under the right conditions, fall—which often seems to be after you parked your new car under it. Watch out for a tree excessively listing to one side—or one that has a large branch that's out of proportion to the rest.

Minimizing the Danger

So you're surrounded by trees, are you? How can you determine if they are healthy and stable, or prone to flatten little Spot's doghouse (with Spot inside)? According to the U.S. Department of Agriculture, there are two steps: First, you have to learn to recognize any dangerous trees; second, you have to take the right corrective actions. Become your own grounds inspector—and pay special attention to your trees. It's best to inspect them in the fall after the leaves have fallen, in spring after the leaves have come out, and after any severe storms. Look at them carefully, on all sides, examining all parts—the main stem, branches and unions, roots, and trunk. Use binoculars to see the taller branches.

When inspecting the trees, keep in mind the following factors: What is the overall condition? A tree in good condition usually has a full crown, good-looking branches, and full-size, healthy leaves. Trees in poor condition have many dead branches and twigs, and small, off-color leaves. Find out the species of your trees, because certain types are more prone to specific defects. Take the aspen trees: They often break at a young age (fifty to seventy years) because of defects that include decay and cankers. Some maple and ash trees in the northeast often form weak branch unions. And finally, how old is the tree and how big is it? Trees are no different than other living organisms: As they get older and larger, they can decay or develop multiple defects.

Now that you've determined which of your trees are naughty or nice, it's time to take action. If you find a naughty tree, there are three corrective actions you can take. First, remove any and all potential targets. The shade it provides may be tempting, but don't park the old Winnebago under the leaning oak tree. Move the kid's play sets and swings from under the large, cracked branch of that maple tree. Don't forget the picnic table under the decayed shagbark hickory, either—unless you've just purchased a large, short-term insurance policy on family members.

Sometimes, it's just not possible to move a target. Homes fall into this category, as does the in-ground pool. If there is a dangerous situation—a dead branch; a large cracked or decayed limb; a weak branch union; twisted, bent, or angled branches; a lopsided branch; or a broken branch lodged in the crown—and the tree is mostly sound, then just prune it. Proper pruning should be done by someone who knows what he is doing, not only for safety during removal, but to ensure future defects aren't being created during the process.

Sadly, sometimes when all else fails, the tree must be removed. This is a big step and not one to be taken lightly. It is the final option. Exhaust all other options before exercising this one. If the tree must come down, especially around houses and other property, it is best done by recommended, insured professionals. And remember to plant another tree in its place—and watch it grow.

Rabid Animals: Why Do You Think They Call It Wildlife?

One of our friends lives on a farm—a place where all sorts of wildlife visit. But one day, the visit was not pleasant. A huge raccoon was chasing our friend's cat down the gravel driveway. It wasn't scared of our friend or his cat. In fact, it was walking drunkenly across the yard—so our friend put the animal out of its misery. The results from the lab were chilling: The raccoon had rabies. It was the second one our friend had found on his farm in two years.

Don't think these rabid animals appear only on farms and ranches. You can meet up with them when you're hiking, camping, hunting, enjoying a picnic in a state park, or even on a city street—in other words, anywhere there is mammalian wildlife. We don't mean the two-legged kind of mammal, although there are some people we know who act rabid. In North America, we mean wildlife such as raccoons, bats, coyotes, skunks, or foxes. And watch it in Mexico and other Latin and Central American countries—there, dogs are the most common carriers of rabies.

Judging the Danger

Rabies is caused by a deadly virus that travels up the spinal cord to the brain. You can contract rabies from the bite or scratch of a rabid animal; or you can become infected by getting a rabid animal's saliva in your eyes, nose, mouth, or an open wound. One rare method of contraction is breathing in infected droplets, usually in a cave housing infected bats. Strangely enough, the beating wings of the bats can aerosolize the bat's saliva secretions—and you breathe in the resulting droplets.

And when we say deadly, we mean *deadly*. According to the Centers for Disease Control and Prevention, rabies kills more than fifty thousand people and millions of animals worldwide each year. It's at its worst in Asia, Africa, and Central and South America. In the United States, rabies has been reported in every state except Hawaii.[2]

Minimizing the Danger

There are ways to keep wildlife away from your home—and not invite a case of rabies to cozy up to you or your pet. Here are a few hints:

✦ Some places experience rabies epidemics, many times in one type of mammal, such as raccoons. Know if you're in one of these areas and be aware of the signs of a rabid animal.

✦ It's important to have your pets and livestock vaccinated against rabies. Just like people, some animals hate needles—but it's better than the alternative. Ask your veterinarian for the best rabies vaccination schedule for your animal. And if at all possible, don't let your pets roam free—especially in areas with possible rabies epidemics.

✦ Don't leave your food or pet food outside overnight. This is like a banquet invitation to wildlife. And keep your garbage in cans with the lids tightly closed.

✦ Don't touch sick, injured, or dead animals. Sick and injured animals in particular may be scared enough to bite you. In fact,

Definitely *Not* Prince Charming

They eat pesky insects. They make pleasant chirping noises at night. Some form of water in a backyard—such as streams, ponds, or even swampy areas—attract these animals. There are even terra-cotta homes for them. We're talking about frogs—those somewhat ugly, often warty, swamp-loving amphibians. And as we all know, they're beneficial creatures.

That's true, but just don't make the same mistake the French made and introduce the North American bullfrog to your backyard pond. *Rana catesbeiana*, as it's known to scientists, is a large frog. We're talking a megafrog—just right for the WFWF (World Frog Wrestling Foundation)—it weighs as much a four and a half pounds and measures up to two feet long.[3]

The North American bullfrogs were introduced into France's Aquitaine region about twenty years ago as a joke, but now they've become a dangerous menace. They eat everything, with a menu that includes fish, smaller frogs, birds, and ducklings. These frogs are extremely voracious and will quickly devastate the local environment. Kiss your koi and maybe even your toy poodle good-bye. And in a twist of Gallic irony, this frog's legs don't even taste good.

If you should be unfortunate enough to experience a bullfrog invasion, follow the instructions issued by the French environment ministry officials: Locate the frogs precisely; mark the area and call for a specialist. Of course, those of you looking for a more organic cure for this invasion can acquire a few of this bullfrog's only natural predators: alligators. And as an added bonus, those reptiles will also keep away trespassers.

no matter how much you think that deer looks like Bambi, or that raccoon like your Uncle Fred at the Fourth of July picnic, don't approach any wild animals. Just watch from a distance.

✦ You usually can't tell if animals are rabid. Sometimes they act friendly or tame; or they don't seem shy or afraid of you. But don't be fooled into thinking this animal can be easily hand-fed or domesticated—you may actually be exposing yourself to rabies. Animals with rabies may have a hard time walking, flying, eating, or drinking. Rabid nocturnal animals (including skunks, raccoons, and bats) may be seen during the daytime. If you see an animal acting weird, don't go near it. Call for help from a local animal control officer, county or state health department official, game warden, law enforcement officer, park employee, or rabies control authority.

✦ If you are bitten by a rabid animal, immediately wash the wound with soap and warm water. Then call your physician or health department and get medical attention immediately. You may also want to call the local sheriff's department to report the rabid animal. DO NOT try to catch it yourself. The medical treatment, if needed, isn't the old agonizing shots in the stomach—it's now five vaccine doses in the arm. Also note what type of animal bit you and the locale in which you were bitten. You'll probably also be asked to report this information to local authorities so they can keep track of any rabies spread.

HOW NOT TO TORCH THE BACKYARD

Backyard Burning: Something's Burning

It's a peaceful country scene. The leaves are turning color; there's a chill in the air. The smell of apple pies and cider mingles with dioxins and furans. Wait! Where did those last two come from? According to studies by the Environmental Protection Agency (EPA) at its Open Burning Test Facility in North Carolina, the open burning of trash in the backyard—a common practice in many rural areas—is potentially one of the largest sources of airborne dioxin and furan emissions in the United States. (Dioxins are from a family called polychlorinated *dibenzo-para-dioxins;* furans are from the closely related family of polychlorinated dibenzofurans, and are often present with dioxins.) All they had to do was burn "typical" household trash in fifty-five-gallon drums to find out the truth about trash burning. In fact, they found that backyard trash-burning emissions put out by a family of four can put as much of these two noxious, toxic compounds into the atmosphere as a municipal or medical waste incinerator serving thousands of people.[4]

And don't think it's all due to burning household hazardous wastes, such as paint, oils, grease, or old tires—things you should never burn anyway, by the way. No, those big, bad, nasty chemical compounds came from the burning of typical household trash: cardboard, food waste, milk cartons, assorted containers (cans, bottles, and jars), paper products (magazines, books, and newspapers), and various types of plastic. Why such a hazardous mess? It's because the chemicals in today's containers and products often come out when you burn them. It's because your backyard burning-in-a-barrel typically occurs at lower burn temperatures and with poor combustion conditions. And it's because no one's there to regularly monitor someone's private backyard emissions. It's all quite different than the average clean-operating, high-temperature municipal incinerator.

Judging the Danger

Dioxins and furans are chemical compounds shown to adversely affect the health of lab animals, which includes developmental abnormalities, hormonal changes, cancer, and immune dysfunction. How much is too much? No one really knows, but based on incidences of accidental exposure, dioxins are nasty. Although studies in people are obviously more limited than studies on those little white mice—who would *want* to volunteer for that test—all the data suggest exposure to these chemicals is not good news for humans.

Dioxins are a group of chemicals belonging to the chlorinated hydrocarbon insecticides. They are no longer manufactured for commercial use, but are a by-product contaminant in the manufacture of other chemicals, often found as an addition to certain items in the average household waste stream. Dioxins enter your body through inhalation or skin absorption—thus the problem with burning your trash. Strangely enough, small amounts of dioxins are produced naturally in volcanoes and by forest fires. But we've probably all heard of them more in association with human disasters: the spraying of Agent Orange in Vietnam; the contamination at Love Canal in Niagara Falls, New York; and on and on.

Minimizing the Danger

Fortunately, the burning of trash in open barrels is banned in most areas of the United States, with exceptions mostly in rural areas. If you live in a rural area, don't burn your trash—whether it's in an old, empty, fifty-five-gallon metal drum or even a pile. And if you *must* burn your trash, try not to breathe in the smoke and burn only small amounts. If possible, pull out the recyclables from your garbage—almost every town has a recycling system in place; and try composting your organic waste in the backyard. Both greatly reduce the amount of garbage you have to toss. Or invest in a more efficient way to burn. Call your county extension or your state's division of the EPA and ask for help. The atmosphere, animals, vegetation, and other human beings will all thank you for it.

Barbecuing: Charcoal Burning Everywhere...

It's a beautiful summer afternoon with no rain in sight. Your friends and family have gathered in the backyard for a picnic. The kids are playing volleyball and badminton; the adults are having some drinks and discussing the latest news and gossip. You check the grill. Excellent—nice and hot. The meat sizzles as it makes contact with the fire. Nothing better than grilling up a bunch of carcinogens for your guests.

Carcinogens? Yes, your high-heat grilling of poultry, fish, or meat can produce cancer-causing substances. They're introduced into the body during eating, and if this becomes a habit, it may increase the chances of you or your guests developing cancer. Anyone for tofu on the grill?

Judging the Danger

According to the American Institute for Cancer Research, the main-stays of grilling, known as "muscle meats"—or high-protein foods—typically form carcinogens when grilled at high heat.[5] You can hear the fat sizzling as it drops onto the hot coals or stones. During this process, the burned fat forms carcinogens, which are reabsorbed by the food when the flames and smoke blacken the meat. And you don't just get one type of cancer-causing substance: At the same time, the high heat produces heterocyclic amines (HCAs)—another type of carcinogen—in the food.

Does this mean you're sure to get cancer after that big, char-broiled steak passes down your gullet? Of course not. But no one knows if there's a magic amount of carcinogens you can ingest and not develop cancer. It might be a little; it might be a huge amount. It probably depends on each unique individual. So take some precautions—just like using a seatbelt when driving. If you're not going to stop grilling, take steps to cut down on the formation of carcinogens.

Minimizing the Danger

There's no need to put the grill on the curb for the recyclers. A few precautions will limit the formation of carcinogens during your barbecue, and they may even make your food taste better. Here are some hints:

✦ Don't just have grilled meats. Use them in moderation, adding grilled vegetables and fruits to the meal—these foods don't form carcinogens. In fact, some fruits and vegetables may play a role in preventing cancer.

✦ Use only lean cuts of meat and get rid of the skin and other fat before grilling. And don't eat the charred portions.

✦ Use tongs or spatulas to turn the meat, thus avoiding piercing it. This will minimize the fat and juices that drip into the fire.

✦ You can reduce the meat's time on the grill by partially pre-cooking it in a microwave.

✦ Marinate your meats before grilling. The researchers don't know why, but this seems to reduce the formation of HCAs. The length of marination doesn't seem to be an issue—it just matters that the meat is marinated.

✦ Here are some safe foods: Try grilling organic vegetables and tofu—marinated correctly, tofu actually tastes good! Vegetables contain extremely low levels of the substances that can become carcinogenic with grilling. To be even safer, avoid charring the vegetables as you cook them. They'll taste better, and there will be even lower levels of carcinogens. And don't forget to roast marshmallows as the heat from the coals dies down.

Wildfires: Bad Burns

Waking up from a pleasant dream in your hammock, you find you have a headache and burning sensation in your nose and throat. You go inside and look in the mirror. Your eyes are red—and so are your nose and throat. Is it a cold, or maybe the flu? Funny. You don't recall being around anyone who was sick. And you don't have allergies. What's going on here?

Summer is traditionally a time of dryness, when the hot sun bakes the land and the temperatures increase to oven level. All it takes is just a spark—from a carelessly thrown cigarette butt to a lightning strike—to set off a raging wildfire. Some wildfires can burn for days or weeks, charring hundreds of acres of grasslands and forests, and burning homes and other buildings. And everyone knows being close to these fires is dangerous—especially the heat, flames, and smoke.

But according to the National Jewish Medical and Research Center, even if you're miles away from a wildfire, you may be at risk for health problems.[6] Winds can push large smoke plumes long distances from the fire. This smoke contains (among other substances) *particulates*, or microscopic pieces of burned wood or ash. Inhaling these particulates can cause numerous health problems, including respiratory irritation and heart and lung problems—especially for those with chronic conditions and weakened constitutions.

Judging the Danger

In addition to particulates, wildfire smoke contains a variety of substances. There are carbon monoxide and carbon dioxide gases, as well as gases from burning man-made and natural products. Fires don't burn just the trees and grass, but anything in their way, including homes. And houses contain plastics, carpeting, wool, cotton, and so forth. A witches' brew indeed.

As the smoke rises, winds may push the plume miles from the fire. Although greatly diminished in intensity, this smoke still contains enough noxious stuff to be a potential health hazard. Those with respiratory diseases such as emphysema and asthma, and/or

The Denver fire companies save homes in the mountains surrounding Loveland, Colorado. (Andrea Booher/FEMA News Photo)

heart problems such as chronic obstructive pulmonary disease are at the most risk from the traveling smoke. Also at risk are the elderly and children. And even if you're healthy, you can suffer irritating effects—red, burning eyes and throat, along with coughing.

Minimizing the Danger

You cannot personally stop a wildfire bent on burning up the land. That's the job of the firefighters who protect our land and buildings—and they do a wonderful job. But they can't stop the winds, or predict which way they will blow—and thus where the smoke plume will travel. No one can stop Nature on a rampage.

What's the best way to avoid this acrid smoke? Here are a few hints:

+ First and foremost, keep an ear to the radio (or your town grapevine) or eye to your newspaper. Be aware of any wildfires in your general geographic location.
+ Determine whether you're downwind of the fire. If there is a danger that smoke will reach you, stay indoors with the windows closed, if it is safe.
+ Consult your doctor if you are exposed to the smoke, especially if you have a chronic lung or heart disease. Take any recommended medications.
+ If the fire comes closer or the smoke problem worsens, consider evacuating the area for a period of time—until the wind changes or the fire is extinguished. Sometimes, the better part of valor is retreat.

YOUR BACKYARD'S LITTLE WILDLIFE

Ticks: I'm Growing Attached to You

There may be hard and soft ticks, but they're just ticks to us. You have to feel sorry for the critters. The female dies after laying over one thousand eggs. The male dies right after mating.

But ticks do come after us. They wait on leaves or grass until you walk by—small, silent, hidden—in woods; overgrown brush; open, grassy meadows; and on lawns. Attracted by the warmth of your body, they hop onto you. Slowly and carefully, they make their way to a good site, attach themselves, and burrow into your skin. From there, they take sustenance from your body's juices; their venom is in their saliva. And these little insect-leeches are everywhere in the outdoors, feeding on the white-footed mouse, the white-tailed deer, birds, and mammals—including us.

The best way to get rid of attached ticks is by using a pair of fine-point tweezers to pull them straight off the skin. Any mouth parts left in the wound may be carefully removed as you would a splinter, or just left alone to come out on their own. Burning attached ticks or smothering them will just increase the amount of saliva they pump into the wound, along with any pathogens they're carrying.

But the danger isn't that you're tops on this insect's blood-sucking menu. There are many other organisms that suck the lifeblood from mammals—from cat fleas to vampire bats. No, ticks are dangerous because they also carry diseases that attack humans. Two of the most well known are Lyme disease and Rocky Mountain spotted fever. And now scientists have discovered ticks can carry a potentially fatal disease called *ehrlichiosis*.

Judging the Danger

The differences between hard and soft ticks are mostly biological. The hard ticks have three distinct life stages (larvae, nymph, and adult); the soft tick's life cycle is not readily distinguishable. Hard ticks have a harder exterior and attach to a host for a long period; soft ticks have softer exteriors and feed for briefer periods. There are different species of each—but it's the hard ticks that spread the majority of the tick-borne diseases to humans.

What are your chances of being bitten by either type tick—or that you'll contract one of these diseases? For those living in certain hard- and/or soft-tick-filled regions, the risk is higher. Here's a run-down of the details:[7]

Could that cute deer in the backyard hold a deer tick in your future? (U.S. Army Corps of Engineers)

✦ *Lyme Disease.* Lyme disease is not actually from the tick itself, but something in its system: the corkscrew-shaped bacteria *Borrelia burgdorferi* transmitted by the bite of the deer tick (*Ixodes scaplularis*; an ixodid means a hard tick as opposed to a soft tick) and the western black-legged tick (*Ixodes pacificus*). Named for Lyme, Connecticut, where it was originally noted, Lyme disease is most often transmitted by deer ticks in the northeastern, mid-Atlantic, and north-central United States, and from the black-legged ticks on the Pacific Coast. Since beginning count in 1982 (the disease was first recognized in 1975), the number of Lyme disease cases reported annually in the United States has increased about twenty-five-fold. Approximately 12,500 cases were reported annually by states in the northeast, mid-Atlantic, and upper north-central regions to the Centers for Disease Control and Prevention between 1993 and 1997 (and one the authors of this book is included in those statistics). Of course, since it's existence became widely known only recently, the earlier cases may have been underreported.

✦ *Rocky Mountain spotted fever.* This is an "old" disease, first recognized in 1896 in the Snake River Valley of Idaho. Originally called the "black measles" because of its blackish rash, it's caused by a species of bacteria, *Rickettsia rickettsii,* carried to humans by another ixodid (hard) tick. It's found not just in the Rocky Mountains, but almost everywhere in the continental United States (except for Vermont and Maine in the past two decades), and even reaches into Canada, Central America, Mexico, and parts of South America. Before the discovery of the antibiotics tetracycline and chloramphenicol in the late 1940s, as many as 30 percent of those infected with *R. rickettsii* died from the infection. Now it's down to 3 percent.

✦ *Ehrlichiosis.* Normally, this bacterial disease—caused by the *Ehrlichia* species—affects cattle, dogs, and other animals, but more recently, it has started to infect people through ticks. There seem to be three types of *Ehrlichia*-related diseases. The first, *E. chaffeensis,* was found in the United States in 1986. This causes human monocytic ehrlichiosis and is found primarily in the southeastern and south-central states, transmitted by the lone-star tick. Human granulocytic ehrichiosis, found in 1994, is transmitted by the black-legged and western black-legged tick. The most recent discovery of tick-carried bacteria, *E. ewingii,* was found in Missouri, Arkansas, and southern Illinois—and more commonly infects dogs. So far, researchers don't know if the disease is new or just newly recognized.[8]

Minimizing the Danger

There is help for these dangerous diseases. First, here are the symptoms:[9]

✦ In Lyme disease, the major symptoms don't show up right away. Some of the initial symptoms are the discovery of a tick imbedded in the skin and, for 60 to 70 percent of humans, developing a bull's-eye rash around the site of the bite (a small rash could develop elsewhere, too). If left untreated for several months, this bacteria can create havoc in your body—eventually causing fatigue, aches, arthritis, paralysis, and permanent damage to the nerves and heart. Antibiotics are used to treat it.

✦ For Rocky Mountain spotted fever, initial symptoms include the onset of fever, muscle pain, and headache; from there, a rash forms. It's hard to diagnose in its early stages, and without prompt treatment, it can be fatal. Effective antibiotic therapy has dramatically reduced the number of deaths caused by Rocky Mountain spotted fever.

✦ All three *Ehrlichia* species manifest themselves with flulike symptoms—fever, malaise, headache, and muscle and joint pain. The symptoms appear seven to ten days after a tick bite, and the disease can be successfully treated with antibiotics. If untreated, serious liver and lung problems develop that can cause organ failure.

And for those of you like us, who love the great outdoors, there are ways to keep these blood-suckers at bay. Here are a few hints:

✦ The biggest problem with ticks is size—they can be as small as a pinhead and still cause a problem. After being in a suspected tick area, check your entire body for small flecks—especially in hidden or hairy areas.

✦ The *Ixodes* (hard) ticks feed and inject their venom by inserting their mouths—not their entire bodies—into the skin of the host animal. And they are slow feeders, taking several days to complete their feast and growing larger the entire time. This slowness gives you a chance to catch up with them. That means doing an all-body check on yourself and your family whenever you come in from the outdoors, especially during the peak tick seasons of spring and summer (May, June, and July).

✦ Wear long pants, long-sleeved shirts, and a hat when you hike.

Don't wear sandals—but hiking boots and socks. Not only will all this protect you from the Sun's ultraviolet rays, but it will also keep most ticks away. And don't forget to use tick repellent—there are some natural ones on the market now, too.

✦ If you develop any strange symptoms after being bitten by a tick—such as a rash, flulike feelings, or a bad fever—see your doctor immediately. In fact, if you've been bitten by a tick, it's a good idea to contact your doctor and carefully bring in the specimen, if possible.

Mosquitoes: They're Everywhere! They're Everywhere!

Some researcher, who must have had time on her hands, came up with a statistic that will turn your hair gray: The mosquito-to-person ratio in the United States is 42,000 to 1.

Everyone knows mosquitoes are among the most annoying of insects. Just when you want to relax outside and watch the summer sunset, clouds of them come out—bent on making you their next meal. These miniature Count Draculas draw blood from your body, leaving behind an itchy welt. This may feel good to scratch, but you'll pay for this pleasure later. And in some of those remote, unpronounceable areas of the world, mosquitoes can carry exotic diseases with equally unpronounceable names. But not here. Not in our civilized First World. Not in the suburbs, either. Here, it's just an irritating bump that itches, then goes away with no consequences. Right?

Unfortunately, in this age of globalization and airline travel, such complacency has gone the way of the dodo. A disease has spread from the Eastern to Western Hemisphere: In 1999, about forty-three people in New York City became ill from a nasty mosquito-borne viral disease called the West Nile virus—first recognized in 1933 in the West Nile region of Uganda and Egypt, where it is most common. No one knows how it got here, but theories include the migration of African birds driven across the Atlantic by storms, the import of an infected bird, an infected person coming to New York, or an infected mosquito making it across the ocean in an airplane cabin.

Whatever the way, the West Nile virus—usually carried by the *Culex pipiens* mosquito, with the most severe cases resulting in encephalitis—is becoming firmly entrenched in the eastern United States. By the wet summer of 2000, around sixteen people in New York City were infected; in upstate and western New York, birds were found carrying the infection, motivating authorities to scramble to paint affected areas with mosquito-killing insecticide. But the bugs are still spreading. Keep that in mind the next time you're in New York and you hear a high-pitched buzz around you. It may not be the whine of a street sweeper, but a mosquito carrying a disease you can do without.[10]

Judging the Danger

The nasty West Nile virus spreads to animals—including humans—through an infected mosquito's bite. The resulting symptoms are almost flulike in nature, including a high fever, headache, and in the most severe instances, *encephalitis,* or the inflammation of the brain lining.

Because birds have been found with the virus, scientists believe the disease will soon cover a much larger area—eventually spreading the virus to more humans. The virus already has been found in more than sixty-three bird species in southern Pennsylvania and Maryland. This includes fifty-three free-ranging birds—which means the disease may move southward along the Atlantic and Gulf Coast states, especially during fall and spring migration. With all that movement, more mosquitoes will pass on the virus. And we're not the only mammals at risk: Eastern chipmunks, horses, raccoons, and three species of bats have tested positive for the disease.

What about the mosquitoes? Scientists discovered it's not just one species of the bugs we have to be wary of—but eight, including those that bite during the day, at dawn, and at dusk. Apparently, no time is safe from these bloodsuckers.

Minimizing the Danger

If you do have flulike symptoms, check with your doctor. In deep summer, there shouldn't be many cases of the flu—it's mostly active in the fall and winter. The good news? Most people recover from the virus after the disease has run its course. However, the very young and the elderly, and those with underlying diseases, are most at risk of dying, with the fatality rate between 3 and 15 percent. If you do get the virus, the best doctors can do is make you comfortable—maintaining oxygen and fluid levels, and monitoring vital signs—things to help your body's immune system fight off the disease.

The easiest way to avoid becoming infected with the West Nile virus is to not let mosquitoes bite you. Right, you say: mosquito bites are a way of life. True, but there are things you can do to minimize the chances of being a mosquito's next meal. Here are a few hints:[11]

+ If you venture outside, especially in wet areas, cover up with light-colored long-sleeved pants and shirts. Protect your neck and head with a hat or bandanna.
+ Use an effective mosquito repellent. There are even some natural ones on the market for people who don't want to douse themselves in noxious chemicals. Use citronella candles when you're out on the patio.
+ Avoid areas where large numbers of mosquitoes are likely to be—including swampy areas, creeks, rivers, and even rainwater in that old tire in your backyard. These critters just love to lay their eggs in stagnant water, so get rid of tin cans, plastic containers, ceramic pots, and other items that can trap water. Clean the gutters along your house. And chlorinate your swimming pools, outdoor saunas, and hot tubs—and don't forget to keep the water drained from their covers. If your backyard has areas of standing water you can't eliminate, find out the best way to kill off any mosquito larvae. Insecticides work, but some may be hazardous to humans and other animals.
+ Be aware of the location of this spreading virus. There are

sites on the Internet that contain this information, such as the United States Geological Survey West Nile Virus Web site.[12]

Fire Ants: Not Necessarily Your Typical Picnic Variety

They don't look like much: just tiny, black, shiny ants. *No problemo.* Step on a few barefoot or wearing sandals and that's the end of it. Ouch. One of them bit you. Ouch. Another bite. And another. How can something so small pack such a punch? You run inside, wiping off any remaining ants on the way and close the door. You're breathing heavy and the bites are burning. Now you know why they call them fire ants. In about two days, you'll notice white pustules from the ant's venom—some that may leave permanent scars. The biggest problem with fire ants is the way they sting and bite: The ant bites with its jaws and pulls a piece of skin up—then whips its abdomen around and stings you. And they do it repeatedly, especially if anything disturbs their mounds or food sources. Put them together with a ripe, juicy person and it's easy to see why humans make it onto the ants' menu.

These imported ants are a menace to all in their path, killing most native insects and harming humans, pets, and cattle with their bite. Fire ants are not native to North America, but are stowaways from South America, first coming to this country in 1918. There are two varieties: black fire ants (*Solenopsis richteri*) and red fire ants (*Solenopsis invicta*)—and they're moving across the southern United States.[13]

Judging the Danger

For those people in northern climates, the temperature has been a barrier to these pests, keeping them well to the south. But new studies of these creatures at the University of Tennessee suggest that a hybrid of these two species can extend its range further north. The scientists thought Tennessee winters would freeze the ants, limiting their northern movement. But this may be changing, since the hybrid can live longer at cold temperatures that its two parent species.

In fact, in laboratory tests only 20 to 40 percent of black or red fire ants survive more than seven days at 32°F (0°C), while 80 percent of the hybrid survived. Does this mean that people in Maine or Minnesota should start preparing for a fire ant invasion? No one knows yet, but tolerance to cold is only one factor. Their northward spread may also depend on certain behavior changes, such as burrowing farther underground during the winter. Maybe these hybrids aren't that smart, which will keep them further south. So for you folks in the north country—don't forgo your picnic plans quite yet.

Minimizing the Danger

The hybrid fire ants are still to the south, so those people living in these areas should be aware of the dangers caused by these critters. Luckily, these ants do have predators. There are even studies by the U.S. Department of Agriculture examining ways to control the ants with parasitic flies. But for those of you who want to have a picnic feast in Florida or take a tea break in Texas, here are a few hints:[14]

- ✦ Wear protective clothing outdoors—especially if you travel in or near infested areas. And don't wear sandals—remember, you're just another chunk of meat to the fire ants. Wear shoes or boots, and tuck your pant legs into your socks.
- ✦ Teach your kids and visitors to your house about fire ants. Let them know these creatures are not to be poked, played with, or prodded—no matter how enticing their mounds of dirt appear. Think of them as hornet's nests on the ground. And remember—they run pretty fast.
- ✦ If you have fire ant mounds, there are several ways to get rid of them. Using ant bait twice a year is a slow method, taking days to a few weeks (follow directions carefully), but it will kill the queen. There are also contact insecticides (again, follow directions carefully). Another, less toxic way is to pour boiling water down the mounds.
- ✦ If you're stung, treat the area with an approved insect bite remedy that deadens pain. The stings are usually not life

threatening, but multiple stings may lead to secondary infections. You can stop any possible infection with an over-the-counter anesthetic that contains benzocaine. You may also want to consult your doctor, just to be on the safe side.

✦ If you or someone you know reacts severely to fire ant stings—which can mean chest pains, severe sweating, slurred speech, loss of breath, nausea, or even lapsing into a coma—contact a physician immediately. And if you are allergic to the ants and you know you'll be around the tiny critters, see your allergist before going out.

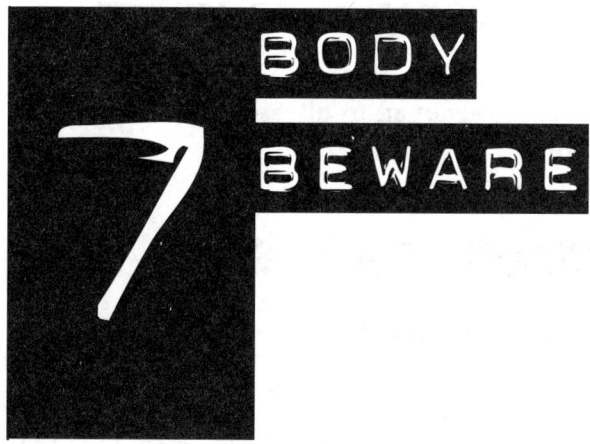

7 BODY BEWARE

I think, therefore I am . . . I think . . .

If your home is your castle, your body must be the shrine. It's just too bad so many people mistake the shrine for a landfill.

Although most of us don't give it much thought, our bodies are made up of cells that band together and work cooperatively to form a living organism. Our bodies can tolerate a wide range of conditions, but there is a narrow, critical balance that must be maintained. Sometimes it's a matter of maintaining your thermostat at the correct temperature: If it gets too cold, hypothermia can set in; too hot, and heat stroke is your lot. Other times, it's eating well: have less salt, keep your edema in control; eat that double burger with all the trimmings, and watch your bad cholesterol climb.

There are dangers you don't have too much control over when it comes to your body. Many of them are very small, very hidden—and there are a vast horde of opportunistic viruses and bacteria just waiting to take over the body, most of them invisible to the human eye.

And pay attention here: in most cases, your immune system is the protector of you, the organism, against some of these more insidious dangers. Anything that weakens or destabilizes this immune system leaves the body open to disease.[1] So treat it nicely and it should be nice to you.

IT'S WHAT'S INSIDE THAT COUNTS

Prions: We're Just Prion Prey

The names sound like something from your worst nightmares or a final exam in advanced biology: scrapie, transmissible mink encephalopathy, chronic wasting disease, bovine spongiform encephalopathy, fatal familial insomnia, Creutzfeldt-Jakob disease (CJD), and the tongue-tying Gerstmann-Straussler-Scheinker syndrome. Humans are susceptible to the last three diseases and several more; animals, to the first four. These infectious diseases are caused by *prions*—and now many scientists believe prions are actually proteins.[2]

These prions (short for *proteinaceous infectious particles*) don't act like any known animal, vegetable, mineral, fungi, virus, parasite, or bacteria. They appear to be proteins—something that should not be infectious. But here they are, out in the open, causing diseases such as the "mad cow" epidemic that started in England in 1986, and continues to this day. Researchers looking back over decades of atypical infectious diseases not linked to any other, "regular" infectors now point to prions as the possible culprits.

One of the more well known human diseases thought to be associated with prions comes in the form of CJD. It's a rapid, fatal brain-deteriorating disease, usually causing dementia and neuromuscular symptoms, that most often affects people between fifty and seventy-five years old. One strain—nvCJD—is thought to be related to the mad cow disease in the United Kingdom, but so far has not been reported in the United States. Like most prion protein-related diseases, the incubation period for CJD is baffling—sometimes only fifteen months, other times thirty years after exposure—with one person in a million seeming to contract it. There's currently no way to determine if a person is infected after a possible exposure—and no treatment or cure.

Judging the Danger

Just when you thought it was safe to think of your cellular proteins as the gentle, minihelpers of your body's enzymatic functions, you find out different. Prions appear to enter a healthy cell and convert normal proteins into the same amino acids (cellular building blocks) that they have—sort of a chip off the old prion block. Everything looks normal, but in reality the prions wait inside the brain's proteins, just biding their time until they make their insidious appearance.

Prions bring about the slow degeneration of the nervous system. For the sheep with scrapie, it's relatively fast—about two to four years until the prion takes over; for humans, it can be up to ten years to see any problem. For this reason, some scientists believe prions may actually be "slow viruses"—the slowness evident in their multiplying habits (making them difficult to isolate), and their slowness in infecting the victim. However they originate, they seem to transform normal, benign protein molecules into infectious, deadly ones by altering the shape of the healthy molecules. Ultimately, infected, prion-bloated brain cells die, releasing other prions into the surrounding tissues, creating gaps in the brain like holes in a sponge (thus, the medical term for prion diseases, *spongiform encephalopathies*). The madness in mad cow doesn't come from being angry, but from being driven mad as the animal loses parts of its brain.

Minimizing the Danger

Prions' newness on the scene makes the danger difficult to assess. In Britain, mad cow disease has become a major problem, as news of the disease spreads to all corners of the island and beyond. The danger comes from how the disease seems to spread: Apparently, the prions that started out in sheep as scrapie made their way to cows—the cattle were fed meals made from sheep offal, the bones and other waste parts of sheep carcasses—and then to humans who ate hamburger from prion-bearing cows.

The United States has banned beef from countries with mad cow disease, and has even banned certain blood donations from

Antibiotics for Two

It's not exactly what you had in that beef sandwich for lunch—it's what the cow had for lunch days before. In so many words, that cow may have had a hefty dose of antibiotics. When you munch down the sandwich, you are chewing down the left-over antibiotics, too. And if some scientists are correct, their overuse creates super-bugs immune to certain diseases—and that could mean you won't be as responsive to antibiotics if you ever need them.

The debate on just how many antibiotics should be ingested by animals and its effect on humans continues. But you wonder if something isn't happening—after all, farm animals in the United States get eight times as many antibiotics as people do. Farmers use the drugs for several understandable reasons—especially to fatten up livestock. But the price may be too high.

Poultry are not excluded: It's estimated that more than 16 million pounds of certain antibiotic drugs in the fluoroquinolone class were used on poultry in the mid-1980s. Now more than 25 million pounds are used. And the connection may be becoming obvious: According to the U.S. Food and Drug Administration, two antibiotics used by poultry farmers may have to be banned. They found that humans who contracted the *Campylobacter* bacteria were developing a resistance to certain fluoroquinolones since the time poultry farmers started to use the antibiotics. This means that if you have a certain type of infection from *Campylobacter*, and you've developed a resistance to the antibiotic, it won't work for you anymore.[3]

infected countries—especially from donors who may have eaten contaminated beef. And the measures are tough: As of 1999, anyone who lived in the United Kingdom or Ireland for more than six months between January 1980 and December 1996 is prohibited for life from donating blood in the United States. Clearly, this is being taken very seriously. By early 2001 the ban was expanded to other European countries as reports of prion infections spread.

The chance, at this point, in the United States of contracting the disease is minute. Still, the best suggestions? You might want to stick with some "safer" foods, like chicken or turkey. So far, no prion disease affecting humans has been found in these animals. Or you can become a vegetarian—especially if you travel, study, or live in Europe. Ignoring steak with your eggs or hamburger with your fries may take some getting used to, but it's better than the alternative.

Bacteria: Nosy Critters

You probably thought that proboscis sticking out from your face was there just to get rid of mucus when you had a cold—or a Mexican dish with too many jalapeño peppers. Not anymore. It's also one of the points of entry for *Staphylococcus aureus* bacteria that can enter the bloodstream and cause serious—and even life-threatening—infections in some people. For 60 percent of us who carry the bacteria in our noses, there are no symptoms. But a recent study of more than two hundred hospital patients with infections found *S. aureus* floating around in their systems. The infections caused by these bacteria can range from minor (such as pimples, boils, and other skin conditions) to serious and sometimes fatal (such as blood infections or pneumonia).[4]

Judging the Danger

No, this doesn't mean you should take the phrase "cut off your nose to spite your face" literally. It just means that there are bacteria that can reside in your nose without causing any harm—or that could cause a definite problem. In fact, for some people, these nose bacteria can start other infections in or on the body. So be aware that these bacteria exist—and if there is a question of which bacterium may be infecting you, bring it up to your doctor. Then she can find out what your nose already knows.

Minimizing the Danger

The inside of a nose is an irresistible condominium setup to these bacteria—either the bacteria refuse to move from the nose, or they move back in after a short absence. Some even built up a quick resistance to antibiotics. One of the ways doctors have suggested getting rid of this problem is, of course, to eliminate the bacteria from the noses of patients to stem the tide of infections. But it's not as easy as it sounds—especially in a hospital setting: Unlike the rapid diagnostic test for strep throat, there is not a quick-and-dirty (or clean, in this case) way to identify the nose-loving bacteria.

In addition, not everyone agrees on how to get rid of the bacteria once they're found. As with so many other bacteria nowadays, certain medications may cause the organisms to become more drug resistant. But there may be hope: many of your nose's *S. aureus* can be treated with a bacitracin, mupiricin, or combination antibiotic-ointment treatments—applied for several weeks at bedtime. Sometimes the treatment lasts for a longer period. Either way, it may clear up a bacterium your nose knows you could do without.

IT'S WHAT'S OUTSIDE THAT COUNTS

SAD: There's No Light When You're SAD

Seasonal affective disorder (SAD) affects many people in the doldrums of the northern winters. Closer to the poles, the Sun's light changes over the season, the direct result of our planet's tilt and orbit around its star. Winter brings fewer hours of sunshine, and, like sad-looking seedlings that don't get enough light, people diagnosed with SAD gain weight, crave carbohydrates, and experience sleep problems, fatigue, and sadness. And with people working longer hours and never seeing any sunlight—even in the summer months—SAD has become something of an epidemic.

Judging the Danger

Scientists are still not sure what causes SAD, but they do know more women than men are affected by the lack of light. Like a bear in hibernation, does the brain's biological clock slow in response to the shorter, darker days? If this is true, it can definitely alter the balance of neurotransmitters, causing changes in body physiology and brain behavior. And if a recent study from Cornell University in Ithaca, New York, is right, light may affect the body clock though the skin, with the blood acting as a messenger for light. If this is true, could SAD actually be a disorder of the blood rather than the brain?[5]

Minimizing the Danger

Although most SAD symptoms are not life threatening, one of the most difficult to overcome is depression. Scientists don't know why, but light plays a central role in helping people cope with depression from SAD. Here are some hints for getting through a tough winter—or even if you just end up on a weird shift at work:

+ *Phototherapy* often works wonders. This doesn't mean staring at snapshots in your photo album; it means a specialized light unit with a full-spectrum fluorescent light. Try glancing at the unit for a few seconds once a minute, and do this for several hours a day. Studies show that mood improves in about two to four days—but you have to continue the treatment throughout the winter. And whatever you do, *do not* use the Sun as an alternative to a light unit. If our star is powerful enough to brighten up an entire planet and the moon, just think how it will destroy your eyes if you stare at it.

+ If you feel depressed, there are medications your doctor can prescribe to get you through the toughest winter months.

SAD and clinical depression may be interconnected, and they can be treated in similar ways.

✦ Some people live in the northern regions in the summer and closer to the equator in winter. The light will improve your mood, but be careful that another type of upset doesn't occur because you dug too deeply into your wallet!

✦ In the winter, rent movies and travel videos that take place in sunny, tropical paradises (but skip *Mutiny on the Bounty*). On second thought, why not visit a nice, sunny tropical paradise for a while?

Influenza: Facing the Flu

What's ninety times smaller than a human red blood cell—so small it can hide between light waves—and in a typical year can cause nearly half as many American deaths as traffic accidents? It's called the *influenza virus*, but you probably know its abbreviated name, the *flu*. The three types of flu are labeled with the first three letters of the alphabet—influenzas A, B, and C—and they pop up like a Halloween prank around November and gradually disappear by April. And as the American population continues to age, the number of deaths due to flu complications will only rise.

Judging the Danger

Just by sneezing or coughing, a flu-struck person discharges millions of virus-filled droplets—which survive about an hour—into the air. Touching a contaminated doorknob or telephone is worse, as the virus can live for several hours on solid objects. Just put your hand anywhere near your mucus membranes—around the eyes, nose, and mouth—and the invasion begins. The virus spreads like wildfire, reproducing in the tens of millions in only twenty-four hours. The resulting flu attacks your respiratory system, giving you a multitude of unpleasant symptoms for five to ten days. People with the flu are contagious from the twenty-four hours before they begin to exhibit symptoms until their symptoms begin to subside.

A Germ by Any Other Name

We all heard the word "germs" when we were young: Wash your hands to get rid of the germs. Don't touch that garbage can—it's filled with germs. Don't put your hands in your mouth—they're filled with germs. The word is actually very broad—meaning a microorganism, or microbe, that causes disease. From there, we can more specifically label almost any entity that does just that—especially viruses and bacteria.

How easy is it to pass germs around? It depends on the germ and the mode of transport. For viruses, colds and flu are at the top of the list as the most easily contracted. Surprisingly, only 10 percent of all cold viruses are truly spread by sneezing—the rest are by putting an germ-infested hand to your face, especially near your nose. The flu virus seems to spread faster through the air after sneezing or coughing, but the majority of people still catch it by touching their face with their contaminated hand. Bac-

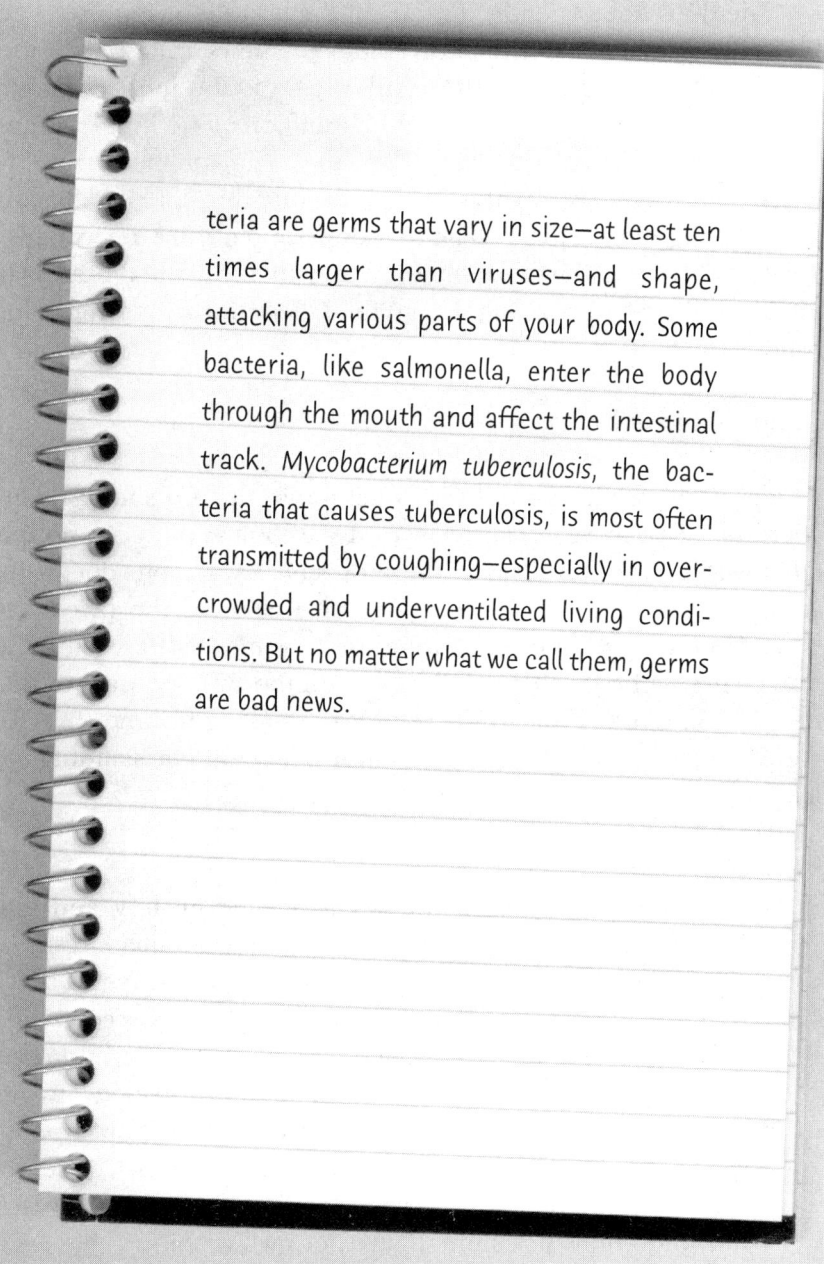

teria are germs that vary in size—at least ten times larger than viruses—and shape, attacking various parts of your body. Some bacteria, like salmonella, enter the body through the mouth and affect the intestinal track. *Mycobacterium tuberculosis*, the bacteria that causes tuberculosis, is most often transmitted by coughing—especially in overcrowded and underventilated living conditions. But no matter what we call them, germs are bad news.

The flu is not a friendly disease. In the twentieth century alone, flu viruses have caused three worldwide epidemics, called *pandemics*. The Spanish influenza of 1918 and 1919 was the most dramatic, killing 20 million worldwide and a half million alone in the United States. Soldiers of World War I bore the brunt of the disease, as more than twenty thousand were killed—one-third of all U.S. casualties during the war. The Asian flu popped up during the winter of 1957 and 1958, killing seventy thousand in the United States. In 1968 and 1969, the Hong Kong flu killed thirty-four thousand Americans.[6]

Minimizing the Danger

The best way to fight the flu is to get an annual flu shot. Anyone over the age of six years can receive one, as long as there are no specific conditions or allergies to the shot (check with your doctor for younger children). Because it takes two weeks for the vaccine to take effect, get one during October or November, if possible. And don't worry—the flu shot will *not* give you the flu: The virus in that needle going into your arm is very dead, making it impossible for you to catch the flu by getting a shot or by sitting, standing, or leaning over someone who just had a shot.

Here are a few more hints to keep the flu at bay:

✦ The immune system is the key to staying healthy, and that means eating well, exercising, and getting adequate rest.

✦ Limit your social activities during the flu season, especially if there is an outbreak, and avoid close contact with people who have the flu. If you eat enough garlic to boost your immune system, you may not have to worry about social functions anyway.

✦ Although it won't look good if Martha Stewart shows up, use paper cups in the bathroom and change towels frequently, especially if someone in your family has the flu. In fact, anyone who is sick should have her own towel.

✦ Keep the humidifier on—it's easier for germs to attack dried-out nasal passages.

◆ Although it's not advisable to do during a blizzard or in sub-zero temperatures, occasionally fling open the windows for a short time to get rid of airborne viruses.

◆ Watch where you put your hands, too—especially if you're well and the person next to you is not. Touching your face is a great way to spread the flu virus to your mucus membranes.

◆ Wash your hands vigorously with warm water and soap for fifteen to twenty seconds, as vigorous scrubbing gets rid of most of the germs. The virus can live for a few hours on doorknobs, water faucets, tissues, toys, towels, steering wheels, and almost any other hard surface touched by a flu-contaminated person.

◆ There are a few medications to ask your doctor about during the flu season. Amantadine and rimantadine are effective against preventing influenza A viruses and may even stop secondary complications. Zanamivir and oseltamivir help the virus from spreading and multiplying, and can shorten the duration of the flu by a few days. (You should consult your physician before taking any medications.)

Mutations: Quick-Change Artists

Sometimes viruses don't act the way humans think they should—but in reality, they are acting just fine. Take, for instance, a solitary virus. One of these small, unseen germs acts like something out of a grade-B zombie horror movie—a genetic entity that exists somewhere between a living and nonliving state. Its only purpose is to make more viruses, killing off the healthy host cells it invades. This is not the way to make friends and influence people—or cells. Actually, it is.

What are some of the most well known viruses? Here's a roll call of the ones you hear about the most: the adenoviruses cause colds; HIV is the virus that causes AIDS; influenza viruses cause the flu; the rubella virus causes German measles; the Ebola virus caused the recent Ebola epidemic in Africa; the herpes simplex viruses cause herpes infections. And rabies, polio, and hepatitis B are all caused by viruses.[7]

An (Aw)Fowl Virus

The Teenage Mutant Ninja Turtles had nothing on the actions of the Hong Kong flu virus in May 1997: A directly transmissible type-A virus jumped from birds to humans, without the usual pig or other domestic animal intervening as a mixing bowl for the viruses' genetic exchange—something scientists always hoped would never happen. Because of the "easy" way it can form and be transmitted, such a virus can cause a huge pandemic in a short amount of time.

The first sign was when a three-year-old boy died of the flu. He caught it from a chicken at a petting zoo—the first time a human contracted this strain from a bird. As more and more people contracted the same virus, Hong Kong officials began to worry. A vaccine, if it could be developed, would take months to test and distribute. And because the vaccines are grown in chicken eggs—and this virus killed chickens—how would scientists develop a vaccine? By late December 1.4 million chickens and other poultry were destroyed in a massive slaughter. By February 1998 there were no new cases—the virus had left behind eighteen confirmed cases with six fatalities. A possible pandemic affecting millions of people had been averted.

Judging the Danger

How does a virus mutate? Take the type-A flu virus—one of the kings of mutation, a master of disguise. This virus periodically experiences a quick-change mutation when a healthy host cell is invaded by two different types of A virus. As their strands of RNA dance and mix together to replicate, they create a new strain of the A virus. With no antibodies built up in humans to fight off the new strain, the virus moves in for the kill. History has shown that *pandemics*—or global epidemics—caused by such sudden mutations have killed millions of people in a relatively short time.

Not only does the shifty A virus mutate and hop from human to human, but it can also jump between species—a rarity for viruses. One of the suspected hosts for this antigenic shift is the pig: Acting like a big mixing bowl, a pig infected by one type-A virus from a human and one from a bird forms a new virus. In fact, looking back further in history, most major pandemics may have originated in China—in which large populations of humans, pigs, and birds coexist.

Minimizing the Danger

When it comes to the effects of a virus, sometimes we just have to accept that control is out of the question—at least at this time. Sure, there are some medicines that slow down the process of the flu, and there are antibiotics to get rid of secondary bacterial infections that often occur after a virus strikes. But antibiotics don't fight off viruses; they kill only bacteria and should not be wasted on viral infections—or else they may not help you when you really need them. But for most viruses (like the virus that causes AIDS), we're still battling in the ring—and there has been progress to a point.

Drug-Resistant Bacteria: Breeding the Superbug

It came into the limelight in the 1970s. Two bacteria became resistant to penicillin: *Haemophilus influenzae*, which causes respiratory infections, and *Neisseria gonorrhoeae,* the bug that causes gonorrhea. These warrior bugs not only had the right arsenal to fight back against the antibiotics, but they actually destroyed the penicillin drug. The mighty gonorrhea bugs were traced to the Philippines and to prostitutes in Vietnam. They had been given regular doses of penicillin as a precaution against the disease. But the overuse of antibiotics killed off the weaker strains and created drug-resistant superbugs. And we're still paying for it, with cases of drug-resistant gonorrhea all over the world.[8]

These superbugs are not superheroes from the comic books— they're the villains. *Superbugs* are what scientists are calling bacteria that now resist many of the tried-and-true antibiotics out there— which gives us fewer resources to fight them. Humans are most affected, and it's humans who have inadvertently bred these bugs. The only thing is, unlike breeding cats, dogs, or horses, these pure-breds aren't something you want to show.

Judging the Danger

Bacteria can become superbugs in several ways. Just like viruses, bacteria have their own mutation moments: Their genes mutate during reproduction, altering the nature of the bug. Like too-tight underwear, some of the alterations don't fit—but once and a while, the change helps the bug resist a certain drug. If that bug multiplies, it has done its job to create extra troops to fight off the drug—and a mutant, drug-resistant army is born.

But mutation may not be enough to develop a widespread resistance to antibiotics. That's where the next weapon comes into play: The bacteria can share their resistant genes with other bacteria. This happens in many ways—for instance, reeling in another bacterium with what looks like a fishing line, then transferring the gene or even vacuuming up scraps of loose DNA that may hold the resistant gene. Whatever the method, don't be mistaken: Certain bacteria are winning various battles—sometimes even becoming resistant to a full arsenal of drugs. When you think that in a single day, *one bacterium can yield 16 billion more antibiotic-resistant bacteria,* you realize this is truly war.

Why is this war being waged? Some scientists believe it's the natural evolution of the bacteria. In other words, the strong survive. Others believe it's us—through our overuse and downright abuse of antibiotics not only for humans, but in animals, too. The more antibiotics we take into our systems, the better the chance that the bugs will win.

Minimizing the Danger

The statistics are mind-boggling: About 160 million antibiotic prescriptions are written annually in the United States alone—which equals about 25 million pounds of antibiotics. We also ship them overseas. And that doesn't even take into account the antibiotics animals get.

No one is saying we should stop using antibiotics. These drugs have saved countless people from all sorts of horrible bacterial infections and have saved numerous lives. But pay attention to the reason you are getting the antibiotic. Again, one fallacy is that you need antibiotics if you have a viral infection. You don't. Antibiotics only work on bacteria—not viruses (although they are often used if a virus causes a secondary bacterial infection).

What can you do to protect yourself against the superbug and keep your body responsive to antibiotics? Remember, it's a war out there. Here are a few tips:[9]

- ✦ Try to avoid taking antibiotics for minor infections that will likely disappear by themselves. But *do* take them when necessary, as prescribed by your doctor.
- ✦ If you have to take antibiotics, take them for the full course prescribed—in most cases, seven to ten days. This will knock off all the pathogenic bacteria. By stopping early, you're creating a monster—essentially inoculating the bug against the antibiotic so it becomes a superbug.
- ✦ After you finish taking the antibiotics, try boosting your body's "good" bacteria (or the lactic-acid bacteria—the ones that may have been destroyed by antibiotics) by eating fermented dairy (yogurt comes to mind), meat, and vegetable products.

Don't Touch It!

So maybe your computer caught a virus—it can only harm the computer. But think again when it comes to those pernicious bacteria.

A few years ago, a study determined that pencils and pens used by doctors and health-care workers are prime places for the spread of bacteria to patients. That made us all stop chewing on our writing instruments. And they're at it again: Scientists at the Tripler Army Medical Center in Honolulu, Hawaii, decided to take the germ-infestation study even further. They collected samples from computer keyboards from patients', nurses', and doctors' computer stations—as well as from faucet handles in the hospital's intensive care unit (ICU). They found enough of a bacterial infestation to use plastic covers, which are cleaned every day, on keyboards in ICU—and are installing noncontact-controlled sinks in the critical-care units. We'll never let anyone touch our computer keyboards again.[10]

✦ Strengthen your immune system by eating nutritiously and exercising moderately.

CREATURES WITHOUT THE COMFORTS

Tiny Critters: Mighty Mites

The Middle Ages were not known for hygienic behavior. People of that era didn't know how disease was spread. One condition surfaced at that time in the form of itch mites—no larger than the "e" in the word "mite." These creatures multiplied under the skin, creating a boil about the size of an egg. Once they matured, they broke out, streaming out of the boils like locusts over a cornfield. Enough of the mites could kill a person: He would literally itch himself to death as secondary infections from the scratching took over.

The itch mite parasite (*Sarcoptes scabiei* of the Arachnids) causes a disease called *scabies* in mammals—including humans, where it is transmitted by skin-to-skin or sexual contact. If you're infected or infested, the spiny female mite burrows just under the top layer of your skin like a crazed mole. And you can see the evidence, too: Right where the mites burrow are white or gray threadlike tunnels. Here, the mites and their feces cause intense itching (the creatures seem to be party animals after dark, because nighttime brings on the most itching). The female soon lays eggs that hatch larvae after three to five days—the reason for the red bumps. While in their temporary human home, the mites' serum leaks from the burrow, forming a crust or scab as it dries—thus, the name scabies. Finally, the larvae head toward the surface to reproduce, squirming back along the burrow to seek mates and start the cycle again.[11]

Judging the Danger

Scabies may have been a problem in the castles and thatched huts of the Middle Ages, but just like the jousting lance, this parasitic disease has pretty much gone by the wayside. But that doesn't mean it

You're Never Alone

Not all mites are created equal. Take the follicle mite: *Demodex folliculorum* is microscopic, with what looks like hairs everywhere. Speaking of hair, these little mites live in your *hair follicles*, the cavities surrounding each eyelash, or in your *sabaceous glands*, the pores on your forehead and nose. And there's nothing you can do about it. Being these creatures' personal ecosystem is a way of life.[12]

These tiny hitchhikers cling to us, their mouth parts piercing our skin. It's a fine relationship: Like a sucker fish to a shark, the mites hang on, feeding on dead skin cells and the oil from our sweat glands. To them, we are the great oil fields of the North Sea. So be careful next time when you rub your eyes or itch your head. You may be wiping out millions.

has completely disappeared. The human mange is alive and well—especially if you come skin-to-skin with an infected person.

If you do see the telltale signs of these tiny mites, you'll often see them as streaks of small, extremely itchy, red spots. They seem to hang out mainly on the webs between the fingers, and on the wrists, elbows, groin, and lower legs. Overall, they can infect any skin

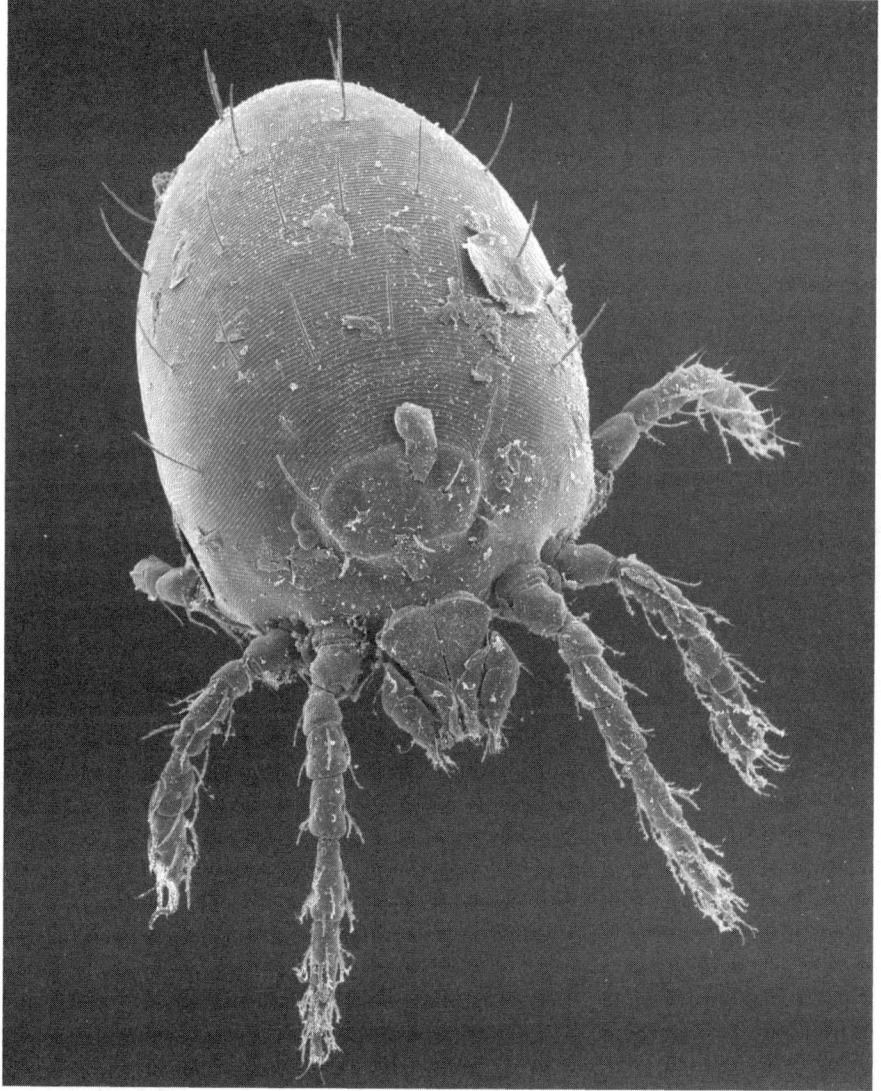

Dust Mite (Copyright Dennis Kunkel Microscopy)

area—except, for some reason, the adult scalp (though infants can be affected at the scalp).

Minimizing the Danger

If you do come down with scabies, it will take—for people who have never had the parasites before—two to six weeks after the infestation to start itching. For those who have already had the critters, it takes only one to four days to begin the itching. And you thought a mosquito bite itched!

Got the itch? Here's how to scratch it out of existence:

+ Visit your doctor. This is because the most effective treatments are available by prescription only—lindane (although this medication is not recommended for pregnant women or very young children) and permethrin. Both are available as lotions that you apply to your entire body, leave on for eight to twelve hours, and then wash off. Follow the directions carefully. Luckily, in most cases, the mites are mightily fooled with one application. You may still itch for a while, since the dead mites persist in the skin until they're absorbed.
+ If some of the itched spots become infected, your doctor may recommend an antibiotic.
+ Because the itching may not start for about a month after you're infested, other members of your household should be treated. Fresh human meat is always a prime target for the mites.
+ *Do not* send your child to school if she is diagnosed with scabies. Don't go to work, for that matter. You have our permission to stay home, at least for a few days.
+ Take all the clothes and bedding you and your family used up to three days before treatment. Put them into the washer with plenty of soap and run them through the hot water cycle. Then, to really get rid of the beasties, dry the clothes and bedding in the hot cycle of the dryer. If you don't want the hot water or air fairies to shrink your delicate silks, cottons, and wools, wash them in cold water and hang them outside on a line—preferably in the sunlight—for several days.

More Mites: A Natural Skin "Treatment"

Once upon a time, an author became entangled with a bunch of chiggers. Also called *red bugs*, they infested said author's sleeping bag while out in the Virginia mountains. There was little doubt the tiny critters had pulled an all-nighter. By morning, the count was thirty-two bites on the stomach alone. Needless to say, said author pulled an all-nighter the next night, sitting up itching.

Chiggers may sound like a cute name for a Mexican restaurant. In reality, they are mites in the larvae stage. If you look close, you can often see the much larger (albeit still relatively tiny) red, eight-legged adults scurrying over pavement and lawns. The adult female lays her groups of eggs in the soil, sometimes up to four hundred eggs in a group. From the eggs hatch the yellowish-orange, six-legged larvae we call chiggers. These critters crawl to the tips of low grass or weeds, ready to hitchhike on any unsuspecting wild, domestic, or human animal host that passes by.[13]

To give them some credit, chiggers infest a host for only about four days. Then they drop off and molt into nonparasitic *nymphs*, or adults, spending the rest of their insect lives feeding off organic matter on the ground.

Judging the Danger

Contrary to popular belief, chiggers don't burrow under your skin or suck your blood. They are more polite than that, preferring just to lightly attach themselves to the surface. From there, their manners need polishing: They secrete digestive enzymes that dissolve your skin tissue. This human-enzyme broth is their elixir—and they suck it up as liquefied tissue. The itchy red welts that accompany your visitors are an allergic reaction to the digestive enzyme.

Chiggers are not known to carry or transmit any disease to humans. Left untreated, the bites can itch terribly for a week or longer. And as with many parasites, the itching may produce sores that become infected, necessitating the use of antibiotics.

Here (Dust) Kitty

We all have them: those fuzzy chunks of dust that roll like miniature tumbleweed across the floor. These dust kitties carry more than just dust. They hold house dust mites—the unkempt, pigpen kings and queens of the mite world. And the dust doesn't hold just the mites—it includes the creatures' fragmented body parts, excretions, and secretions. Why so much stuff? Do the math. The minuscule female mite lays about one egg a day for thirty days. It may take an egg a month to develop into an adult, but there are plenty more eggs out there—and they multiply exponentially.

As is often the case, we are the reason the dust mites are attracted to our homes: These scavengers love to feast on our dead skin cells. Since we each shed about five grams of skin cells per week—and one gram feeds thousands of mites for months—our homes are virtual banquet halls for the creatures. And the eating is good—estimates are that more than half of all homes in the United States have a dust mite infestation.

About 4 percent of humans don't get along with dust mites. Many people have an allergic reaction to the mites' lack of hygiene. Sneezing is the most prevalent symptom; second is an aggravation of an asthmatic's symptoms as he breathes in the mites' tailings. Solutions for the sneezing include frequent changing of bedding, the use of nonfibrous bedding (mites love natural fibers), and vacuuming regularly. In the case of dust mites, the problem is easy to prevent if nonwashable bedding items such as pillows, mattresses, and box springs are encased in allergy-proof covers. And washing bedding every week can remove dust mite allergens, as long as the water is at least 130°F (54°C).

Minimizing the Danger

There are ways to throw off the hitchhiking insects. Here are a few hints:

✦ If you walk in chigger-infested areas (sometimes parks or recreational areas will have warnings), protect yourself by using a tick repellent on your clothing and exposed skin—especially around your feet, ankles, and legs. If you're allergic to the repellents, try special herbal or hypoallergic sprays available at many drug or health food stores.

✦ If you meet up with a bunch of chiggers, take a soapy bath. Applying an antiseptic to the welts will also greatly relieve the itching.

✦ If you live in a chigger-prone area, keep your lawn mowed. Not only will your neighbors be happy, but the chiggers will have fewer places to jump from.

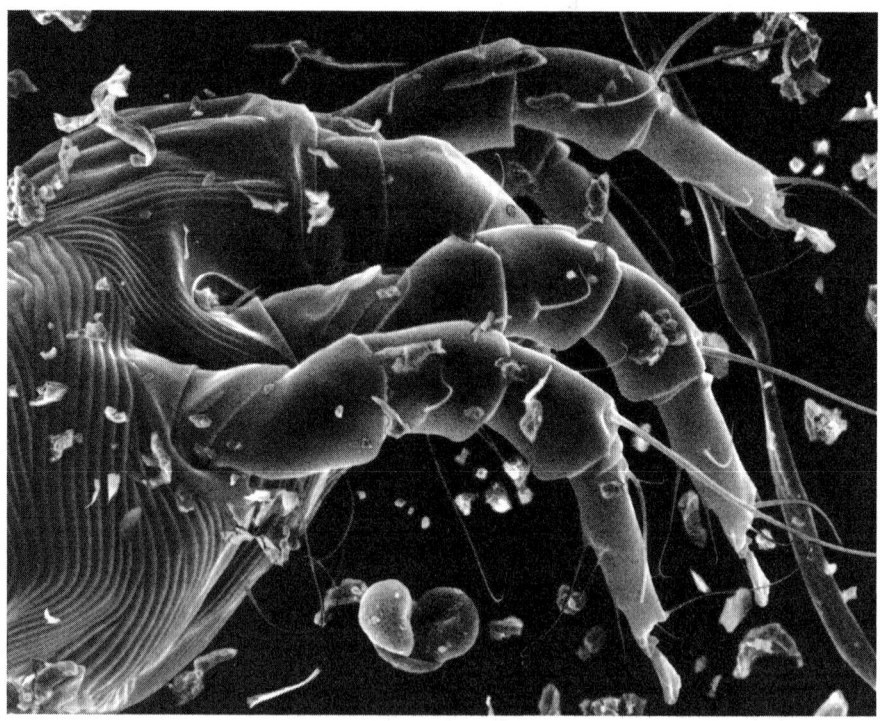

Chigger (Copyright Dennis Kunkel Microscopy)

Lice: Keeping Your Head

Having a lousy day? You will if you're infested with tiny creatures that have been known for more than nine thousand years: the crawling, blood-sucking, wingless, little sesame-seed-sized beasties with legs called *lice*. Some cultures really liked these bloodsuckers. The Aztec king Montezuma paid his subjects to pick mite eggs, called *nits*, off other peoples' bodies—the ultimate in being nit-picky. He would then dry and save the nits in his treasury, for whatever reason. Perhaps people were worth their weight in nits? Or was this Montezuma's *real* revenge?

This "mechanized dandruff," as the United States government officially calls lice, loves your hair, a place with the perfect temperature and humidity, and an endless supply of food—your scalp. They use their six clawed legs to cling to human hair. And we should consider changing the common phrase "multiplying like rabbits" to "multiplying like lice": A female louse can produce from 50 to 150 eggs—that's six to ten nits a day. The eggs hatch in five to ten days and the critters begin chewing on your scalp immediately.[14]

Judging the Danger

Lice, or *Pediculus capitis*, are tiny creatures that can invade the best of homes. Although there are no official statistics on how many people are infested every year, schools across the country have been reporting an increase in infestations. A louse infestation can spread like wildfire in such close quarters, spreading as kids in school butt heads, roll around with each other, and share combs, brushes, hats, or other headgear. In fact, except for the common cold, infestation by lice is more common than all other communicable childhood conditions combined. The annual bill for treatment comes to about $370 million, with as many as 20 million people infected.

There are many reasons why most of us detest the off-white, rust, or gray critters (they often camouflage themselves in a person's hair). The lice can cause considerable skin irritation as they feed on your scalp, sipping on your blood every few hours like a mint julep.

Thank goodness they can't hop or jump. But when they *do* move, they're quick little buggers, crawling through our hair at speeds of up to five miles per hour.

Minimizing the Danger

You'll know if you're infested with lice—you can actually feel and see them crawling on your scalp. Here are some ways to stop the lousy lice:

✦ The old-fashioned way may be the best: Shampoo with olive oil, then remove the nits by hand. There are actually people in Boston and New York who charge fifty dollars per hour to train parents to do just that.

✦ Try washing your hair with an over-the-counter lice-killing shampoo (pediculicide). Follow the directions on the bottle. Most have you go through two treatments, usually about eight to ten days apart. And comb your hair with a special louse or nit comb every day for about two weeks to help get rid of the lice and nits.

✦ If you don't want to use the strong chemicals in lice-killing shampoos in your hair—after all, they are pesticides—there are some alternatives. (And of course, with the passage of time, even your average louse can become a superlouse, unaffected by medications.) There are certain products with enzymes that are nontoxic to humans, such as protease, lipase, cellulase, and amylase—some of which cause the lice's exoskeletons to literally fall apart. We see this in nature all the time, such as the enzymes in a Venus flytrap that break down a trapped fly.

✦ And finally, don't ever blame your pet for a lousy day— human lice like only humans.

Biting Bugs: Got Itch?

What's the number-one bug everyone thinks of when we say the word "itchy"? Yes, it's the unsightly, multi-eyed, needle-mouthed mosquito. And when they say bloodsucking, they mean it: This parasite drinks blood. The insect's mouth comes in many parts: Four stylets pierce the skin and make a hole. Another part pumps an anticoagulant into the victim's (that's us) bloodstream. This mix stops our blood from clotting, eliminating the possibility that our blood will stop them from feeding, and gives us a nasty, itchy welt as our immune system responds. The last part acts like a sump-pump, sucking the blood up. As the mosquito feeds, it swells so much that its skin stretches. In fact, its skin becomes so thin that you can see the blood you've donated to the mosquito cause.[15]

Second on the to-itch list are fleas, the tiny, flat, narrow, wingless insects that can not only quickly move through hair, but can jump hundreds of times their body length—more than a foot. They go through four stages of development: from egg, larva, and pupa to the adult, the one that enjoys using us as a blood meal. And with more than two thousand species of fleas known, it's a wonder all mammals haven't gone extinct from the itching. Luckily, most fleas have specific hosts they prefer to munch on.

Judging the Danger

When mosquitoes see a mammal, they act like a used-car salesman beelining for a potential customer. But they don't think of kicking the tires or slamming the doors—they immediately go for bare skin or right through that thin shirt you're wearing. The concern with these creatures is not only the itch, but the mosquitoes' roles in spreading disease: They are carriers of many often-heard-of diseases, such as malaria, yellow fever, and the West Nile virus. Some folks try to eliminate the swarms, using chemicals, light oil, or gas dumped in standing water. The future bloodsucking larvae—hanging from the water surface to absorb oxygen—sink and drown. But then you have the problem of oil in your water—something of concern to people with well water. Spraying an area from the air is also often a solution in the warmer, more humid areas of the country. But these insects still show up like an unwanted relative popping up on your honeymoon.

Unlike swarming mosquitoes, fleas love to really bunch up. And they seem to thrive in humid places such as Hawaii, coastal California, the Gulf Coast, and the Atlantic seaboard south of Maryland. (Who wouldn't like those places?) Flea breeding is perfect there year-round—and with about one hundred fleas producing a half million baby fleas in one month, odds are some of these bugs could set up camp in your home.

Minimizing the Danger

The usual way to get keep these insects at bay is to stay inside. But that's not practical for all of us. And what about the bugs that sneak in the front door when you pick up the mail? Here are a few tips to keep mosquitoes away if you venture outside:

- ✦ Be aware the most mosquitoes come out in profusion around sunset and sunrise; still others, such as some in South America, feed during the day. And day or night, mosquitoes really, really like wet, mushy, swampy, damp areas.
- ✦ For people who like the outdoors during the summer, try a screened porch. If you have a wet area in your yard, there are special doughnutlike chemical wafers that you can put in standing water to kill off the nymphs.
- ✦ Mosquitoes are most attracted to the carbon dioxide in your breath, certain of your odors, and the heat given off by your body. If you do any hiking—or other outdoor activities—this doesn't mean you have to show up in knight's armor to keep the bugs away. A bug repellent with Deet in it works. The higher the dosage of Deet, the longer the repellent protects you—but don't over-apply it. For those of you who search for a more natural alternative, there are plant-oil-based products you can usually find in outdoor clothing and supply stores, although the more natural products may not protect for as long as a Deet-based product. We've also tried wearing mosquito netting/hats—they work fine to keep the creatures off, but are not the best to see through if you're on a birding expedition.

It's easy to see why a pet would bring on a flea infestation: Fleas can hide in the animal's fur, laying up to fifty eggs per day on your pet. The eggs soon fall from the animal into your carpeting, beneath the cushions in the furniture, and anywhere else your pet puts its posterior. If you do see the little jumping insects on bedsheets, dogs, cats, or sundry other places, try the following:

✦ Vacuuming the house can remove many of the eggs, larvae, and pupae—all life stages of the flea. We're not sure if it's the noise or not, but vacuuming also causes the preadult fleas to emerge sooner from their insecticide-resistant cocoons. After vacuuming, seal the vacuum bag in a garbage bag and throw it in your outdoor trash container.

✦ For a light infestation, there are chemicals you can purchase at department or pet stores. For a more natural approach, there is something at most garden stores called Neem—a powerful and relatively safe natural insecticide. Some people also swear by dusting any flea-ridden places in their homes with *diatomaceous earth*—the fossilized skeletons of ancient sea animals (organic farmers often use this to kill off insects in their gardens).

✦ For absolute flea takeovers, sometimes the only way to win is to fumigate your home with chemical bombs available at some department or pet stores, or from your veterinarian. Make sure you and your pet stay out of the house during the bombing.

✦ Once the fleas seem to be gone, vacuum every other day to keep help remove the eggs that may have been left behind in the carpet. And remember to throw the bag away each time— or the fleas will hatch inside, causing another flea fiasco.

The Hitchhiker

The mosquito must have a brain the size of a nanobot (for you non-Borg and *Star Trek* fans, that means really, *really* small). Take some mosquitoes in South America—please. As they fly around in their usual helter-skelter way, they can be caught by a botfly. After it captures the mosquito victim, the botfly glues its eggs to the insect prisoner's abdomen—then in a moment of compassion, lets the mosquito go. Nanobrain mosquito thinks it's gotten away with something, so it goes on its way, seeking the usual body emissions from an unsuspecting mammal.

Not only will the mosquito do its usual, spitting saliva to give us itchy bites, but it also leaves a gift from the botfly. As the mosquito feeds, our own heat causes the botfly eggs to hatch. The quickest larva wins, wasting no time crawling into the fresh bite wound. There, it sets down roots, using two mouth hooks to anchor itself, and

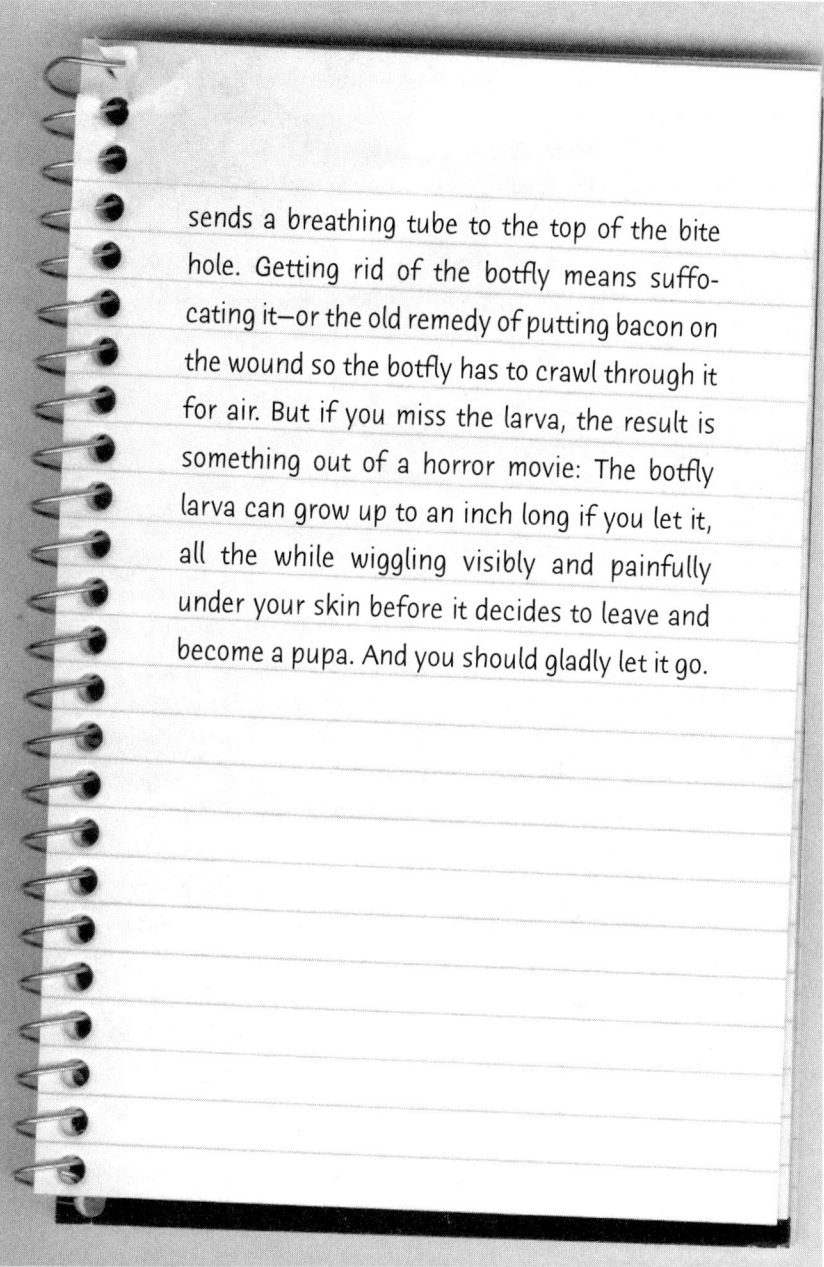

sends a breathing tube to the top of the bite hole. Getting rid of the botfly means suffocating it—or the old remedy of putting bacon on the wound so the botfly has to crawl through it for air. But if you miss the larva, the result is something out of a horror movie: The botfly larva can grow up to an inch long if you let it, all the while wiggling visibly and painfully under your skin before it decides to leave and become a pupa. And you should gladly let it go.

NO PLACE LIKE HOME?

Home is where the heart is—and everything else,
it seems . . .

Surely you're safe in your home. After all, most people spend a good part of their time there. Not only is it familiar, but with all the modern improvements, it's very safe. Right?

Unfortunately, the opposite is true. Most accidents and problems occur in the home, mainly because we're there most of the time. In fact, studies have shown that for people over seventy-five, the home is the most dangerous place in the world.

There are, of course, the obvious dangers, such as tripping on rugs, falling down, accidents with electrical or gas appliances, chimney and other fires, slipping in the shower or tub, acts of nature, not programming your VCR properly and ending up with *I Love Lucy* reruns, or setting your breakfast Pop Tarts on fire. But what most people don't realize is the number of hidden dangers that lurk in the castle called "home." For example, 80 percent of food poisoning doesn't happen in restaurants, but at home. There are germs, bacteria, and fungi everywhere, from the moldy basement to the sink sponges and cutting boards. Don't forget those dust kitties and mites, either—or that innocent-looking pet. No matter how you cut it, the home can be a battlefield for the uninformed.

WHAT'S HAUNTING *YOUR* HOUSE?

Pesticides:
A Walk on the Wild (Chemical) Side

You've just finished spraying your pristine lawn with a weed killer. After admiring its lush, dandelion-free greenness, you put away the can and sprayer, wash your hands, and go inside for lunch. Little do you know that you've just contaminated your castle with potentially dangerous chemicals—ones that can be particularly harmful to your children. And what you also don't realize is that the chemicals will linger in your home for almost an entire week.

A recent study found that weed killers and other pesticides applied to lawns can be tracked into the home by people and pets up to a week after the treatment.[1] And there was an interesting distribution of the pesticide, too: In homes with carpeted entryways, the level of pesticide was higher than in other parts of the house. Bare floor entryways had lower levels of pesticide. In general, rooms with bare floors had lower levels of tracked-in pesticide than those with carpeted floors.

Judging the Danger

The study followed what you track into your house—herbicides that can cause irritation to the gastrointestinal tract, skin rashes, and dermatitis. The long-term effects are unknown, but exposure, whether short- or long-term, to pesticides in general may increase the potential health risks to everyone living in a house. Those at highest risk are infants and toddlers, who normally spent a lot of time crawling or lying on the floor—especially in homes with carpets. Their toys may also pick up pesticide residues—and these are objects that infants normally put in their mouth.

What are some of the hazardous chemicals in pesticides? Try dimplylate (better known as the extremely toxic diazinon), chlorinated hydrocarbons (suspected carcinogen and *mutantagen*—something that causes a cellular mutation—that accumulate in food and in your fatty tissue), and organophosphates (toxic and poisonous). Not only can't you pronounce most of these, but many times you can't see the damage they can do until someone becomes ill.

Minimizing the Danger

What can be done to prevent the spread of pesticides into the home from outside? The most obvious is to avoid using pesticides in the first place. But we realize such a request is not reasonable for many people who either have to use them (some insects do radically encroach around homes) or insist on using them. If that is the case, here are a few hints to keep pesticide encroachment in your home to a minimum:

✦ Have all family members and guests remove their shoes before entering. You can keep several pairs of soft, one-size-fits-all slippers in the guest closet for visitors.

✦ Keep adults and children off the lawn right after application.

✦ Put carpets or rugs in every entryway. This will cause the pesticides to accumulate on the carpet, limiting the amount that reaches other areas of the house.

✦ Clothing used during the application of pesticides should be removed before entering the house. You may want to do this in a garage (keep a clean set of clothes out there) so you don't give the neighbors a show.

✦ Don't forget to keep pets off the lawn right after application. Not only are most of these chemicals bad for your pet, but Fluffy and Spot also like to roll on the ground. Not good.

✦ Don't use chemicals on your lawn in the first place. Most lawns don't really need them. Try composting and spread the results on your lawn. Call your county's cooperative extension to get alternatives to pesticides.

Nothing to Sneeze At

American homes have been invaded. That's right, invaded. The results are allergic reactions and worsened asthma symptoms for adults as well as children. And asthma is ranked as the most common chronic childhood disease in the United States.

Who are these invaders? They're allergens, invisible by-products of common household dwellers such as bugs. And houses in the United States are crawling with bugs, according to a first-ever national survey by the National Institute of Environmental Health Sciences (one of the National Institutes of Health). In particular, they studied dust mites and cockroaches, whose allergens are known to worsen asthma symptoms and allergies. In other words, there may be a good, though hidden, reason for your coughing and hacking.[2]

Not my home, you say. It's clean. I haven't seen any dust mites or cockroaches, much less tiny allergens. Well, you might not see them, but there's a good chance they're present. The survey sent a questionnaire to 830 homes—from rural to urban—asking questions about issues related to allergies and asthma, including time spent outside and inside the home, amount of smoking, cleaning habits, and history of insect infestation. Five hundred of these homes were visited and inspected, with dust samples taken for analysis. The results were then extrapolated to the entire United States population.

It wasn't pretty—or even very clean. Forty-four million homes, about 45 percent, had dust mite allergens present. About 22 million, or 23 percent, had levels of dust mite allergens associated with allergen sensitization. And 15 percent of the homes had dust mite allergen levels known to increase the symptoms of asthma. Six million homes, about 6 percent, had cockroach allergens present in the beds. More than 1.2 million, representing over 10 percent, had enough allergens to worsen allergies.

Just in case you think this problem is limited to inner cities, the survey found problems in rural and suburban homes as well. Apparently, like politicians the week before elections, these allergens are everywhere. The next step in the ongoing study is to examine the allergens related to other bugs, fungi, and pets. We bet many of us won't get a clean bill of health on those sundry items, either.

✦ Sometimes pesticides can come in through your windows—
especially if the neighbor puts chemicals on her lawn. Just
close the windows and get out of the house for the day.
Remember, if you can smell it, your lungs are absorbing it.
And you may not want to be exposed to it.

Hot Tubs: A Waterworld for Germs

It's Saturday afternoon, and you're relaxing in your indoor hot tub.
Ahh . . . The warm water swirls around you, relaxing those tired mus-
cles. You sip a glass of cold white wine. Just the thing after a hard week
of work. Later, as you're getting ready to go out for dinner, a wave of
tiredness sweeps over you. You cough repeatedly. That night, you wake
up sweating, running a fever. For several days, you lose weight, even
though you're not trying. What's going on here?

Recent studies have found people who regularly use indoor hot
tubs run the risk of developing lung disease. Two types of nontu-
berculosis mycobacteria (NTM)—specifically *Mycobacterium avium*
and *Mycobacterium fortuitum*—have been found in the hot-tub water
and in the air of homes of people diagnosed with this disease. Scientists think these invisible organisms are distributed into the air by
the swirling action of the hot tubs. And since these hot tubs are
inside, there is no ready mechanism such as the wind to get rid of
the bacteria. You inhale the critters all the time, greatly increasing
your chances of illness.[3]

Judging the Danger

NTM organisms normally live in brackish ocean water, such as tidal
pools. But hot tubs are also nice homes for them. They wouldn't be a
real problem, except for the action of the hot tubs: The jets that make
the nice, relaxing, swirling action are responsible. Jet-formed bubbles
float up, burst, and send tiny, bacteria-filled water droplets into the
room as a mist. From there, without anything to stop them, the bacteria drift throughout the room and into the rest of the house.

This type of lung disease is easy to misdiagnose. Symptoms are

Tracing Legionnaires' Disease

Of course, we couldn't get away with just one disease from contaminated bubbles rising from whirlpools and sundry other mist-driven devices. There's another bacteria that causes infection, one that became a media star in 1976 when it caused an outbreak of pneumonia among attendees of a convention of the American Legion in Philadelphia—the *Legionella* bacteria that causes Legionnaires' disease.

Even after all these years, the Centers for Disease Control and Prevention states that about eight thousand to eighteen thousand people come down with Legionnaires' disease (or *legionellosis*) in the United States each year. And because between 5 and 30 percent of the people who contract it die, that's significant enough for a warning. The insidious bacteria that leads to this disease, *Legionella pneumophila*, breeds profusely in warm, stagnant water, especially in places associated with mists. That includes air-conditioning cooling towers (but not household or car air-conditioning units),

[continued on next page]

whirlpool spas, and showers—even potting soil has been blamed—in places such as homes, offices, hospitals, and public places. A person who breathes any of those bacteria-infested mists comes down with fever, chills, and a cough in two to ten days; some have muscle aches, headaches, tiredness, loss of appetite, and sometimes diarrhea. Tests will show that the patient's kidneys are not functioning properly and chest X rays will show pneumonia, so the best way to know if the disease is definitely *Legionella*-induced is to test for the bacteria itself.

The one good thing—if it can be considered "good"—is that the disease usually occurs as a single, isolated case, not as an outbreak. When there is an outbreak, it can usually be traced back to such items as a cooling tower or a mister of some type. So watch it if you're middle-aged or older—and especially if you smoke cigarettes or have chronic lung disease or a suppressed immune system: You're more susceptible. In most cases, the antibiotic erythromycin is administered to treat the disease.[4]

similar to other granulomatous lung diseases, such as sarcoidosis or the well-known tuberculosis. And when misdiagnosed, patients often continue to use the hot tubs in their homes, further exposing themselves to the bacteria—and worsening the symptoms.

So far, only a handful of cases have been traced back to an indoor hot tub. But as more people install these tubs for leisure in this stress-filled world, exposure will increase—as likely will the number of cases.

Minimizing the Danger

If you have an indoor hot tub, here are a few hints to protect yourself (and please note: NTM is not contagious and you cannot be infected by another person):

✦ Learn to recognize the symptoms of this lung disease. They include a cough, weight loss, tiredness, night sweats, and fever. If the symptoms are severe, consult your doctor. You may need a course of antibiotics (sometimes three or four types all at once), corticosteroids, or a combination of the drugs. You will also have to stop soaking up the suds on Saturday nights.

✦ For those with a mild case of NTM, move the hot tub from inside to an outside setting, so the wind will blow away the bacteria-ridden bubbles.

Lead Poisoning: Leading It Out

Many of us are familiar with the dangers of lead poisoning. Look what happened to the Roman Empire. And Ludwig van Beethoven. And no doubt a litany of others throughout the ages that drank or ate from lead-tainted pipes, mugs, or dishes.

The horror stories about lead abound. Even though lead levels in the blood have dropped about 80 percent over the past twenty years, there are still more than a million children who have way too much lead in their blood—enough to endanger their health. The scariest

Advice for the Pool Shark

Doctors in the U.K. have found another hidden source of lead poisoning: pool chalk. No, not the chalk we all used in school, but those small cubes used to chalk up the cues during a friendly game of eight ball. Those cubes just aren't as friendly as they seem.[5]

A three-year-old girl brought the problem to the forefront: She was taken to the doctor with a suspected upper respiratory tract infection. Symptoms included poor diet, no interest in solid foods, and only drinking milk. Blood tests determined that she was anemic and she was given iron supplements. The tests also detected an abnormally high level of lead in her system. When the parents told the doctor that the child had a history of eating nonfood substances such as dirt and concrete, they searched the house to find the source of the lead.

Testing the water, dust, soil, paint, and plaster proved negative. Months later, the girl's lead level went up again, and she was sent to the hospital. At this time the parents mentioned that the girl was often seen with pool chalk cubes in her mouth. Bingo. The pool chalk

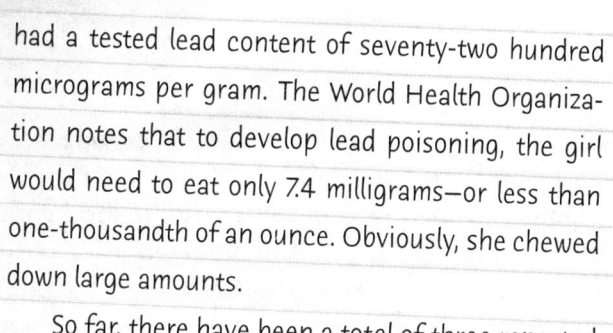

had a tested lead content of seventy-two hundred micrograms per gram. The World Health Organization notes that to develop lead poisoning, the girl would need to eat only 7.4 milligrams—or less than one-thousandth of an ounce. Obviously, she chewed down large amounts.

So far, there have been a total of three reported cases of lead poisoning due to pool chalk—one in the U.K. and two in the United States. Though rare, it does illustrate the need to be aware of all potential sources of lead in the home, especially when children are present. And the lead-infested chalk doesn't even have to be ingested to cause lead poisoning. The fine dust formed when using the chalk will contaminate everything around it, such as the clothes of the user, the surrounding furnishings, and the pool table itself. So if you have children and a pool table, purchase and use only lead-free pool chalk. And play safe if you don't have a good shot.

part is that they may not have any symptoms; but what they *do* have is highly problematic. If not detected early, lead poisoning can cause serious brain and nervous-system damage. It can even lower the IQ of young children if they ingest dangerous amounts before the age of five. Also at risk are pregnant women and their unborn children.

Judging the Danger

Lead poisoning is an insidious problem. In today's world, common sources of lead are some paints, contaminated soils, water that has been routed through lead pipes, and some food containers (mostly cans) and plumbing solders. And although lead is bad for everyone, children are particularly susceptible to this type of poisoning.

Our exposure to lead has gone down over the past two decades. It was removed from residential paints in 1978, and fuels—hence, unleaded gasoline—in 1982. Lead poisoning was caused by the paint flakes being chewed on by infants and toddlers; it was also entering the systems of children playing outside—lead particles from cars' combustion process fell on lawns nearest the streets. But everyone is still trying to get all the lead out.

Minimizing the Danger

The best ways to avoid the danger of lead is to get the lead out—period. Here are a few hints:[6]

+ If you're remodeling a home built before 1960, it will more often than not contain heavily leaded paint; even houses built before 1978 can have lead problems on indoor and outdoor painted surfaces. (In fact, a great deal of child lead poisoning is from young children chewing paint off windowsills, door frames, and other easy-to-chew spots in older homes.) If you plan to sand, scrap, or use heat guns, remember that you will be releasing the lead into the air. The best way to handle the lead is to contain it. The Consumer Product Safety Commission may be able to help; or call a local contractor to do the work for you.

✦ Be careful of food cans from other countries. Oftentimes, they still use lead in their solder.

✦ Terra-cotta pottery is beautiful, but in some places, especially overseas, it is made with lead that easily leaches into liquids. Lead glaze is often the culprit—it can be durable, but it's dangerous. Unless you're sure lead-free glazes have been used on that expresso mug, you should avoid putting acidic or hot foods in it.

✦ Beware of handmade or hand-painted ceramic items (check with the maker to make sure it is lead free, or read the literature that often comes with the item), imports (especially from Mexico, China, India, and Spain), any ceramic piece that leaves a grayish, chalky residue after you wash it, and antique pieces.

✦ If you think you or your child has been exposed to lead, don't hesitate to see your family practitioner.

Computers:
Why We're Really Sick of Computers

It's been a long day at the computer. True, you telecommute and you're at home—but it's still been a long day. Finally, your report is finished and you can relax. If only the headache, itching, and nasal congestion would go away. No time for a cold. It's probably just eye strain—and you thought that new, larger monitor was supposed to fix that problem. Sometimes you wonder if your job is making you ill. And sometimes you wonder if the computer itself is making you sick. Oh, well. Time for dinner, then you'll relax by playing a new computer game. The symptoms continue long after you go to bed.

You're not alone in thinking your computer is making you sick—and now researchers have uncovered evidence that your suspicions may be correct. A recent Swedish study discovered that emissions of a chemical compound from the computer monitor's plastic may be detrimental to your health. Manufacturers add triphenyl phosphate to the plastic—not only to monitors but to other products as well—as a flame retardant. This substance is a known

Speaking of (Cat) Allergies

It's a superstition that's been around for ages: A black cat crossing your path will bring you bad luck. Now researchers may have found out this is true—at least for people with allergies.

While cats in general can trigger asthma and other allergic reactions in some people, a recent study of more than three hundred allergy-prone people found exposure to dark-colored cats brought on more symptoms—mostly wheezing and sneezing—than light-colored cats. And no, they didn't subject the poor patients to timed intervals of cat exposure in laboratories. Instead, the researchers discovered that allergic patients who owned dark-colored cats were six times more likely to have moderate to severe allergy symptoms than people who owned light-colored cats. In addition, despite an earlier study suggesting that male cats cause more human allergic reactions than females, this report found no such evidence.[7]

The reason still has scientists puzzled, although they suspect the darker-colored cats may produce more allergen in their salvia and skin. Or maybe the cats have some other, previously unknown antigen. Now scientists want to measure the allergen levels on different colored cats to find out what is going on.

For now, if getting rid of dear old black Sassy-cat isn't an option, at least keep him out of the bedroom. For noncat owners, be aware that allergens from a cat can reside on its owner's clothes—and can trigger an allergic reaction. Be especially aware of those who own dark-colored cats, or people who seem to be under the spell of their cats—catering to the feline's every whim. Unfortunately, that would encompass just about every cat owner in the world.

allergen, causing headaches, nasal congestion, and itching in some people. As the monitor heats up during operation, it emits the chemical compound. At present, no one knows how much exposure will trigger a reaction. And while computers may be obsolete the day after you buy them, older computers are apparently safer: The study showed that new computers emit more triphenyl phosphate than older ones.[8]

Judging the Danger

In the Swedish study, the new computer monitors' normal operating temperatures ranged from 122° to 131°F (50° to 55°C). As a result, there was a measurable level of triphenyl phosphate in the area dubbed the "breathing zone"—the two-foot area in front of the screen. The levels of the chemical compound dropped significantly after the monitors were in continuous operations for eight days. That's the good news.

The bad news? The level remained ten times higher than normal background level—even after the equivalent of two years of normal use. In a small, enclosed environment like a home office, this is a significant long-term source of allergens. And buying a different monitor is not the solution, since nearly all manufacturers use this same flame-retardant compound.

Minimizing the Danger

How can you avoid this form of computer sickness? A combination of increased airflow in the room and sitting farther away from the monitor might help alleviate symptoms. But the researchers caution that even with more ventilation, the compound may remain a potential health hazard. Until manufacturers begin using a flame retardant that does not cause allergic reactions, limiting the time spent at the computer might be the best solution. Or buy an old computer and bring it up to speed. Perhaps eliminating the computer and going back to the quill pen might work—except for those allergic to feathers.

Food Poisoning: Guess Who's Coming to Dinner

It was a hot, sunny day in September when our intrepid author-motorcyclist decided to go to a nearby motorcycle rally. He made it there in an hour, with plenty of time to visit the booths filled with all sorts of stuff he really didn't need for his motorcycling lifestyle. After a while, he noticed his growling stomach and stood in line for the offered fare. Mostly a vegetarian, he had only a choice of meats. Hey, it's only one meal, he thought. The rest of the day was uneventful, and he rode home with a smile and a new pair of leather gloves.

But this was no ordinary meal. That night, his stomach no longer growled—it felt like it was tied in knots. Soon, watery diarrhea set in, along with severe cramping, nausea, fever, and headache. Like all good macho motorcyclists, he toughed it out for three days, thinking it might be the flu. On the third day, feeling weak from dehydration, he took himself to the hospital. The prognosis: Food poisoning from *Campylobacter* bacteria—now not-so-lovingly known as "the time he got campy."

The state health department called soon afterward (they receive all such reports from hospitals to stop outbreaks) to determine just where he contracted the bacteria. That's when he found out the bacterial contamination can be caused by improper cooking. Sure enough, it was from his meal at the rally. Needless to say, our author now eats even more vegetarian cooking than ever before—and always packs his own lunch.

Judging the Danger

You may not *want* to guess who's coming to your next dinner. It may be food poisoning, a group of medical conditions that result from chowing down the wrong food. It could be one of a litany of harmful bacteria: *Staphylococcus aureus*, *Salmonella*, *Clostridium perfringens*, *Campylobacter*, *Listeria monocytogenes*, *Vibrio parahaemolyticus*, and *Bacillus cereus*. And we can't forget *Escherichia coli*. Et tu, *E. coli*?[9]

Contrary to what you learned in high school biology, not all bacteria are bad. Some bacteria in our stomachs help break down milk into milk sugars. In fact, fewer than 20 percent of the many thousands of known bacteria are actually bad. But bad is bad. It's estimated that between 24 and 81 million cases of food-borne diarrhea occur each year in the United States, and they cost between $5 and $17 billion in medical expenses and lost time on the job. These harmful bacteria grow rapidly at room temperature, moving from food to people, from person to person, or from people to food.

How are you usually exposed to these bacteria? We can't list all of them, but here are a few of the more well-known ones:

✦ *Staphylococcus aureus.* Our respiratory passages, skin, and superficial wounds are breeding grounds for this bacterium. So are certain foods prepared by hand—potato salad, ham salad, and so on. Cooking may destroy the bacteria, but not the toxin it leaves behind. And it just loves to drop its toxin if you leave the salads out at room temperature for long periods of time. Your symptoms will be nausea, vomiting, and diarrhea within four to six hours, but you'll have no fever. (This bacterium has also changed over the years: Doctors used treat this infection with penicillin; but now more than 95 percent of these infections defy penicillin, and stronger antibiotics must be used. It's possibly a prime example of the development of a superbug—bacteria that eventually develop resistance to certain antibiotics.)

✦ *Salmonella.* This bacterium gets a good deal of coverage in the media—and for good reason. The most common sources are high-protein foods such as meat, poultry, fish, and eggs. You can destroy the bacteria at temperatures above 150°F (65°C); you can control the growth by refrigeration below 40°F (4°C). But it's often spread by insufficient cooking or contamination from contact with utensils that were not properly washed after use with the raw products. You won't like the symptoms here, either—diarrhea, nausea, chills, vomiting, and fever within twelve to twenty-four hours.

✦ *Clostridium botulinum.* This is botulism—one of those horrible bacteria we always fear, and for good reason. It's usually caused by our own hand. Only about one out of every four hundred cases of food poisoning is from botulism, but it's still important: It causes death in 30 percent of cases, and it's almost always caused by home-canned foods. The bacterium can exist as a heat-resistant spore, producing a neurotoxin in under-processed, home-canned food. The usual way to detect it is by a bulging can or top or a strange odor. But not all give a tell-tale sign. So never taste a home-canned food before heating, and boil the food for ten minutes to destroy the toxin. And if you don't listen to us, you will definitely hate the symptoms: Blurred vision, respiratory distress, and possible death.

Minimizing the Danger

You don't have to "get campy" or any other bacteria from food poisoning. And you don't have to supersterilize your kitchen—common sense will do. First, assume that all foods may cause a food-borne illness—then you won't be taking any chances of getting sick. Here are a few hints to stop the bacterial spread:

✦ Mom always said cleanliness is next to godliness—whatever that may be. When it comes to cooking and food, this is essential. Always wash your hands, food preparation surfaces, and used utensils before and after handling raw foods. (And if you walk into a restaurant and it looks as if they've been cooking on the floor, go somewhere else to eat.)

✦ Cook food to the proper internal temperature; if you have one, check big cuts of meat with a food thermometer. Serve hot foods immediately or keep them heated above 140°F (60°C); keep refrigerated foods below 40°F (4°C). Try dividing larger cooked food portions into smaller portions in the fridge to lower the temperatures more quickly—and so as not to raise the temperatures of the surrounding, already-cooled foods.

It's Super(heated) Water!

Time for a nice cup of tea. If you're like a lot of people, the quickest and most convenient way to heat the water is to place it in the microwave. But beware. There is a danger lurking in the microwave—and it doesn't have anything to do with radiation.

Sometimes, when heating water (or other liquids) in a microwave, it doesn't seem to boil, no matter how long you heat it. There are no bubbles. The natural thing to do is to heat it some more. *Don't do it.* That liquid may be *superheated*—already above the boiling temperature, but without the telltale sign of bubbles. And if you take the superheated water out of the microwave, then stir or add the teabag or coffee—watch out! The water can erupt, spraying extremely hot water everywhere—including in your face and on your body.

To avoid this superheating problem, take a few precautions. First, and it may sound simple,

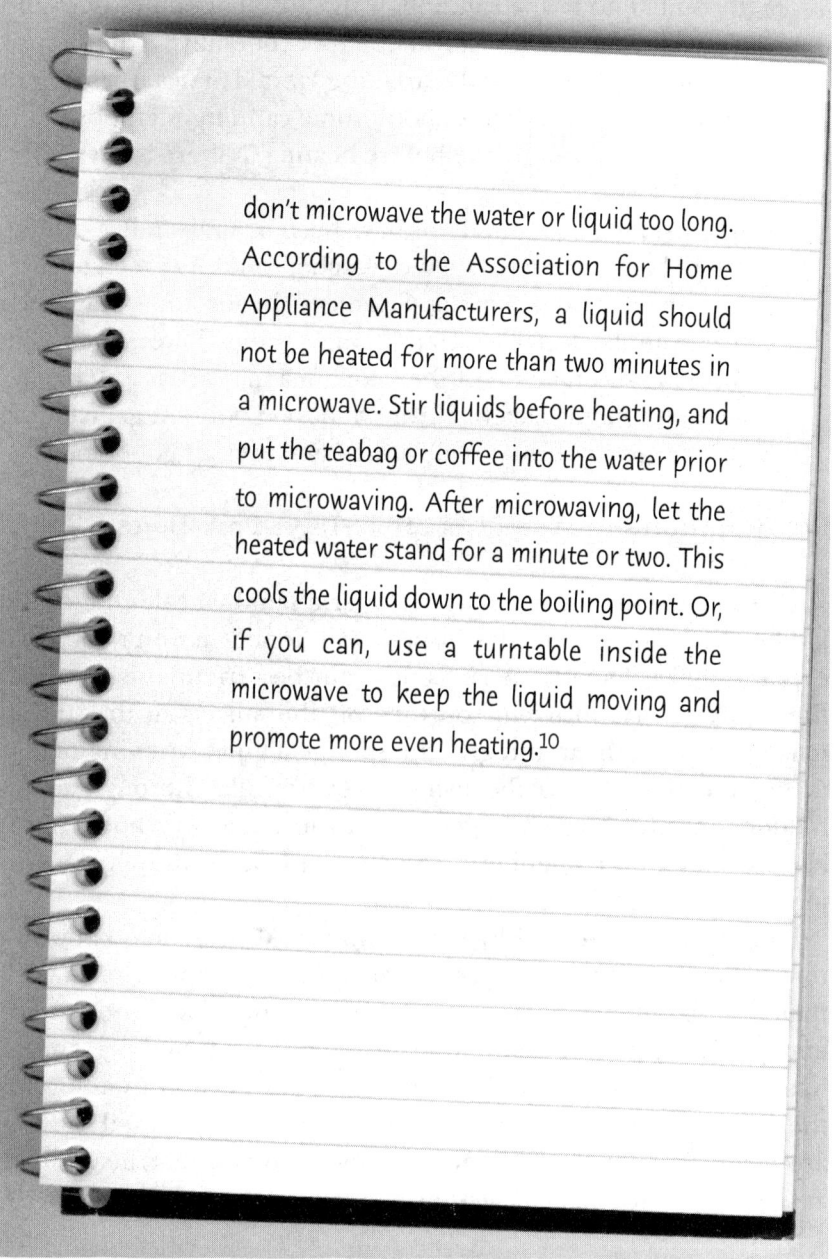

don't microwave the water or liquid too long. According to the Association for Home Appliance Manufacturers, a liquid should not be heated for more than two minutes in a microwave. Stir liquids before heating, and put the teabag or coffee into the water prior to microwaving. After microwaving, let the heated water stand for a minute or two. This cools the liquid down to the boiling point. Or, if you can, use a turntable inside the microwave to keep the liquid moving and promote more even heating.[10]

✦ If you like to home can, follow the correct boiling times and procedures. Call your local county cooperative extension or get on the Internet and search the United States Department of Agriculture bulletins about home-canning methods.

✦ Don't taste canned food before heating; if there is any doubt, throw it out.

✦ Interestingly enough, there have been several studies coming out of Japan that indicate the catechin in strong green tea may help deter food poisoning. Scientists already know that green tea is antibacterial, and additional studies have shown that drinking several cups of the strong tea may act as a sterilizing agent for many bacteria involved in food poisoning, including *Staphylococcus*. It can't really hurt—and it tastes good, too.

Common Household Items: D-Day for Bugs

You're in the kitchen, cleaning up after a family meal. One of the kids was sick and had to stay in bed. You hope you don't get whatever they have. The phone rings. It's your best friend, raving about the newest movie in town. You turn off the faucets in the sink to make it easier to hear and give the sponge a good wringing before taking the phone into the living room to talk. Although it was hidden, an infectious pathogen has just invaded your body. It was lying in wait on the telephone, the kitchen faucets, the sponge—or maybe all three.

Many diseases spread by direct contact. Most people know not to breathe in another person's sneeze or cough droplets, or to wash their hands after touching an ill person. But that's not always enough. Some pathogens are transferred by an infected person to a handy surface, where they remain alive and infectious, waiting for the next human host to walk by. Some diseases transmitted this way are relatively mild, such as the common cold and diarrhea; others are more serious, like *Salmonella*.

Judging the Danger

What are the chances of picking up an infectious disease from a common item found around the house? It depends on a number of factors: the type and number of infectious agents present, the type of surface, the ability of the infection to transfer efficiently, and the "dose" needed to start the disease. Not so easy to tell when you remember the little buggers are invisible to the naked eye.

How do these insidious organisms spread? A recent study looked at the disease transfer of a bacteria and bacterial virus from common household items to a person's hand. The two culprits, *Serratia rubidea* (similar to *E. coli*) and PRD-1, a bacterial virus, were easy to find in certain places. Faucet handles were particularly good at transferring these pathogens, with an efficiency of 28 percent for the *S. rubidea* and 34 percent for the PRD-1. Phone receivers were also good, with readings of 39 and 66 percent transfer, respectively. Once the infectious agent was on the hand, the study found that 34 percent of both pathogens could be transferred from a contaminated fingertip to the lower lip. No wonder your mother told you not to bite your fingernails.[11]

There's another reason why you may not want to answer your phone anymore—or rather, let anyone else answer it. Your electronic contact with the outside world can easily spread the diarrhea-causing bacteria *Salmonella*. The pathogens exist in a person's stool—and if that person didn't wash his hands properly after defecating, you could have an infection on your hands, so to speak. After all, your unsanitary friend could contaminate the receiver with a tiny amount of their feces. The next person to use the phone—more than likely, you—would pick up approximately 107,104 of the pathogens and transfer 36,383 to her mouth. Those are numbers that easily trigger the disease in you, the new host.

And it's not only the bacteria that love to hang around your home. Viruses are particularly insidious, since they can survive for a period ranging from hours to days on hard surfaces. To compound the problem, the number of microscopic viruses found in an infected person's fluids is large—and the dose needed to contract the disease is very low. Take a diarrheal rotavirus that an infected person introduces to the surface of a phone. If only 10,000 viruses were present on the surface, the next person on the phone would pick up 6,580 on their hand, with approximately 211 viruses ending up on a fingertip. Just a touch to the lips would transfer 72 viruses to the new host—easily resulting in many trips to the bathroom for the unfortunate victim.

Don't think that those clean-appearing faucet handles are benign, either. They are rich sources for pathogens—particularly the faucets in the kitchen, where viruses can survive for several hours. Consider the cold virus: The mucus of an infected person has large numbers of these viruses, and the number needed to infect another person is extremely small. Just touch a kitchen faucet handle contaminated by someone with a cold and you could pick up 1,037 of the viruses. Without thinking, you could eventually transfer 11 viruses to your mouth, eyes, or nose—enough to bring on a miserable cold and days in bed watching soap operas.

And don't forget household sponges. Watch out for these items: They come in pretty colors; they're efficient; they're never changed. And they may contain up to 320,000,000—yes that's 320 *million*—bacterial pathogens just waiting to hop onto your hands. Although the transfer of pathogens from a sponge is very low (about 0.0009 percent), the large numbers mean about 2,912 bacteria can be transferred to your hand. Approximately 93 would attach themselves to your fingertip—and from there, 32 bacteria would be transferred to your mouth. If the bacteria on the sponge were *E. coli*, this would be enough to infect a person with this disease. Some ways to avoid this situation are to use new sponges more often, buy the types with bacteria-killing compounds built in, or microwave used sponges for one minute to kill all the bacteria.

Minimizing the Danger

The bottom line? If someone in the house has an infectious disease, remember that it can easily be transmitted to others via the surfaces of common items such as phones, faucets, and sponges. And if these

Making It to the Top

Not every household chemical can reach the "chemicals we love to hate list" of the Texas Department of Health.[12] Killer chemicals have to be pretty good to get such recognition. It's too bad people pay more attention to the Oscars than to this list:

1. Air fresheners. Try smelling when your nasal passages are coated with an oil film—or a nerve-deadening agent. Yes, that's what you'll often get if you spray your bathroom with that new pine scent. And we should also mention the formaldehyde (highly toxic, known carcinogen) and phenol (can cause all sorts of rashes, burns, and hives on the skin, not to mention cold sweats, convulsions, and other problems) found in some fresheners. Please, just open the window a crack.

2. Ammonia. Watch your eyes, respiratory tract, and skin with this one. And whatever you do, don't add ammonia to bleach (a strong corrosive, by the way)—no matter what Aunt Mattie says. The combination creates fumes that can be deadly!

[continued on next page]

3. Carpet and upholstery shampoo. These creations often use highly toxic substances to overpower your rug stains, such as perchlorethylene (known carcinogen that can damage your liver, kidney, and nervous system) and ammonium hydroxide (a corrosive that's irritating to the skin, eyes, and breathing passages).

4. Dish-washing detergents. Watch out for children here—the chlorine in the dry formula is the number-one cause of child poisonings.

5. Drain cleaner. Watch out for children here, too. These nasty concoctions contain lye (caustic enough to cause burns to the skin and eyes, and tears up your esophagus and stomach if you swallow it), hydrochloric acid (an extreme corrosive that damages everything it touches), and trichloroethane (eye and skin irritant and nervous-system depressant).

6. Furniture polish. Contains petroleum distillates that are highly flammable. They've also been linked

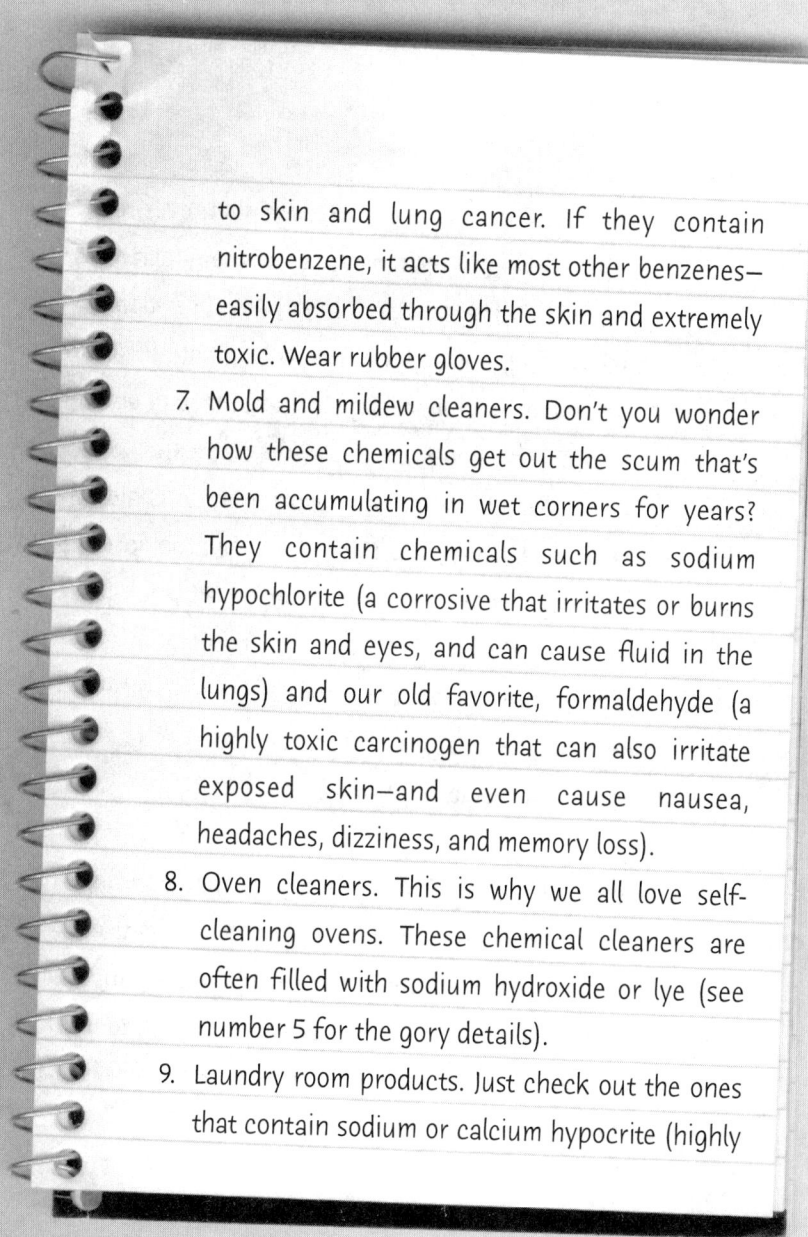

to skin and lung cancer. If they contain nitrobenzene, it acts like most other benzenes—easily absorbed through the skin and extremely toxic. Wear rubber gloves.

7. Mold and mildew cleaners. Don't you wonder how these chemicals get out the scum that's been accumulating in wet corners for years? They contain chemicals such as sodium hypochlorite (a corrosive that irritates or burns the skin and eyes, and can cause fluid in the lungs) and our old favorite, formaldehyde (a highly toxic carcinogen that can also irritate exposed skin—and even cause nausea, headaches, dizziness, and memory loss).

8. Oven cleaners. This is why we all love self-cleaning ovens. These chemical cleaners are often filled with sodium hydroxide or lye (see number 5 for the gory details).

9. Laundry room products. Just check out the ones that contain sodium or calcium hypocrite (highly

[continued on next page]

corrosive and can irritate or burn skin, eyes, or even your lungs), linear alkylate sulfonate (can be absorbed by the skin and is a known liver-damaging agent), and sodium tripolyphosphate (it's a skin and mucous-membrane irritant that can also be absorbed through the skin from clothes).

10. Toilet bowl cleaners. Our favorite chore is also hazardous: Many cleaners have hydrochloric acid (highly corrosive) or hypochlorite bleach (a corrosive that can irritate or burn your eyes, skin, or breathing tracts)—and if you use other chemicals with some of these cleaners, you can create fatal chlorine fumes.

The solution? Avoid buying products that contain the worst of these chemicals. Find more natural alternatives—they're out there—such as organic cleaners that use citrus or herbal cleaners. Your family, your pets, your body, and the earth's landfills will thank you for it.

items are used repeatedly, the probability of transmitting the disease goes up even more. So play with your own toys if someone else nearby is sick. Your immune system will thank you for it.

SICK OF BUILDINGS

Sick Building Syndrome: House Calls . . . Literally

Most of us spend a lot of time indoors. Between work, mealtimes, sleeping, recreation, and other activities, we're inside more than out, particularly in winter. The result of this equation? You have a species that, unlike any other, is intimately cocooned within an artificial dwelling. That's all right. We need shelter from the elements. And no one said shelter had to be uncomfortable, either. But the very home or building we spend so much time in—where we feel safe and secure—can literally make us sick. It's something experts call *sick building syndrome* (SBS).

Although SBS can be caused by a multitude of things—from pollutants in the air to chemicals emitted by certain plastics or glues in a building—there is a new culprit: A toxic fungus called *Stachybotrys chartarum*. It could be in your house or place of work right now—but you can't see it or smell it. You'll know it by the symptoms it causes however: fatigue, headaches, lack of focus, shortness of breath, or just general uneasiness.

Judging the Danger

What types of buildings are at risk from this fungus? In a nutshell, any that have sustained some form of water damage, such as flooding, leaking, condensation, sewer backups, or broken pipes. *S. chartarum* spores are always present in the soil, so they can be tracked into buildings either through human or natural mechanisms. Combine the spores with water, and you have instant fungus infestation.

Many times water damage can be hidden, such as in the ceiling or

The Odd Couple

"Turn off the TV and go outside and play." Our parents told us that for years—and they may have been right, after all. Except the *parents* who stayed behind in the house should have listened. A recent study finally uncovered a hidden danger of watching sitcoms, game shows, talk shows, and the other forms of mindless entertainment—such as political debates—on the "boob tube." Passive television watching is the only midlife recreational activity positively linked to developing Alzheimer's —a disease of the brain that brings about personality changes, memory loss, dementia, and death.[13]

Almost 25 percent of the over-eighty-five population are affected by this debilitating disease, as are 5 percent of those over sixty-five. The study surveyed 193 patients who either probably or possibly had Alzheimer's, along with 358 of their friends, acquaintances, and neighbors who had no sign of the disease. The subjects were asked how much time they spent in twenty-six different recreational activities, including physical, passive, and intellectual. It turned out the healthy folks had been more active in all three categories during their midlife years—from ages twenty to sixty. Those with Alzheimer's had been less active in all the categories—except when it came to TV viewing, the prime sport in which they had been most active during those years.

In the United States, the average person watches four hours of television per day. That's a good deal of time spent in a nonlearning, semiconscious state. Apparently, our brains continually develop through activity and learning—even as we get older. Scientists don't know at this point if midlife inactivity (along with more TV activity) is a risk factor for Alzheimer's, a consequence of early symptoms of the disease, or a combination of the two. In any case, it makes sense to turn off the tube, get outside, and take a walk, garden, or read a book—anything to keep the mind and body active and this disease at bay.

behind walls—or even near your air conditioner. Here, the fungus can grow undetected. Surfaces that make a nice, comfy home for *S. chartarum* include insulation, wood, paper, ceiling tiles, wallpaper, sheetrock covering, and even natural-fiber carpets. When visible, this fungus has a black appearance; it is powdery when dry and shiny when wet.

Minimizing the Danger

How can you avoid a *S. chartarum* infestation and its form of sick building syndrome? Here are some hints:[14]

+ If you have had any water damage and/or manifest some of the symptoms, start with a thorough inspection of your building—especially those areas that you know have sustained water damage.
+ If the water problem is a continuing one, such as a leaky roof, correct it to hinder any further growth.
+ If you do find areas with fungus, find out the safety procedures for working with toxic natural substances. Consult an expert. Even though you may appear to have removed the fungus from a surface with a disinfectant, there may still be some traces left within the material that will start to grow again. Many times the best option is to completely remove the contaminated material.

Carbon Monoxide: Don't Take a Breath

It's an insidious killer. Silent, colorless, tasteless and odorless, it can stalk your home and strike without warning. You won't even know it's present until it's too late. "It" is carbon monoxide (CO), a toxic gas that can be found in even the best-kept homes—a result of malfunctioning or improperly used fuel-burning appliances.

Small concentrations of this gas make you feel as if you have the flu, but minus the fever. Larger concentrations can result in unconsciousness, brain damage, and death within minutes. Every year in the United States alone, carbon monoxide poisoning affects hundreds of people, and nearly three hundred people die needlessly in their homes as a result.

Judging the Danger

Carbon monoxide gas is produced when any type of fuel—such as oil, gas, wood, charcoal, or kerosene—is burned. If your home has a fuel-burning appliance—and what one doesn't?—you have a potential source of CO poisoning. This includes the furnace, fireplace, gas water heater, gas stoves, woodstoves, and unvented kerosene and gas space heaters. Leaking chimneys and clogged vents can also contribute to the problem. A properly operating appliance, appropriately vented to the outside, will introduce only tiny amounts of CO into the home.

However, if there is a problem with either the appliance or the vent, larger amounts of this toxic gas can rapidly accumulate, particularly in today's newer airtight structures—and especially in the winter, when the windows and doors are normally closed. As you breathe in the carbon monoxide, the molecules of gas migrate from your lungs into your bloodstream, where they are attracted to hemoglobin. There, they displace oxygen, binding themselves to these structures. This is a bad thing. As you breathe more and more carbon monoxide, more oxygen is displaced, and you literally suffocate from the inside out.

Carbon monoxide poisoning can strike anyone, even physically healthy people. Some, however, are particularly susceptible to this deadly gas, including infants, unborn babies, senior citizens, and anyone with respiratory or coronary problems.

Minimizing the Danger

To avoid carbon monoxide poisoning, understand the warning signs. Low concentrations of this gas produce fatigue in healthy people and chest pain in those with heart disease. Higher concentrations result in impaired vision and coordination, headache, nausea, irregular breathing, and dizziness. And as we stated above, carbon monoxide symptoms can mimic those of the flu, without the fever. If your symptoms disappear when you go outside, then reappear when you go back inside, you do not have the flu, but may be experiencing CO poisoning. Never ignore these symptoms. Better safe than sorry—or dead.

If there is the slightest suspicion that you, or others in your household, are being poisoned by this gas, open the windows and doors, turn off any fuel-burning appliances, and leave. Go to the nearest emergency room and tell the physician that you suspect CO poisoning. They may be able to confirm this using a carboxyhemoglobin blood test.

To avoid ending up in the ER—or worse, the morgue—there are a number of things you can do. The following has been adapted from the Environmental Protection Agency:[15]

+ Have your entire heating system inspected, cleaned, and serviced every year by a trained professional, preferably just before the heating season. This includes furnaces, water heaters, ranges and ovens, dryers, fireplaces, space heaters, and wood stoves. All vents and chimneys should also be inspected.
+ All fuel-burning appliances should be installed by professionals using the manufacturer's instructions and following any local building codes.
+ Periodically examine your chimneys and vents for stains, rust, or improper connections.
+ Operate appliances in accordance with manufacturer's directions.
+ Look for signs of improper appliance operation, such as a burning or unfamiliar odor, sooting, and decreased performance.
+ Replace unvented space heaters with vented models.
+ Never leave a car running in the garage, even if the garage door is open.
+ Never burn charcoal in the garage or anywhere indoors.
+ Don't service fuel-burning appliances if you don't have the requisite training and tools.

✦ Never operate unvented gas-burning appliances in a closed room. Avoid sleeping in a room that is heated with an unvented space heater.

✦ Don't use a gas oven or range for home-heating purposes.

✦ Never use gasoline-powered engines in enclosed spaces. This includes chain saws, generators, snowblowers, lawn mowers, and so forth.

One other thing you can do to avoid carbon monoxide poisoning is to install Underwriters Laboratories–approved CO detectors. Put the primary detector near the sleeping area; a second detector may be located near the main heating source. Remember, never ignore a CO detector's alarm, and understand that a detector is no substitute for a properly operating heating system and other fuel-burning appliances.

Radon: Just Like a Scary Movie

There is something evil that can infiltrate your house. No, not cable television. This evil enters from the soil and rock surrounding your home, through the water you drink and bathe in, and the very air you breathe. This evil has a name: It's called *radon*. A radioactive gas, radon is invisible to our senses, and the only way to detect its presence in your home is to use specialized equipment.

When radon infiltrates a house, it can sometimes reach high concentrations. Environmental and medical studies have found that breathing in radon can be a health risk, primarily as a cause of lung cancer. It is estimated that radon exposure causes thousands of deaths each year. The surgeon general has warned that radon is the second leading cause of lung cancer in the United States; only smoking causes more deaths from this disease. The combination of smoking and high radon levels in the home makes your risk especially high. Both the Environmental Protection Agency (EPA) and the National Academy of Sciences' Institute of Medicine have declared that radon exposure in the home is a public-health problem.[16] So just because it's invisible doesn't mean it's nice.

Judging the Danger

Radon is a naturally occurring gas produced by the radioactive decay of radium. In this process, solid radium loses what is called an *alpha particle*, composed of two protons and two neutrons, forming radon gas. Eventually, this gas experiences its own radioactive decay, losing an alpha particle and forming the radioactive element polonium. It is this element, a product of radon in the air and in people's lungs, that can cause trauma to lung tissue, eventually leading to lung cancer.

So where does it come from? The element uranium is the first, or parent, element in the string of events that eventually produces radium and radon. While uranium decays slowly, with a half-life of 4.4 billion years, radon is quick, with a half-life of only 3.8 days. (A *half-life* is the amount of time that it takes for one-half of a given amount of an element to decay.) So radon decays and produces polonium very quickly, compounding the hazard.

However, just the presence and amount of uranium in the soil in your area does not directly determine how much radon gas will be present in your house. True, the higher the amount of uranium in an area, the higher the potential for high levels of indoor radon. But some homes in areas with high uranium amounts in the soil have low levels of indoor radon, and vice versa. Even houses located next to each other may have vastly different levels of radon.

The amount of radon in a given home is determined by a number of other factors. For example, how easy it is for the newly formed radium and radon atoms to leave the mineral grains of the rocks and enter the pore space between the grains or the fractures in the rocks? This determines how much of these radioactive elements will be able to move inside. How much water is present in the pore space (soil moisture content), how much pore space is there (soil porosity), and how interconnected are the pore spaces (soil permeability)? Radon moves much faster in air than water; more porosity means more space for radon to enter; and more permeability means that the radon can move rapidly through the soil. All of this means that homes in areas of drier, highly porous and permeable soils, such as hill slopes, coarse glacial deposits, and the bottoms of canyons, have the potential for higher levels of indoor radon, as opposed to those located in wet, less porous and less permeable soils.

Another factor has to do with the house itself. Normally, radon near the surface of the soil just escapes into the air. But place a house on that soil, especially one with a basement, and the dynamics of radon movement change. The radon may move toward and into the house because of increases in soil permeability around the basement; the difference in air pressure between the house and soil; and the presence of openings such as uncovered soil in crawl spaces, cracks, utility entry points, and seams. Most homes obtain less than 1 percent of their indoor air from the surrounding soil. However, a house with many openings to the soil, a poorly sealed foundation, and low indoor air pressure could potentially draw up to 20 percent of its indoor air from the soil. Even if the soil has only moderate radon levels, the indoor concentration of this gas may be very high.

The water system is another potential entry point for radon. Those homes that obtain their water directly from the ground, such as through wells and small public waterworks, have a higher potential for radon than those that get their water from sources such as lakes, rivers, and large municipal systems. Radon in the water enters the indoor air during activities such as clothes washing, dish washing, or taking showers.

Minimizing the Danger

You can get an idea of your general radon problem by consulting a radon potential map. This type of map is created using a combination of data, such as the uranium or radium level in the soils and rock, the location of fractures, the moisture content and permeability of the soils, radon measurements of local soil air, and any existing indoor radon data. Not all of this information is available for every area, so radon potential maps from different areas may have been created using different combinations of data.

One such map was created by the EPA: the Map of Radon Zones for the United States (it can be viewed on the Internet at www.epa.gov/iaq/radon/zonemap.html). This particular map was produced using indoor radon measurements, geology data, aerial radioactivity, soil permeability, and foundation types. It is used by national, state, and local organizations to focus their resources and implement radon-resistant building codes. Note that the radon level is measured in picocures per liter (pCi/L), a standard of radiation measurement where 1 pCi is equal to the decay of approximately two radioactive atoms per minute.

However, these maps can only give you an idea of the potential for an indoor radon problem. The only way to know your actual indoor radon level is through in-home testing. The EPA and surgeon general recommend testing all homes below the third floor for radon. The tests are easy and inexpensive. Look in the Yellow Pages of your phone book under "Radon Testing" for companies that service your area or check out the EPA Web site for a link to state radon contacts. All houses that have a radon level over 4 pCi/L can—and should—be fixed. There are ways to reduce high radon levels that won't bankrupt you, so there's no excuse for putting it off.

JUST WHEN YOU THOUGHT IT WAS SAFE...

. . . It All Comes Tumbling Down

You've managed to duck the falling tree limbs. There are no asteroids coming your way. And those mites don't seem as mighty as they used to be—especially since you vacuum regularly now. You're snug as a bug in your house. Then you hear it. It's that creaking, groaning noise again. It sounds like something is slipping in the bedroom. The next thing you know, there's plaster everywhere and the house seems to be falling down. In fact, it is—your house is caving in! There was no earthquake—one of the major reasons for house collapse—this happened all on its own. Or did it?

Or maybe you're reading this book one night when something seems to pop. Then you hear something sizzling like a pan of hot fajitas, but dinner's been over for hours. The lights go out, but you still see something bright. Over in the corner, right by that frayed wire coming from your table lamp, a small fire is starting to burn. You *knew* you should have paid attention—and now your entire house is going up in flames because you didn't hire an electrician to check out your wiring before you moved in—or you didn't get that wire fixed.

Yes, you may have survived all the other dangers around you—but there are others that can affect you and your family: your house collapsing around you or burning to the ground.

Judging the Danger

According to a member survey from the American Society of Home Inspectors, the most frequently found problems in a home are structurally related. And it's everything from crumbling foundation walls, wooden joists being eaten by termites, and even rotten floors. Even new homes aren't immune, with horror stories of shoddy workmanship leaving sloping floors, bowing walls, or fractured, leaking basement walls.

But that's not all. Another problem on that list—noted by close to 20 percent of the respondents to the survey—improper electrical wiring. That includes insufficient electric service to the house, no overload protection, and poor wiring techniques done by amateurs to "fix" earlier problems. Add to that a faulty electric cord or a defective appliance and your house can go up in a blaze. Yes, those minute electrons we can't see may help our refrigerator to hum, but they can also raze a house in a flash.

Minimizing the Danger

Here are some hints if you fear your walls are falling in around you:

+ If the house comes close to collapse because of hungry termites—and plenty of the critters go unnoticed—there are people to contact to get rid of the pests. Try the National Pest Management Association, a Virginia-based trade association representing more than four thousand pest control companies, or the Termite Action Group, another group that offers information for the homeowner.[17]

+ If a part of your home is losing plaster, bulging, or cracking, call your town building inspector or a licensed building contractor.

+ Periodically check your house—maybe during your swing of "spring cleaning"—for signs of rotting wood, bowed floors, or sagging walls. Any of these could be a sign of a larger structural problem.

+ Also periodically check your foundation—or the slab the house is built on—for cracks or water.

Electrical safety is just as important as your house's structural safety. Try some of these safety rules in the home to prevent torching your house:[18]

+ Some electrical problems can be cured with a twist of a screw or a bending of a wire. But before you do anything with your electricity—TURN OFF THE POWER! Better yet, call an electrician.

+ Cooking fires are all too common. If you're prone to forgetting things, keep a timer on when you're cooking something. Don't leave food cooking—especially in or on the stove—and go out to the store or elsewhere. Keep an eye on what you're cooking. Burning food can be the first step to burning down the house.

+ Never touch an electrical appliance while your hands or feet are wet or while you're in any water (such as the tub). And don't even think of turning on the sink while you have the plugged-in hair dryer in your hand. Water is a conductor of electricity.

+ Don't use an appliance, lamp, stereo system, or television— in other words, any electrical device or appliance—that has a frayed cord or a cracked or broken plug. Get it fixed by a competent electrician, or replace it.

+ Don't try to repair any electrical appliance if you aren't trained in the electrical trade. It may look easy, but there are tricks of the trade you should know, especially with the more advanced technology used today in appliances and sundry other electric devices. Let the pros fix that broken refrigerator—not your cousin Lou who once saw a special on electricity on public television.

✦ Pay attention to any spark, tingle, or shock you receive from an electrical device, lamp, or appliance. Pull the plug immediately and let a trained electrician fix the problem. And if you feel any tingle or shock from metal in your home—such as a pipe or the kitchen sink—contact an electrical contractor as soon as possible. It could mean you have faulty wiring in the house. And it will be your fault if you don't get it fixed (pun intended).

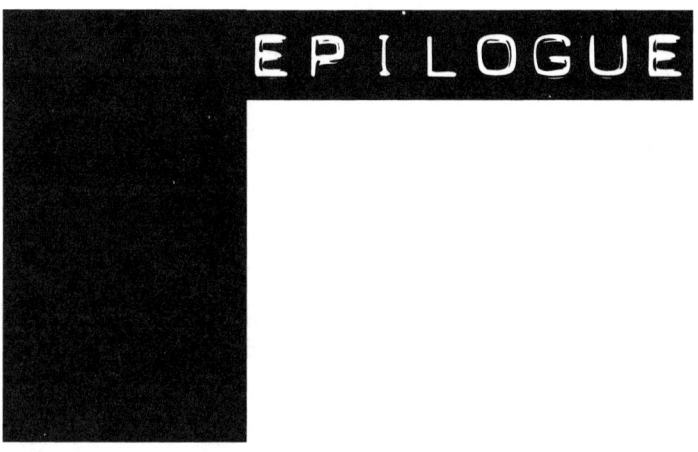

EPILOGUE

Yes, it's true. The world—from the micro to the macro—can be a dangerous place. But it can also be awe inspiring, beautiful, and enjoyable if we take the time to learn about it. Hopefully, this book has helped you discover a great deal about the perils that lurk around us, how to prepare for and/or prevent them from happening, and how science is continually discovering new phenomena that may or may not pose new dangers.

Humans seem more frightened of the unknown than of actual dangers themselves. And as we've said before, knowledge is power. You can contact us, the authors, at pbarnessvarney@hotmail. com. We'll try to answer any questions you have—sorry, but we can't help you with your paranoia. That's something you'll have to work out for yourself. And always remember, as your mother said, "Be careful out there."

ENDNOTES AND EXTRAS

These endnotes are a compendium of research gathered over the years: people interviewed, and articles torn from magazines and journals. Added in these pages are the newest form of research—information from the Internet. We've provided the best Web sites from our research just in case you want to investigate further—general sites, our own notes, and some extra sites and books you might want to explore.

But such a list comes with a caveat: The addresses of these Web sites often change. If an address listed here doesn't work, use a search engine to find the current address.

General Resource:

www.fema.gov/library—One of the best repositories of disaster information on the Internet.

www.riskinstitute.org—The clearinghouse for the Public Entity Risk Institute.

www.colorado.edu/hazards—The always-useful site of the Natural Hazards Research and Applications Information Center in Boulder, Colorado.

CHAPTER 1. THE VIOLENT EARTH

1. For some of the best data on earthquakes, visit earthquake.usgs. gov, the site for the United States Geological Survey.

2. Help for natural disasters in the United States is usually handled by the Federal Emergency Management Agency (FEMA), at www. fema.gov.

3. G. S. Fuis et al., "Crustal Structure and Tectonics from the Los Angeles Basin to the Mojave Desert, Southern California," *Geology* 29, no. 1 (January 2001): 15–18.

4. S. J. Kenner and P. Segall, "A Mechanical Model for Intraplate Earthquakes: Application to the New Madrid Seismic Zone," *Science* 289, no. 5488 (September 29, 2000): 2329–31. You can also try the Centers for Earthquake Research and Information at the University of Memphis (www.ceri.memphis.edu/public) for more information about the possibility of a New Madrid earthquake.

5. Find out more about this study from the University of Colorado at Boulder news service at www.colorado.edu/Carillon/volume36/stories/3-3madrid.html.

6. To see a copy of the world's first earthquake hazard map, go to the Global Seismic Hazard Assessment Program at seismo.ethz.ch/GSHAP/index.html—a color rendition of the world's hot spots for quakes.

7. See the FEMA Web site at www.fema.gov/nwz00/nwz00_51.htm.

8. Check out the United States Geological Survey's National Earthquake Information Center at wwwneic.cr.usgs.gov.

9. To see how to handle earthquakes and other natural disasters, go to the FEMA Web site (www. fema.gov/library/eqinfo.htm).

10. Los Angeles City Fire Department, "Los Angeles Fire Department Earthquake Handbook" (1997) coded by Bud Gundersen, LAFD (Ret.). Or check out the great primer for surviving an earthquake at the Los Angeles City Fire Department's Web site (www.lafd.org/eqindex.htm).

11. There are may Web sites with information on tsunami warning systems. Try the Intergovernmental Oceanographic Commission at ioc. unesco.org/iocweb/activities/tsunami.htm, the International Tsunami Information Center at www.shoa.cl/oceano/itic/itic.html, or the National Oceanic and Atmopheric Association's own Pacific Tsunami Warning Center site at www.nws.noaa.gov/pr/ptwc.

12. Underwater landslides have been a big interest lately, especially since the underwater landslide in Papua New Guinea in 1998. This section refers to several papers given at the American Geophysical Union's fall

2000 meeting. Two helpful presentations are: H. G. Green et al., "Landslide Hazards Off of Santa Barbara, California," *EOS Trans. AGU*, fall meeting suppl., Abstract OS21H-10, v. 81 (2000): 48; and J. C.Borrero et al., "Tsunami Inundation Maps for Santa Barbara and Santa Monica Bay," *EOS Trans. AGU*, fall meeting suppl., Abstract OS71C-11, v. 81 (2000): 48.

13. See the FEMA Web site at www.fema.gov/library/tsunami.htm.

14. See the FEMA Web site at www.fema.gov/library/volcano.htm.

15. Thomas Simkin et al., "Volcano Fatalities—Lessons From the Historical Record," *Science* 291, no. 5502, (January 12, 2001): 255.

16. Landslide information can be found at the United States Geological Survey's National Landslides Hazards Program Web site at www.usgs.gov/html_files/landslides/program.html.

17. See the FEMA Web site at www.fema.gov/library/landslif.htm.

18. From the United States Geological Survey's National Landslides Hazards Program Web site at www.usgs.gov/html_files/landslides/program.htm.

Extras

earthquakes.usgs.gov—A plethora of information about earthquakes.

geohazards.cr.usgs.gov/eqint/html/zipcode.shtml—The United States Geological Survey's "Zip Code Earthquake Ground Motion Hazard Look-up Page"—just put in your zip code and the site gives you the predicted seismic ground motion for your location.

www.eqnet.org—A cooperative effort between several United States hazard organizations, this site is maintained by the University at Buffalo's Information Service at the Multidisciplinary Centers for Earthquake Engineering Research.

observe.ivv.nasa.gov/nasa/exhibits/tsunami/tsun_start.html—NASA's informational guide to tsunamis.

www.grid.unep.ch/preview—The United Nations Environment Program offers a way to locate relevant Web sites from about one hundred organizations dealing with reports, data, and early warning information on natural disasters.

CHAPTER 2. OCEAN AND CLIMATE FEARS

1. See California's Department of Boating and Waterways Web site at www.dbw.ca.gov/sneaker. htm.

2. Information on rip currents from the Florida Division of Emergency Management is available at www.dca.state.fl.us/bpr/Response/Plans/Nathaz/HazWX/Marine/marine.htm.

3. From North Carolina State University's Sea Grant program, Coast-Watch, www.ncsu.edu/seagrant/coastwatch.

4. From the International Coastal Cleanup site, www.cmc-ocean. org/cleanupbro/index.php3, a global project of the Center for Marine Conservation (CMC) in Washington, D.C.

5. Ibid.

6. S. C. Jiang et al., "Potentially Harmful Human Viruses In Coastal Waters," *Applied and Environmental Microbiology*, 67 (January 2001): 179–84.

7. From the Web site of the Environmental Protection Agency, www. epa.gov/ost/beaches/2000fact.html.

8. From the local news, KABC, Orange County, California, May 2000. See abcnews.go.com/local/kabc/news/37470_5282000.htm.

9. From the Florida Museum of Natural History—a place where they know about sharks (www.flmnh.ufl.edu/fish/sharks/attacks/howwhen. htm).

10. The International Shark attack file is at www.flmnh.ufl.edu/fish/ sharks/isaf/isaf.htm

11. Ibid.

12. P. R. Epstein, "Is Global Warming Harmful to Health?" *Scientific American*, August 2000, 50–57.

13. Check out the United Nations' Intergovernmental Panel on Climate Change at www.ipcc.ch.

14. This group's site is at www.nacc.usgcrp.gov/. It gives you a good idea about what changes mean—and, site-specifically, what can be done to help plan for future climate change.

15. E. R. Easterling et al., "Climate Extremes: Observations, Modeling, and Impacts," *Science*, September 22, 2000, 2068–74.

Extras

web.mit.edu/afs/athena.mit.edu/org/g/giving/spectrum/spring98/sea walls.html—"Seaside Debate" is a good article to check out on the problems with using seawalls to manage beach erosion (from the Massachusetts Insitute of Technology's *Spectrum*, story by Eve Downing).

www.aloha.com—Go to a good source for beach and ocean hazards—Hawaii. This site will lead you to the state's "Common Hazardous Beach & Ocean Conditions" page.

www.cdc.noaa.gov—The National Oceanic and Atmospheric Administration's CIRES Climate Diagnostic Center's primary goal is to understand climate variations—from months to centuries—to predict climate change.

enso.unl.edu/ndmc—The Web site for the National Drought Mitigation Center at the University of Nebraska–Lincoln, including a drought monitor.

www.ozone.org/heatstress—The Physicians for Social Responsibility and Ozone Action, a national environmental group, for those who want to read about the increased frequency of extreme weather events—especially as potential impacts of human-induced global warming.

CHAPTER 3. WEATHER WARY

1. Ben C. Bernstein, National Center for Atmospheric Research, personal communication with the author, 1998.

2. Jan Null, "Winds of the World," *Weatherwise* 53, no. 3, (May/June, 2000): 52–53.

3. L. J. Cooke et al., "Chinook Winds and Migrane Headaches," *Neurology* 54 (January 25, 2000): 302.

4. From the Washington State Boating Safety Officers Association Web site at www.boatwashington.org.

5. From the National Oceanic and Atmospheric Association, 205.156.54.206/om/severeweather/index.shtml.

6. From the NOAA's National Weather Service site at www.nws.noaa.gov/HAW/day1/storm_surge.htm.

7. Ibid.

8. Federal Emergency Management Agency (FEMA), at www.fema.gov/fema/trop.htm.

9. This is information right from a place that experiences plenty of dust storms, the Arizona Department of Public Safety's "Dust Storms a Summer Danger," www.dps.state.az.us/news/1999/nr99003.htm; or try www.edsweather.com/Almanac1998/arizona_dust_storms. htm.

10. Try the National Lightning Safety Institute, found on the Web at www.lightningsafety.com.

11. From the National Center for Atmospheric Research, www.ncar. ucar.edu.

12. From NASA's Science site at science.nasa.gov. You can also check out the Global Hydrology and Climate Center at www.ghcc.msfc.nasa.gov, a joint venture between NASA and academia to study the global water cycle and its effect on the climate.

13. "Rainmakers," *Discover*, November 1998, 34.

14. L. Elkins, "Meteorologists Help Hospitals by Matching Weather With Illness," *Times* (London), November 25, 2000.

Extras

www.boatwashington.org/downbursts.htm—Washington State Boating
    Safety Officers Assoication's page on boater safety.

www.srh.noaa.gov—Try the National Oceanic and Atmospheric Associa-
    tion's southern regions headquarters—this page will lead you to other
    weather sites around the country.

www.fema.gov/mit/tsfs01.htm—"Taking Shelter from the Storm: Building a
    Safe Room Inside Your House," FEMA Publication 320 (booklet and con-
    struction plans), at the Federal Emergency Management Agency Web site.

www.outlook.noaa.gov/tornadoes—Information on tornadoes from the
    National Oceanic and Atmospheric Administration.

www.esig.ucar.edu/sourcebook—A compilation of weather statistics in the
    Environmental and Societal Impacts Group's *Extreme Weather Sourcebook.*

Patricia Barnes-Svarney and Thomas E. Svarney, *Skies of Fury: Weather Weird-
    ness around the World* (New York: Simon & Schuster, 1999).

Y. H. Ohtsuki, ed., *Science of Ball Lightning* (New York: World Scientific Pub-
    lishing Co., 1988).

CHAPTER 4. HAZARDOUS SPACE STUFF

1. Information on coronal mass ejections (CMEs) from NASA's SOHO spacecraft site, sohowww.nascom.nasa.gov/explore/faq/cme.html—SOHO is the craft that watches the Sun and takes many of the CME images.

2. R. Cowen, "Stormy Weather," *Science News* 159 (January 13, 2001): 26–28.

3. "Planet Earth on the Move," BBC News Online, February 5, 2001, news.bbc.co.uk.

4. R. Binzel, personal communication with the author, 1998. Also try the Near-Earth Object Program at NASA's Jet Propulsion Laboratory Web site neo. jpl.nasa.gov.

5. For a complete rundown of this study, try www.nearearth objects.co.uk.

6. The English study is C. Bhattacharjee et al., "Do Animals Bite More During a Full Moon? Retrospective Observational Analysis," *British Medical Journal* 321, no. 7276 (2000): 1559–61; the Australian study is S. Chapman and S. Morrell, "Barking Mad? Another Lunatic Hypothesis Bites the Dust," ibid., pp. 1561–63.

7. From ABC News Online, October 20, 2000, abcnews.go.com/sections/world/DailyNews/stratfor.html).

8. The SOLACE study is conducted at NASA's Goddard Space Flight Center's EOS Project Science Office, online at www.gsfc.nasa.gov.

9. H. Mueller et al., "Effect of Different Possible Interstellar Environments on the Heliosphere," *EOS Trans. AGU,* Spring Meeting Suppl. #U22A-04 (2000).

Extras

www.sec.noaa.gov/SWN and www.spaceweather.com—Two great space weather sites to keep you up to date on the Sun's daily activities.

www.lpl.arizona.edu/spacewatch—The Lunar and Planetary Observatory's SpaceWatch group's Web site.

neo.jpl.nasa.gov/news.html—NASA's Jet Propulsion Laboratory's near-Earth objects Web site.

www.nearearthobjects.co.uk—Britain's answer to the study of near-Earth objects, from the National British Space Center.

impact.arc.nasa.gov/index.html—Another NASA site offered by the Ames

Space Science Division, called the "Asteroid and Comet Impact Hazards" site.

satz.space.noa.gr/~daglis/asi2000.html—This is NATO's Advanced Study Institute's site "Space Storms and Space Weather Hazards."

Patricia Barnes-Svarney, *Asteroid: Earth Destroyer or New Frontier?* (New York: Plenum Publishing, 1996).

CHAPTER 5. TRAVEL-TIME TERRORS

1. Deep vein thrombosis has become a major concern—especially for people on longer airline flights. Thus, the British medical journal the *Lancet* has had many papers on the subject. Two in particular about DVT issues are excellent: B. Bendz et al., "Association Between Acute Hypobaric Hypoxia and Activation of Coagulation in Human Beings," *Lancet* 356, no. 9242 (2000): 1657–58; and R. A. Kraaijenhagen et al., "Travel and Risk of Venous Thrombosis," *Lancet* 356, no. 9240 (2000): 1492–93.

2. For you travelers, what better place to get scuba and travel advice at once than from Hawaii? Try Dr. Alex del Rosario's "Travel Medicine" Web site at www.discoveringhawaii.com/SF_Medicine/SCUBADiving/Scuba DivingFlying.html

3. From the Centers for Disease Control and Prevention Web site, www.cdc.gov/travel.htm.

4. Ibid.

5. From the Health Physics Society Web site at www.hps.org.

6. From Diana Fairechild's great site, www.flyana.com. She's also the author of *Jet Smarter: The Air Traveler's Rx.* (Anahola, Hawaii: Flyana Rhyme, 1999).

7. From the National Center for Infectious Diseases, part of the Centers for Disease Control and Prevention, www.cdc.gov/travel/diseases.htm.

8. Ibid.

9. Ibid.

10. A worldwide site for the eradication of polio, with plenty of information, is at www.polioeradication.org, sponsored by the World Health Organization.

11. From MSN's Women Central site, June 6, 2000, womencentral. msn.com/health/articles/week1.asp.

12. From the National Center for Infectious Diseases, at www. cdc.gov/travel/diseases.htm, or try www.cdc.gov/travel/foodwater.htm.

13. Ibid.

Extras

www.umdnj.edu/ntbcweb/—The site of the National Tuberculosis Center

CHAPTER 6. BACKYARD PERILS

1. From the United States Department of Agriculture Web site at www. pueblo.gsa.gov.

2. From the Centers for Disease Control and Prevention, www.cdc.gov/ncidod.htm.

3. From ABC News Online, April 4, 2001, www.abcnews.com/sections/world/dailynews/france010403_bullfrogs.htm.

4. From the federal Environmental Protection Agency at www.epa.gov. You can also check out: P. M. Lemieux et al., "Polychlorinated Dibenzofurans from the Open Burning of Household Waste in Barrels," *Environmental Science and Techology* 34, no. 3 (2000): 377–84; available online at pubs.acs.org/journals/esthag.

5. From the American Institute for Cancer Research, www. aicr.org.

6. From the National Jewish Medical and Research Center, www.nationaljewish.org.

7. From the Centers for Disease Control and Prevention, www.cdc.gov.

8. R. S. Buller et al., "*Ehrlichia ewingii,* a Newly Recognized Agent of Human Ehrlichiosis," *New England Journal of Medicine* 341, no. 3, (1999): 148–55.

9. From the Centers for Disease Control and Prevention, www.cdc.gov/ncidod/dvrd/ehrlichia/Index.htm.

10. From the New York State Health Department, www.health.state.ny.us/nysdoh/westnile/index.htm.

11. From the Centers for Disease Control and Prevention, www.cdc.gov/ncidod/dvbid/westnile.

12. One of the best sites to track the West Nile Virus and other wildlife problems is the United States Geological Survey's National Wildlife Health Center's West Nile virus page at www.nwhc.usgs.gov/westnil2.html.

13. Fire ant research is being conducted at Ames Plantation in Grand Junction, Tennessee, in cooperation with the University of Tennessee. Check it out on the Web at www.amesplantation/org/FireAntResearch/fireantres.htm.

14. B. M. Dreees and S. B. Vinson, "Fire Ants and Their Management" [online] Texas Agricultural Extension Service, Texas A&M University System, entowww.tamu.edu/extension/bulletins/b-1536.html. The National Agricultural Library of the U.S. Department of Agriculture also has a great site, www.invasivespecies.gov/profiles/fireant.shtml, with some more or less technical articles on fire ants.

CHAPTER 7. BODY BEWARE

1. Howard Hughes Medical Institute, "The Race Against Lethal Microbes" (Chevy Chase, Md.: booklet, 1996).

2. Almost any news broadcast or magazine article from news magazines covered the mad cow disaster in Europe around mid-March 2001. This is a compendium of information from them and from government agencies such as the Centers for Disease Control and Prevention. For more details on mad cow disease, try www.cyber-dyne.com/~tom/mad_ cow_disease.html and www.mad-cow.org, both from the Sperling Biomedical Foundation in England. To discover more about Creutzfeldt-Jakob disease, try the CJD Foundation at www.cjdfoundation.org.

3. From the United States Food and Drug Administration, www.fda.gov/fdac/features/2001/101_chic.html.

4. G. Mirkin, "Treatment of Staph Aureus in Nose," October 1, 2000, www.drmirkin.com/morehealth/G167.htm.

5. The Society for Light Treatment and Biological Rhythms in San Francisco, California, has a wonderful site concerning SAD and other biological rhythm concerns at www.websciences.org/sltbr/ or www.sltbr.org.

6. The authors did a great deal of research on the flu for the Discover Changel Web site, www.discovery.com. Our resources included the Centers for Disease Control and Prevention.

7. Some of the more well-known viruses are watched by the World Health Organization (WHO) in Geneva, Switzerland. The WHO is on the Web at www.who.ch.

8. P. Radetsky, "Last Days of the Wonder Drugs" *Discover*, November, 1998, 76–85.

9. From the Centers for Disease Control and Prevention, www.cdc.gov/antibioticresistance.html.

10. S. Bures et al., "Computer Keyboards and Faucet Handles as Reservoirs of Nosocomial Pathogens in the Intensive Care Unit," *American Journal of Infection Control* 28, Special Issue (2000): 465–71.

11. There are two places to find information on mites: One is a natural—Heartland Products, Inc. (for pets) at www.hartlandnatural.com. The other is at the great site of the Central District Health Department in Boise, Idaho, at www.cdhd.org/CommunicableDisease.

12. Here's another good mite site at Ohio State University: ohioline. osv.edu.

13. From the University of Kentucky's Cooperative Extension, www. uky.edu/Agriculture/Entomology/entfacts.

14. Try Heartland Products, Inc. at www.hartlandnatural.com.

15. For some of the best and most up-to-date information about mosquitoes, try the University of California at Davis' MosquitoNet at mosqnet. ucdavis.edu. Or you can try the site jointly run by the Associated Executives of Mosquito Control Work in New Jersey and the New Jersey Mosquito Control Association: www-rci.rutgers.edu/~insects/njmos.htm.

Extras

B. Dixon, *Power Unseen: How Microbes Rule the World* (New York: Oxford University Press, 1996).

L. Garrett, *The Coming Plague: Newly Emerging Diseases in a World Out of Balance* (New York: Penguin, 1995).

S. B. Levy, *The Antibiotic Paradox: How Miracle Drugs Are Destroying the Miracle* (New York: Perseus Press, 1992).

F. Ryan, *Virus X: Tracking the New Killer Plagues* (New York: Little Brown & Co., 1998).

CHAPTER 8. NO PLACE LIKE HOME?

1. See this study at pubs.acs.org/hotartcl/est/99/research/ es980580o_rev.html at this American Cancer Society site.

2. From a National Institute of Environmental Health Sciences study available at www.niehs.nih.gov/ocs/news/bedding.htm.

3. From the National Jewish Medical and Research Center, www.nationaljewish.org.

4. Find information about Legionnaires' disease from the Centers for Disease Control and Prevention, www.cdc.gov/ncidod/dbmd/disease info/legionellosis_g.htm. There are also many journal articles about the bacterium *Legionella,* including: T. J. Dondero Jr et al., "An Outbreak of

Legionnaires' Disease Associated with a Contaminated Air-conditioning Cooling Tower," *New England Journal of Medicine*, 302 (1980): 365–70 (This article was written four years after the famous outbreak that gave the disease its familar name.); F. J. Mahoney et al., "Communitywide Outbreak of Legionnaires' Disease Associated with a Grocery Store Mist Machine," *Journal of Infectious Diseases*, 165 (1992): 736–39; and D. B. Jernigan et al., "Outbreak of Legionnaires' Disease Among Cruise Ship Passengers Exposed to a Contaminated Whirlpool Spa," *Lancet* 347 (1996): 494–99.

5. P. I. Dargan et al. "A Case of Lead Poisoning Due to Snooker Chalk," *Archives of Disease in Childhood*, 83 (2000): 519–20; available online at adc.bmjjournals.com. This problem was also reported several years earlier in the news, so watch that pool chalk—especially around young children.

6. From the United States Environmental Protection Agency, www.epa.gov/lead. You can also find out a great deal about lead from the National Lead Information Center at 800-424-5323. You may also want to try some of these sites:

www.hud.gov/lea/leadhelp.html—An e-brochure from the Housing and Urban Development agency on how to help yourself from the dangers of lead.

www.ncsl.org/programs/esnr/pbdir.htm—A lead-poisoning prevention directory from the National Conference of State Legislatures.

7. From Reuters Health Online, about a black-cat-and-allergies study done at the Long Island College Hospital October, 26, 2000.

8. H. Carlsson et al., "Allergenic Flame Retardant Triphenyl Phosphate in the Indoor Environment," *Environmental Science and Techology*, 34 no. 18 (2000): 3885–89; available online at pubs.acs.org/journals/esthag.

9. From many references in the United States Food and Drug Administration, www.fda.gov; the New York State Health Department, www.health.state.ny.us/nysdoh; and the National Institutes of Health, www.nih.gov.

10. Louis Bloomfield is a professor of physics at the University of Virginia and the author of *How Things Work: The Physics of Everyday Life*, 2d ed. (New York: John Wiley & Sons, 2001). His Web site has information on superheated water in the microwave—and plenty of other interesting items: rabi.phys.virginia.edu/HTW/microwave_ovens. html. You might want to also check out the Food and Drug Administration's site: www.fda. gov/cdrh/consumer/erupted.html.

11. From the American Society of Microbiology, www.asmusa.org/pcsrc/gm2000/16554.htm.

12. From the Texas Department of Health, www.capitol-city.com/tdh/indextdh1.html.

13. R. P. Friedland et al., "Patients with Alzheimer's Disease Have Reduced Activities in Midlife Compared with Healthy Control-group Members," *Proceedings of the National Academy of Sciences* 98, (2000): 3440.

14. From the American Phytopathological Society, www.apsnet.org.

15. For good information about carbon monoxide poisoning, try the Environmental Protection Agency, www.epa.gov/pubs/senseles.html. There's also the *Fire Fighters Safety* magazine's article, "Carbon Monoxide: The Silent Killer," available online at www.safety-network.com/ffsm/carbon.htm.

16. Radon information can be obtained from the United States Geological Survey Web site at energy.cr.usgs.gov/radon/georadon/1.html and the Environmental Protection Agency site at www.epa.gov/iaq/radon.

17. Try the National Pest Management Association at www.npma.org or the Termite Action Group at www.termiteactiongroup.com for more information on getting rid of termites.

18. For information on home wiring hazards (and remedies), check the Electrical Safety page (part of the Electrical Contractor Network): www.electrical-contractor.net/Electrical_Safety_Page.htm; and a great text by the National Electrical Safety Foundation: pamphlet GSA #2403, "A Home Electrical Safety Check," available through the Federal Consumer Information Service at www.pueblo.gsa.gov/press/nfcpubs/homeelec.txt. You can also call almost any electric utility company for brochures on electric safety in the home.

Extras

www.epa.gov/iaq/pubs/sbs.html—Try the EPA for information on sick
building syndrome.

INDEX